Technology an advanced language learner

R/B2

Edited by Tim Lewis and Annie Rouxeville

Centre for Information
on Language Teaching and Research

Titles in the series 'Current Issues in University Language Teaching'

* no longer available

Acknowledgements

The editors would like to thank the AFLS Editorial Board and the referees for their helpful suggestions in the preparation of this volume.

First published in 2000 by the Association of French Language Studies in association with the Centre for Information on Language Teaching and Research, 20 Bedfordbury, London WC2N 4LB

ISBN 1 902031 66 0
2004 2003 2002 2001 2000 / 10 9 8 7 6 5 4 3 2 1

Printed in Great Britain by Copyprint (UK) Ltd.

CILT Publications are available from: **Central Books,** 99 Wallis Rd, London E9 5LN. Tel: 020 8986 4854. Fax: 020 8533 5821. Book trade representation (UK and Ireland): **Broadcast Book Services**, 2nd Floor, 248 Lavender Hill, London, SW11 1JL. Tel: 020 7924 5615. Fax: 020 7924 2165.

Contents

Threat or promise?
The impact of technology on language learning

Tim Lewis and Annie Rouxeville
University of Sheffield

1 Introduction

There are few academic disciplines in which the impact of technology has not been significant. But its role in second language learning is qualitatively different from that which it plays in most other areas of the academy. Language learning alone may claim that its primary object – speech itself – first became fully available to practitioners of the discipline long after its foundation, thanks only to a technological advance: the invention of sound recording.

Since then, the relationship between technology and language learning has grown ever closer, broader and more complex. Audio recording has been succeeded by video recording and both continue to evolve, as technology itself moves from the analogue to the digital age. Information technology now offers an entirely different set of choices and opportunities than those which existed two decades ago. Indeed, by virtue of its ability seamlessly to combine media, it appears set to supplant the technologies which preceded it. The impact of technology has not always been – and doubtless will not always be – benign (one thinks inevitably of the false dawn offered by audio-visual and audio-lingual methods in the 1960s). But language teachers have – to their credit – always exploited with alacrity – sometimes with too much alacrity – the possibilities it appeared to offer. Indeed the relationship of technology to second language pedagogy has developed to a point where some commentators are beginning to wonder which is the tail and which the dog

(Hewer, 1996: 235). The advent of the e.world has so fundamentally changed the ways in which we live and work, that it must surely bring about a corresponding shift in learners' needs and objectives. (It may be, for example that most international communication will take place not face-to-face by the oral/aural channel, but remotely, by e-mail, webconference, or mobile phone.) Our approach to the learning and teaching of languages will also change, as too will our understanding of language itself – in the light of the mass of linguistic information which powerful modern computers enable us to compile and analyse. However, a key lesson to be drawn from the chequered history of technology in language learning is that its use will only be effective within the framework of a sound pedagogical theory and if teachers and learners receive appropriate and adequate guidance in how to exploit it most apppropriately and effectively. In the words of Brian Hill:

> *One of our biggest failings throughout education has been our consistent inability to manage innovation successfully. It is the biggest challenge to be faced as we look towards the millennium. It has its roots not just in questions such as the selection, financing and introduction of equipment, but, even more importantly, in the need to improve our understanding of how people learn effectively from video, CD-ROM or satellites and in the need to provide more effective training for those who are asked to participate in the process of innovation.* (Hill, 1996: 227)

The good sense of Brian Hill's warning is beyond question. It cannot help but draw our attention to a deficiency which – if not peculiar to UK Higher Education – is nonetheless particularly marked here. For the development of our understanding of how learners and teachers can use technology effectively relies crucially on the opportunity to conduct and to publish research in the field, often of an applied nature. Sadly – with a few honourable exceptions – in seeking to foster the effective use of educational technology to second language learning, higher education in the UK labours under several entirely self-imposed handicaps. The first is the fact that the experimental use of technology for language learning takes place predominantly in Language Centres, where conditions are significantly different from those which obtain in academic departments. Many Language Centre staff are employed on a casual, part-time or fixed-term basis. Few are required by their contracts to undertake research. They may indeed be actively prevented from doing so –

even where their research focus is squarely on the language learner – on the grounds that this would amount to a diversion of resources. Many will be ineligible for the award of research leave, whether from their employers or from external funding bodies (such as the AHRB). Many will find that their employers refuse to return their research under the Research Assessment Exercise.

A number of the contributors to this volume hail from Language Centres and therefore – in large part – work under the conditions outlined above. It is greatly to their credit that they have devoted time and energy to the research that went into this volume and that they have succeeded in producing contributions of such quality. Let us hope that, as an example of highly fruitful collaboration between Language Centres and Modern Languages Departments – both in its writing and in its editing – this book can offer a path towards a more enlightened attitude to research into the use of language learning technology on the part those who manage higher education in the UK and elsewhere.

Such is the array of technological applications available to us for language learning and teaching that no single volume could hope to offer an equal degree of coverage to all of them. Moreover the pace of technological change is such that any claim to be giving an account of the 'state of the art' would be outdated before it was published. This book therefore does not pretend to offer a panoramic survey of how technology is being used – or can be used – for the learning and teaching of languages. Instead, it goes some way to meeting the need for pedagogic guidance so clearly identified by Brian Hill, by offering a series of accounts by practising language teachers of their learners' use of the new technologies. These are primarily descriptive. All are located within a framework of pedagogic theory and practice. They do not cover the whole range of the technologies, or of the applications now available to us. There is, perhaps surprisingly, no essay on computer-based testing, an area which seems rich with potential. Nor is there anything on ICALL. But what we do have, in this collection, is an indication of those uses of the old and new technologies which language teachers themselves see as most worth investing their energies and expertise in. Often they deal with fairly simple applications, which may reflect the limited amounts of time most practising language teachers have in which to develop new strategies and prepare materials. If we disagree with their priorities, we should perhaps consider why it is that they have chosen as they have and what – if anything – needs to be done to counteract that. As editors, we shall content ourselves in this introductory paper, with sketching the history of some of the main branches of technology use in second language learning and seeking to identify, often with the help of informed commentators, some of the outstanding issues which remain to be addressed in connection with each of them.

2 Audio and language labs

As one of the older technologies of which language learners today still make use, there is a temptation to regard audio as 'old hat'. Indeed, even those whose business has long been to manufacture and maintain language laboratories now fight shy of the term, preferring to refer to themselves simply as educational or telecoms companies. Moreover, it can be argued that audio as a medium is somehow unnatural, in that it deprives us of the myriad visual cues which help us to understand our partners in face to face conversation, when they are speaking and which enable us to monitor the reception of – and to modify – our own utterances, when we are speaking. It has been claimed (Kellerman, 1990: 272; Little, 1998: 39) that only in very few real-life situations – in telephone use, in listening to the radio or to loudspeaker announcements, or in the dark – are we required to communicate without visual clues. Unnatural as audio-only communication may seem, there is however, every indication, from the high sales volumes of audio books to the proliferation of mobile phones that it is an integral – and possibly even an expanding – part of our daily activity. Many people nowadays would regard themselves as simply too busy to sit down and watch a video of any length. But those same people will often be prepared to try to learn a language by listening to audio recordings while doing something else (e.g. at the wheel of a car). More seriously, in many parts of the world, where the funding allocated to language learning cannot or does not match that to be found in the average university in the industrialised world, audio is likely to continue for the foreseeable future to be the primary means by which language learners will have access to second languages spoken by native speakers. For this reason, if for no other, the use of audio continues to merit some consideration, though it is advisable to make the crucial distinction between audio as a medium and the language laboratory as one manifestation of it. In a brief, but extremely thoughtful and well-informed historical survey of the use of audio for language learning, Peter Green has charted the ups and downs of the language laboratory in the UK. First introduced into a school in Salford in 1962, to a rhapsodic commentary by the school's headteacher, it met its widespread demise as a learning instrument by the mid-1970s, as a result, firstly, of the demolition by Chomsky of behaviourist theories of language learning, and secondly – but no less importantly – of a series of empirical educational research findings which showed a) that pupils disliked the passivity forced on them by language labs and b) that the latter were no more effective in producing proficient linguists than the traditional methods which they had ousted (Green, 1996: 215–218). One argument in favour of the continued use of audio recording at advanced levels (which may however disappear with digitisation) is that audio cassettes can be much more accurately manipulated by the learner than video cassettes. For those who believe in the merits of transcription as a learning exercise at advanced level (and there is a high correlation between dictation skills and general language proficiency as measured, say, by a C-test), audio currently has no rival. Unsurprisingly, therefore, though language labs may have come and largely gone,[1] Green sensibly points out the major benefits of audio recording and concludes that 'language teaching nowadays is almost unthinkable without cassette tapes for pronunciation and listening practice', while 'the humdrum cassette recorder [is] firmly established as a basic language teaching aid' (Green, 1996: 220–221).

3   Television and video

When, in the early 1980s, university language teachers awoke fully – more or less simultaneously – to the promise of desktop computing and live satellite TV, it seemed at first that the latter might have more to offer – in terms of its ability to provide authentic L2 input for advanced learners, which could be developed into stimulating teaching material with relatively little effort. Time makes fools of us all. It has been clear from the early 1990s that the many faceted potential of networked computing as a learning medium would outstrip that of all other technologies. Though off-air video can provide learners with some of the visual cues (about both the speaker and his/her subject) which can aid understanding, it is neither problem-free nor a panacea. While computers have become unimaginably smaller, faster and easier to use than the (often mainframe) machines of two decades ago, the selection and elaboration into readily usable form of off-air video demands just as much time and effort as it did then. Visual images, however well chosen, attractive and motivating, date rapidly, imposing the need for constant renewal of resources. Above all, any one seeking to develop video resources for anything other than classroom use faces the problem either of seeking copyright clearance for the material they wish to use, or of shooting in-house, both of which are costly and laborious. The latter requires professional expertise. The late 80s and early 90s saw the publication by committed academics – often as collaborative projects – of a number of video-based courses or video resources. (One thinks particularly of the AFLS *Vidéogrammaire* project, of the SUFLRA-produced *Lyon à la Une*, of *Thèmes* and the other courses produced at Oxford University by Peter Dyson *et al*. See References.) But the flow now seems to have largely dried up, leaving the field largely restricted to well-resourced professional volume producers such as the BBC. This tendency is understandable but the result is a virtual monopoly coupled with an unquantifiable black market. This is not a healthy situation. Brian Hill, offering an otherwise largely positive appraisal of commercially produced language learning programmes, nonetheless points out some of the outstanding problems (Hill, 1996: 226–7):

• some courses fail to meet the learning objectives expected of them by producers and/or learners;

• the drop-out rates of independent adult learners using such programmes is very high;

• in the day to day hurly burly of the classroom, many teachers still fail to fully avail themselves of existing resources;

• an incomplete understanding of the relationship between understanding, practice and learning – a confusion of 'listening for gist' with 'listening for learning' – has led to some programme makers to present material too rapidly, with insufficient opportunity for practice.

If purpose-made video is not without its problems, nor is the staple of many advanced language courses, namely off-air recordings. In this respect, one of the claims made for video – namely that it apes real communication by offering visual cues – reveals itself to be highly questionable. The research reported by Kellerman in this area (notably that by Reisberg *et al*) indicates quite specifically that it is actually the ability to see the lips, mouth and jaw of the speaker which produces significantly higher comprehension scores on the part of listeners (Kellerman, 1990: 276). In media circles, there is – unfortunately for language teachers – a tendency to scorn 'talking heads', which means for example that most documentaries are narrated by voices off. Even news bulletins are read to an accompaniment of filmed footage, the images of which do not always correspond to the spoken word.[2] Despite these reservations, video still remains a major resource for second language learners and teachers. In this volume, Jim Coleman charts the various ways in which it has been and can be effectively exploited, while Anne O'Keeffe examines its use for conveying pragmatic and sociocultural information to learners.

3.1 Videoconferencing

One possible solution to the problems raised in connection with the use of off-air video may be to explore the opportunities offered by videoconferencing, especially when this is undertaken in conjunction with, say, an e-mail exchange and given a specific focus. The latter may be vocationally oriented – the encounter may take the form of a job interview or sales presentation, or it may encourage the exploration of cultural identities, by means of the exchange of sample 'culture packages' between paired classes in different countries, to be opened onscreen. English readers will be happy to learn that such packages, especially when received from France, regularly contain gastronomic and even alcoholic delicacies. A choice is available between ISDN-based videoconferencing, which uses standard telephone lines and desktop video conferencing, using a PC connected to the Internet. While the former will give the kind of high quality images that are appropriate for second language learning, line rental charges remain expensive. Internet-based video conferencing, though free of charge to Higher Education Institutions, is dogged by slow refresh-rates, which means that the information it offers about articulation is of poor quality and arrives with a time delay. Nonetheless, experiments with desktop videoconferencing are being pursued both in secondary and higher education and those responsible for them have reported improvements in a range of aspects of language use (pronunciation, intonation, fluency and accuracy), as well as gains in confidence and motivation on the part of their learners (Butler and Fawkes, 1999: 46–7). Unfortunately, they also indicate that videoconferencing ideally

7

requires dedicated space and technical support both in-house and from the manufacturer. Clearly a sympathetic senior management and a supportive supplier are indispensable for this kind of initiative.

3.2 The video camera

As an alternative to simply watching video, Broady and Le Duc report two initiatives in which students were encouraged to use video cameras to record collaboratively produced situational scenarios and news reports. Both exploited the opportunity this offered for participants to reflect on their performances (including viewing video recordings made by themselves and others). Learners found both projects to be motivating and felt that their confidence in using French had been raised. The conclusions arrived at by Broady and Le Duc may serve as guidelines for those wishing to experiment with project work using video recording. They are (adapted for brevity):

- It is important that learners see themselves as communicating in video, rather than producing examples of the target language for video.

- Learners must feel in control of the technology.

- Learners should be given explicit responsibility for group management tasks, such as setting deadlines, defining task specifications, allocating roles, to help them to focus quickly on the task in hand.

- Learners must evaluate themselves. Video recordings can help in this. Learners can develop evaluation skills gradually by watching and commenting on other anonymous learners' video recordings.

- Learners require a clear framework for the use of their imagination, to fuel their language learning. (Broady and Le Duc, 1995: 77)

4   Information and communication technologies

If audio and video, in their various manifestations, continue to serve as useful aids to language learning and teaching, it is now clear that the information and communication technologies can do much more than that. The sheer potential of computing in the field of languages is evidenced by the volume and dynamism of activity being invested in the devising and evaluating of new software and applications. This has manifested itself in an unceasing proliferation of acronyms. IT (Information Technology) has given way to ICT (Information and Communication Technologies) to reflect a significant enhancement of the role and potential of computers brought about by networking. Equally CALL (Computer-Assisted Language Learning) has spawned such variants as TELL (Technology Enhanced Language Learning) which has subsequently mutated into WELL (Web Enhanced Language Learning) to express a related shift in focus. More seriously, the sheer volume of publication devoted specifically to ICT-related applications in language learning indicates that it is on this sector that the vast majority of linguists with an interest in education technology have decided to concentrate their energies. Europe alone has two journals of international stature *Computer Assisted Language Learning* and *Re CALL*) in the field, while a third (the *CALICO* journal) is published in the United States. Both in Europe and North America associations of those interested in using computing for learning languages have been formed (EuroCALL and again, CALICO). The former holds annual conferences of which it publishes the edited proceedings. In none of the other branches of language-related technology are such developments to be found. Moreover, interest in the use of technology for second language learning remains bewilderingly scant in the Applied Linguistics community as a whole, on this side of the Atlantic. Only *System* lives up to its self-description as 'An International Journal of Educational Technology and Applied Linguistics'.

4.1 Computer assisted language learning

Given the impact of global networked computing, and the kind of fundamental changes it seems set to bring to the ways in which we both live and learn, one may be forgiven for wondering if the days of what we must now call 'traditional CALL' are numbered. We should remember however, that CALL, unlike the language laboratory before it, has actually made a spectacular recovery from what was in effect a very bad false start (Hewer, 1996: 229). We should not underestimate either its resilience or its flexibility. Nor should we ignore its key strenghs. Sue Hewer identifies these as:

• the ability to provide learners with instant feedback

• the ability, by means of branching, to offer learners the opportunity of navigating their own way through a set of learning materials

- the ability to conceal or reveal information, thus surprising the learner.

Catherine Pope, in 'Learning from jumble', explores the pedagogic implications of using software which exploits the computer's ability to displace – rather than actually conceal – information. She concludes that, suitably used, it can increase confidence and competence and promote learner autonomy. In fact, text reconstruction and manipulation tasks demand a complex cognitive response from the learner, which may mean that, though based on a very simple operation, they are pedagogically preferable to the branching activities that we as teachers might instinctively prefer. This at least was the conclusion of Legenhausen and Wolff, in a comparative review of two pieces of software based on these two principles (Legenhausen and Wolff, 1990: 12). The comparative study conducted by Liam Murray focuses on a different set of distinctions. Murray examines student attitudes when confronted – on the one hand – with agentive (here, text-based) and – on the other – with instrumental (multimedia) CALL software. He shows how students' evaluative sensitivity is heightened by their use of the various kinds of software and how this influences their perception and expectations of other CALL materials.

Though convinced of the value of CALL, one reservation about the volume of effort being expended in the field must be voiced. Essentially, this concerns just how well that energy is being directed. The work of Mike Levy, for one, casts some doubt on this. Exploring the role of instructional design theory in CALL development, Levy surveyed 104 key CALL practitioners worldwide. He discovered that only 17.6% of new CALL applications were derived from a 'higher level theoretical framework', while 18.6% were devised in response to a 'lower-level task or problem'. (A further 14.3% were derived from existing CALL applications.) Levy concludes that traditional instructional design principles, in which media selection is the penultimate step in a nine-part sequence, are probably inappropriate for CALL development. But his observation that 'responses to the CALL survey represented the whole spectrum, from highly structured, linear, systematic processes to largely unstructured, iterative ones' should be heeded as a warning (Levy, 1997: 51). Levy concedes that instructional design can be a dynamic process, which entails both the transformation of existing goals and the discovery of new ones. But he concludes that a sizeable number of current CALL practitioners are technology-led proceduralists whose work has no coherent theoretical support. He contrasts this group with the formalists, who give primacy to theory, even though this may limit their opportunities to exploit technology to the full. Levy himself argues for a dynamic concept of 'fit' between theory and technology (Levy, 1997: 54).

4.2 The Internet

If traditional CALL – conceived and designed within an appropriate theoretical framework – continues to have a role as an aid to language learning, two other developments in computing seem likely to do much more than this. The first of these is the Internet, which is by its very nature the interactive communication tool *par excellence* for language learners. The plethora of possible uses of the Internet are charted in Mark Warschauer's edited volume *Virtual Connections*. There is little sense in repeating the exercise here, except to say that the possible applications include the use of e.mail (for interaction between teachers and students, between individual students, or between whole classes), bulletin boards, newsgroups, mailing lists, discussion forums, real-time conferencing and MOOs (multiple-user domains, object oriented: i.e virtual edifices around which learners can navigate and in which they encounter and interact with other cybernauts) (Warschauer, 1995: *passim*). Some of the purposes to which these applications have been put are: supporting student writing, project work of various kinds, including the exploration of cultural stereotypes, the creation of a slang dictionary, shared story creation, dialogue journals and cyber surveys, as well as the delivery of entire courses. In the present volume, Caroline Sheaffer-Jones explores how a bulletin board may be used to improve the written communication of advanced learners of French, by fostering a constructive community learning environment.

In Europe the major Internet-based language learning project of the last decade was the International E.mail Tandem Network, established in 1994 by Helmut Brammerts of *Ruhr-Universität Bochum*, on which pioneering work was undertaken by language teachers from ten European countries, including the University of Sheffield, the *Universidad de Oviedo* and the *École Nationale Supérieure des Télécommunications* in Paris. The project was later joined by the Centre for Communication and Language Studies of Trinity

College Dublin, which brought considerable expertise in the theory of learner autonomy to it and did more than any other body to publicise its activity.

In 1997, Jane Woodin highlighted the extent to which the Internet made computer mediated communication across language boundaries not merely compatible with – but increasingly central to – communicative learning activity at advanced levels. Woodin's empirical study, 'E-mail tandem learning and the communicative curriculum' charts an e-mail tandem exchange between native speakers of Spanish and English who are learning each other's language, focusing particularly on the activities of 6 English non-specialist learners of Spanish. She seeks to assess the success of their learning experience by means of 6 indicators (wording adapted, for reasons of brevity) (Woodin, 1997: 23):

- exposure to language (the quantity of e-mails written and received);

- active learning (asking for information and commenting on that received);

- negotiation of meaning (establishing a relationship with a partner);

- error correction (how much do they seek and give this?);

- use of cultural information (in an end-of-semester presentation);

- re-use of language provided by partner (also seen as evidence of active learning).

Surveying the group, Woodin concludes that certain factors made for success in this particular batch of e.mail tandem learners (Woodin, 1997: 27). They were:

- prior experience of living in the other culture;

- integrative motivation (i.e. a personal interest in the L2 and its culture);

- the possession of basic e-mail skills.

The main problem she reports was a sense of 'dehumanisation', in that 4 out of 6 participants in the project felt that they were dealing with a machine, rather than another person (even where the content of their messages strongly suggested the contrary). This she explains in terms of Trent Batson's comment that, in the networked classroom 'communication is with the screen in front of you, in your private social space, not with a person many feet distant, out in public space' (cited in Woodin, 1997: 27). However, it may also be that this feeling was a function of personality, since all four of these learners also identified themselves as people who liked working alone.

Woodin insists on the high level of interpersonal, organisational and linguistic skills required for successful e.mail tandem learning. It is clearly of primary benefit to learners whose language proficiency is already advanced. Nonetheless, she argues, it offers a bridge between the necessary artifice of the language classroom and the real world of language use. As an approach to advanced level learning, it is clearly communicative, because it entails (wording adapted for brevity):

• the use and understanding of authentic language;

• real communication;

• the development of learner autonomy;

• the deployment of a full range of communicative competence (including the use of communication strategies to solve any problems in the transmission of information);

• the elaboration of a new form of language use: e-mail discourse (Woodin, 1997: 31).

The present volume contains two tandem-related contributions. Lesley Walker examines the strategies for collaboration between learners that make for a successful e.mail tandem partnership, while Jane Woodin and Liz White chart the uses made by learners of a bilingual (Spanish/English) discussion forum.

4.3 The World Wide Web

The Internet is such an obvious and powerful instrument for collaborative language learning that, to some extent, the World Wide Web proper, for all its glamour, can seem somewhat anticlimactic. Despite the interactivity of many World Wide Web sites, it is after all Internet applications, rather than the Web, which have converted the computer from an information provider into a communications tool. Moreover, a survey conducted by Couzin and Falbo-

Ellis on actual Web use in Higher Education revealed that 'much of its potential still remains to be exploited' by both learners and teachers (Couzin and Falbo-Ellis, 1999: 190). In particular, they found that:

- most institutions had as yet made little use of telematic resources, despite investing in infrastructure and hardware;
- the commonest use of the Web was as a source of materials by teachers (rather than learners) and that cases of its interactive or communicative use were very few;
- most training in Web use had been by individual, rather than institutional, initiative;
- the major obstacle to its more effective use was the lack of staff training. (Couzin and Falbo-Ellis, 1999: 186 [wording adapted]).

Sue Hewer describes Information Technology as 'a medium for solutions' rather than a solution in itself, which means that 'it is what people do with it that determines its worth' (Hewer, 1996: 229). Of no aspect of the new technology is this more clearly the case than the World Wide Web. Its role as an information source may not seem particularly dynamic, but one should not by any means underestimate the volume, range and specificity of the information on the Web. This can be of particular use for subject-specific project work by advanced language learners, especially those specialising in other disciplines. They will often find that there is a dearth of second language texts on their particular specialism, in their home university library in UK. In such cases, the Web is the only obvious source to which they may have recourse. Even an hour spent giving hands-on training in the use of search engines can pay rich dividends in enhancing the quality of the work they are able to produce. But the use of the Web as an information source brings with it a significant problem. One of the features of the Web is that it allows one to copy text onto one's own computer. Learners are aware of this and sadly, cannot always resist the temptation to plagiarise in producing project essays, however stern the warnings one issues. Readers whose learners are already using the Web will be familiar with the problem. Those who are planning to encourage their learners to do so will need to build appropriate safeguards into their assessment procedures.

Information and news gathering is only one of five different kinds of use of the Web by language students charted by Mark Warschauer (Warschauer, 1995: *passim*). The other four are:

• research in bibiographies and databases;
• virtual travel (which can be particularly useful for those preparing for a period of residence abroad);
• finding and using interactive language learning sites;
• publishing student work.

Equally, Couzin and Falbo-Ellis in their lively and extremely informative article offer a succinct account of the advantages and disadvantages of Web use, as well as listing interactive learning sites and offering advice on how teachers can use downloadable freeware, such as *Hot Potatoes* to create their own interactive learning materials. Their appendix includes a list of 'Useful Web Resources for Language Teachers', including the address of the WELL (Web Enhanced Language Learning) project (see References), with which they are associated (Couzin and Falbo-Ellis, 1999: 192). Both it and the WELL project home page are quite simply a must-read for any one interested in the interactive use of the Web. In this volume Uschi Stickler and Elke St John, for their part, explore how Web-based transcripts, used in conjunction with off-air recordings of news broadcasts, can minimise the effort required for materials development by teachers and give students themselves more responsibility for monitoring the effectiveness of their own learning.

To all intents and purpose and for all its so far unfulfilled potential, an interest in the www is no longer optional. Robert Godwin-Jones, for one, is adamant that sooner or later all language teachers will be expected to take advantage of what the Web has to offer and warns that 'those who don't get ahead of the curve and find ways to get the technology to make sense in their discipline will down the road find themselves using pre-formatted, pre-digested, one size fits all models which make little sense for language learning' (Godwin-Jones, 1998: 2). For Godwin-Jones, the key strength of the World Wide Web is that it enables creative thinkers to invent new paradigms, in whatever discipline. To language teachers, he offers the following rationale:

Fundamentally we want to use technology to supplement what we do in the classroom and to help in doing what we can't do very well now (share multimedia, collaborate long distance, make authentic materials comprehensible). But we also want to use technology to help us think 'out of the box', to experiment with approaches we'd never thought of before (Godwin-Jones, 1998: 2).

4.4 Corpora and concordancing

If the Internet has resulted in a sea change in the relationship between computing and language learning, another development in computing may yet produce even more fundamental changes in our understanding of language itself. This is the ability of computers to compile and analyse large-scale language corpora. Such corpora provide factual information about the nature of language that was simply not available to traditional linguists, who relied heavily on intuition. Corpus-based approaches to second language learning have been publicly advocated for more than a decade now. Their application to the learning of modern foreign languages has been held back somewhat by the fact that until fairly recently, corpora in languages other than English were not widely available, nor were the multilingual concordancers capable of dealing with parallel or comparable corpora. This is no longer the case.

The impact of computer-based language corpora will be wide-ranging and is to some extent unpredictable. At the most basic level, corpora may be used to raise the language awareness of learners, particularly in the area of lexical selection (see Wichmann, 1995: 61–62). Small-scale corpora in specialist technical domains are also demonstrably useful for the teaching of languages for special purposes (see Beeching, 1997: 374). There is also evidence that hands-on concordancing of language corpora by learners may facilitate the acquisition of new vocabulary by mimicking 'the effects of natural, multicontextual lexical acquisition – reading – but in a more concentrated and efficient way' (Cobb, 1997: 314). Corpora are more than simply another language learning tool, however. Insights gained from corpus linguistics are likely to change fundamentally the ways in which languages are learned. Let us take as our starting point the organisation of the syllabus. The pioneering work, in this respect, was done by Dave Willis. In *The Lexical Syllabus: a New Approach to Language Teaching*, Willis, who worked in collaboration with the team assembled by John Sinclair at the University of Birmingham, explains with impeccable logic why this should be so. He takes as his starting point 'the glaring inadequacy of pedagogical grammars' and quotes both N.S. Prabhu and William Rutherford as acknowledging that 'we cannot begin to offer anything like an adequate description of the language on which to base a pedagogical grammar' (Willis, 1990: iii). If that is so for English, then how much worse must the situation be for other languages. Willis notes that similar conclusions have been drawn by both interlanguage theorists and classroom researchers, as well as by countless practising teachers, whose frequent laments give voice to the realisation that what is taught in the classroom (input) is very different from what is learned in the classroom (intake).

Willis therefore argues that the language to which learners are exposed should be:

a) *graded*, to avoid the demotivation that may result from meeting undue difficulties too early;

b) *selected*, so that learners are exposed to the patterns and meanings they are likely to meet outside the classroom;

c) *itemised*, so that important features of the language experience of learners can be highlighted and the potential learning outcomes from such experience can be identified and signposted.

For language syllabus designers, these are relatively uncontentious requirements. Yet – as Willis himself concedes – they run counter to the communicative approach which stresses the use of authentic, naturally occurring language. In support of his arguments, Willis convincingly points out that 'the 700 most frequent words of English account for around 70% of the English we speak and hear, read and write' and that 'the most frequent 1,500 words account for around 76% of text and the most frequent 2,500, for 80% of text' (Willis, 1990: vi). It seems clear that the frequency of lexical items, as measured by the corpus, should be the guiding principle for the organisation of the syllabus into levels and that is what Willis proposes, arguing that, in doing so, he satisfactorily resolves the contradiction between syllabus design principles and the teaching methodology associated with the communicative approach. Two contributions to the present volume deal with aspects of corpus use outlined above. While Marie-Noëlle Guillot explores the direct application of concordancing as a learning tool, Marie-Madeleine Kenning focuses instead on the use of corpora to inform syllabus design.

In fact, the insights derived from corpus lexicography may have wider applications even than this. Michael Lewis, for one, has expanded its influence to the sphere of teaching methodology and for much of the last decade has advocated a 'Lexical Approach' to language teaching (Lewis, 1993: *passim*), based on the view of learning as non-linear and language as primarily composed of lexical items (words, collocations, fixed expressions and semi-fixed expressions), which, 'when combined, produce continuous coherent text' (Lewis, 1997: 7). In this he draws support, not only from corpus linguistics, but also from SLA research, such as that by Weinert, which suggests that 'classroom learners (...) show extensive and systemic use of chunks', or prefabricated formulaic items 'to fulfil communicative needs in the early stages of learning' (Mitchell and Myles, 1998: 12). All of this represents a serious and mounting challenge to the post-Chomskian consensus view that the fundamental aspect of language is syntax. It offers a significant challenge to the dominance of the communicative approach. It should at the very least produce a re-evaluation of our understanding of how languages are learned and its longer term impact may be to change our understanding of language itself.

5 Conclusion

If current views of language learning and teaching are under threat from language handling technology, so too, John Sinclair believes, are the language professions themselves. For Sinclair, the threat stems from the spread of digital technologies, which he sees as devaluing and potentially rendering obsolete the traditional expertise of teachers, translators and applied linguists. In part, his warning stems from a long and successful career in corpus linguistics, which makes him sceptical about the claims to scientific status of theoretical linguistics:

> As one explores a corpus, constantly finding things that are recognised immediately but that do not yet have a place in the body of language knowledge, one may begin to wonder why so much of the obviously important structuring is not recorded in published descriptions, nor

retrievable by simple introspection. This especially applies to structures which pivot on lexical words (now often called 'lexicogrammatical' structures). Gradually, one's confidence in the adequacy of established descriptive methods is eroded. (Sinclair, 1999: 36)

Sinclair contrasts the relative lack of success experienced by linguists in producing adequate descriptions of the nature of language, or of the ways in which learners actually learn it, with some of the successes experienced by those using information processing models, which he regards as likely to supplant linguistic ones in the exploration of language and perhaps also in second language pedagogy:

The threat to us all is that in a growing number of applications of language, linguistic skill and knowledge may be marginalised or ignored; the reason for such policy is that better results can apparently be obtained quicker without reference to language expertise. And why not to language teaching as well? (Sinclair, 1999: 43)

One has to concede that Sinclair has a case. But so too do those who counter the claims of Natural Language Processing, by pointing out that it has so far fed very few developments in the actual delivery of second language learning. A marrying of the linguistic and information-processing disciplines is to a large extent already occurring. Is that a threat or a promise? With you, dear readers, lies the answer to this question.

References

Beeching, K. (1997) 'French for Specific Purposes: The Case for Spoken Corpora', *Applied Linguistics*, 18: 374–394.

Birks, R., Rouxeville A. and Schonfelder L. (1998) *Vidéogrammaire*, Paris: Didier/Hatier.

Bishop, G., Dyson, P. and Worth-Stylianou, V. (1995) *Dossiers France Télévision*, London: Murray.

Broady, E. and Le Duc, D. (1995) 'Learner Autonomy and the Video Camera: A Wider Role for Video Recording Activities?', *Language Learning Journal*, 11: 4–77.

Butler, M. and Fawkes, S. (1999) 'Videoconferencing for Language Learners', *Language Learning Journal*, 19: 46–50.

Cobb, T. (1997) 'Is there any measurable learning from hands-on concordancing?' *System*, 25: 301–315.

Couzin, G. and Falbo-Ellis, V. (1999) 'The WWW: Creating an Interactive and User-friendly environment for language learners', in D. Bickerton and M. Gotti (eds) (1999) *Language Centres: Innovation Through Innovation, papers from the 5th Cercles Conference*, Plymouth: Cercles, pp. 183–192.

Danaher, M. and Danaher, P. (1998) 'The Benefits of Language Laboratories for Learning Japanese as a Foreign Language', *Language Learning Journal*, 18: 50–55.

Dyson, P. and Worth-Stylianou, V. (1991) *Actualités TV – Presse*, Walton-on-Thames: Nelson.

Godwin-Jones, R. (1998) 'How can Language Teachers use the Web to help Students Learn?', *Language Learning and the Web*.
Available at: <URL http://www.fln.vcu.edu/cgi/l.html> [Accessed 15 February 2000].

Green, P.S. (1996) 'The Tape Recording Revolution', in E. Hawkins (1996) *30 Years of Language Teaching*, London: CILT, pp. 211–222.

Hare, G. (1988) 'Using the World Wide Web as a Resource in Modern Language Studies', *Language Learning Journal*, 18: 42–46.

Hewer, S. (1996) 'Information Technology', in E. Hawkins (1996) (see above), pp. 229–236.

Hill, B. (1996) 'Moving Text – TV, Video and Satellites', in E. Hawkins (1996) (see above), pp. 223–228.

Kellerman, S. (1990) 'Lip Service: The Contribution of the Visual Modality to Speech Perception and its Relevance to the Teaching and Testing of Foreign Language Listening Comprehension', *Applied Linguistics*, 11: 272–280.

Legenhausen, L. and Wolff, D. (1990) 'CALL in Use – Use of CALL: Evaluating CALL Software', *System*, 18, 1: 1–13.

Lewis, M. (1993) *The Lexical Approach: The State of ELT and a Way Forward*, Hove: Language Teaching Publications.

—— (1997) *Implementing the Lexical Approach: Putting Theory into Practice*, Hove: Language Teaching Publications.

Levy, M. (1997) 'Theory-driven CALL and the Development Process', *Computer Assisted Language Learning*, 10, 1: 41–56.

Little, D. (1998) *Technologies, Media and Foreign Language Learning*, Dublin: Authentik.

Sinclair, J. (1999) 'New Roles for Language Centres: The Mayonnaise Problem', in D. Bickerton and M. Gotti (eds) (1999) (see above), pp. 31–50.

Mitchell, R. and Myles, F. (1998) *Second Language Learning Theories*, London: Arnold.

Walker, A. *et al* (1986) *Lyon à la Une*, Edinburgh: University of Edinburgh Press.

Warschauer, M. (ed.) (1995) *Virtual Connections*, Honolulu: University of Hawaii Press.

The WELL project home page is at: <URL http://www.well.ac.uk> [Accessed 15 February 2000].

Wichmann, A. (1995) 'Using Concordances for the Teaching of Modern Languages in Higher Education', *Language Learning Journal*, 11: 61–63.

Willis, D. (1990) *The Lexical Syllabus*, London: Collins Cobuild.

Woodin, J. (1997) 'E-mail tandem learning and the communicative curriculum', *ReCALL*, 9, 1: 22–33.

Notes

1. Even the language laboratory should not perhaps be completely written off. As an intelligent recent study by Mike and Patrick Danaher suggests, carefully designed activities, reinforced by an appropriate level of teacher support can produce positive reports by undergraduate learners on the use of labs (Danaher and Danaher, 1998: *passim*. See below).

2. We are indebted for this insight to an unpublished research proposal by Elspeth Broady.

Video in university language teaching

James A. Coleman
University of Portsmouth

Introduction

It is twenty years since satellite television and the videocassette made it
possible for university language teachers to build learning activities around
recordings of genuine target-language speech. It is more than ten years since
technology married video to the computer, allowing the teacher similar
control over authentic spoken interaction as printing has for centuries allowed
over the written word. Spoken interactions between native L2 speakers,
captured in full visual as well as aural detail, have for two decades been
exploited as text for comprehension, as model for analysis and imitation, and
as stimulus for language teaching and learning within a communicative
approach. As technological advances today cross a new threshold, putting
unlimited, easily manipulated, digitised video at the command of every
teacher and learner with a networked personal computer, technical questions
are definitively relegated to the background, and it seems appropriate to take
stock of methodological issues. This chapter will seek to provide an overview
of the ways in which video is used today in university foreign language
learning. It will examine the rationale for bringing authentic spoken texts into
the classroom or resources centre, evaluate the advantages and drawbacks of
using video, analyse the different types of video document, and explore the
many pedagogical techniques for exploiting video in receptive and productive
activities to develop all four language skills and to motivate students to learn.

1 The technical and historical context

A historical review shows how technological development is accelerating. The first experiments in recording images using photosensitive materials took place in the late eighteenth century, and Daguerre's first black and white photographs were produced in 1831. Although the first colour photo was made in 1861, it was 1941 before colour film for still photography became generally available. Black and white moving pictures originate in 1891, and the Lumières' first film projection from 1895. Both relied, as film and video still do, on a series of still pictures, projected in rapid succession (24 frames per second for film, 25 for video), giving an appearance of continuous movement thanks to the persistence of retinal impressions sending nerve impulses to the brain.

The drawback with film is that it requires time for processing. The introduction of no-processing Polaroid photographs in 1947 was followed, in the early 1950s, by the first video recorders. They adopted the technology of sound recording, storing electrical signals from a television camera as magnetised patterns on the iron oxide coating of a plastic tape. The patterns regenerate the original signal when played. Videotape recording is immediate, requiring no further processing and allowing instant replay. The convenience was further enhanced by the replacement of reel-to-reel videotape by cassettes in the 1970s, but slowed by the co-existence of competing formats (VHS, Betamax) and different ways of encoding chrominance and luminance (NTSC, PAL, SECAM). It was at this time that university classrooms began to acquire video equipment – although for many years afterwards the inconvenience or unavailability of replay equipment reduced classroom video use.

Even in cassette, videotape remains a linear medium, and the early combinations of computer and video, where segments of tape could be selected by computer programs, were severely hampered by the time taken to disengage the tape, wind it forward or backward, and re-engage the heads: today's classroom teachers, of course, still primarily reliant on videotape, face the same problem. The Laservision disc and then the CD-ROM brought intermediate solutions for a professional market willing and able to lay down permanently its own video recordings, but required dedicated equipment. In the last few years, CD-ROM production has come within the scope of university budgets, as CD-ROM drives have become standard features on personal computers. And happily, with digital video recording and storage replacing analogue (for an analysis of the different processes, see Coleman & Rollet, 1997), and the widespread installation of data projection facilities, we will soon have in the classroom instant access to any part of our own purpose-made or off-air recordings.

Access to transmissions has also become easier. The dedicated satellite dishes installed in the 1980s may continue to serve for some years yet, but will be increasingly supplemented by bought recordings, digitally encoded terrestrial and cable broadcasts, and by the internet, where pioneering sites such as *Tagesschau* have shown that streaming video has applications in language learning, and not just in pornography: television and computer technology have converged. However, with digitisation comes encryption, and access to some digital broadcasts on satellite or cable may become restricted to subscribers within national boundaries.

A history of video in university language teaching has yet to be written. The BBC has been delivering language courses for seventy-five years, and it is they who pioneered or popularised many approaches to video use. Jack Lonergan (Lonergan, 1984) and Brian Hill's Brighton team helped spread the expertise to higher education. In the 1990s, the Open University first offered language courses, and its video course components too have been influential. Dedicated academics have produced advanced level materials – most notably the Scottish Universities' *Lyon à la Une* (1986), the first ever university language course based on a corpus of authentic spoken interactions recorded on video. But market forces have made commercial publishers prefer lower-level materials, and no doubt as universities increasingly welcome less proficient entrants, UK-originated courses such as Renée Birks' *Le Français en gros plans* will prove their worth. In less than fifteen years, the combination of moving pictures and computer control has gone from infancy (Coleman, 1987b) to maturity.

The residential model of a university, invented in Europe over eight centuries ago and dominant throughout the last millennium, is rapidly giving way to a dispersed model, with traditional course delivery supplemented by an intranet and by online learning environments such as WebCT. Internet-based desktop videoconferencing has reached an acceptable standard, and will be allied to the tandem approach which is itself probably the most significant methodological development of the decade now finishing to become a familiar part of adult language learning in all institutional contexts. Video is a natural, inevitable part of the new learning process. Reflecting on what language teachers do with video now can provide some insight into its enduring potential.

2   The theoretical and methodological context

Video is a tool. Like any other tool, it must be used with an appropriate technique, to achieve a desired outcome, as part of an understood process. To use video in language teaching is no different in nature from, say, using a brace and bit in woodwork. In the latter case, the objective is a round hole, the technique involves choosing sizes, angles and relative pressure, and the whole process requires some knowledge of the properties of wood and iron, and of how the density and grain of the wood must be taken into account to optimise the result. My analogy stops there: the point is that to appreciate the techniques which have been devised and developed for using video in language teaching and learning, one must first understand what are the goals and what is the nature of the process.

Theoretical approaches to second language acquisition (SLA), and related pedagogical considerations, have evolved at a different pace from video technology, but have profoundly influenced its use. Textbooks which summarise theoretical developments (e.g. McLaughlin, 1987; Ellis, 1994; Mitchell and Myles, 1998) tend to start no later than the 1950s, since this is when scientific research into foreign language learning began to become widespread, although naturally discussion of the process and objectives of language learning is as old as recorded history (Kelly, 1969), and has been tied to public policy and actual classroom practice for over a century (see Stern, 1983: 75–116 for a summary). It would be false to assume that developments in SLA theory have been quickly and universally translated into innovations in teaching practice, particularly in higher education, where practitioners may lack theoretical knowledge and pedagogical training, and the aims of language teaching were often closer to those which Kelly's (1969) historical survey defines as literary and scholarly rather than to objectives

Kelly would term 'social' and which nowadays are generally labelled 'communicative'.

Within a communicative approach, the adjective can apply to both the outcomes and the methods (Brumfit, 1984). The aim of communicative language learning is that the learner shall be able to use the target language, productively and receptively, in speech and in writing, to communicate with native and non-native speakers in real situations. Definitions of such communicative competence (Canale, 1983; Canale & Swain, 1980; Bachman, 1990), typically embrace a number of component competences: grammatical, sociolinguistic, discourse, strategic, interactive, and sociocultural. The mastery of the forms of the target language, of the linguistic, cognitive, affective and sociocultural meanings expressed by those forms, is seen as an intuitive mastery, enabling the learner to give maximum attention to communication and minimum attention to form, to use the target language creatively.

So what of the method within which video as a tool, and the techniques for its exploitation, are embedded? One key phrase is *extensive and intensive meaningful interaction in and with the target language*. You learn a foreign language (L2) by using it repeatedly in meaningful interactions: by listening, by speaking, by reading, by writing. So the target language or L2 is used not only by the teacher as the means of classroom management, but also between learners in social interaction. Most of the activities described in this chapter assume a monolingual L2 classroom, and therefore intermediate or advanced learners. Little, Devitt & Singleton (1989) underline, however, that interaction with the target language, in purely receptive mode, can be equally fruitful. Thus, receptive, productive and interactive use of the target language can enhance language learning, depending on the learner's psychological involvement with the material. Authentic material can in its turn enhance this psychological involvement.

Definitions of 'authentic' vary, but, broadly speaking, an authentic document is one produced for a purpose – a communicative, social purpose – other than to be used in language teaching. The definition applies equally well to writing or recorded speech, to television adverts or magazine adverts, to newspaper articles or television interviews, and even to cinema, although, as Eisenstein asserted, 'Film is by its very nature calculated deceit'.

While there may be interesting typological distinctions to be made between video documents – soaps or news broadcasts are scripted, for example, while interviews are normally not, but may nonetheless be semi-scripted, or at the least influenced by the presence of the camera – such distinctions are best subordinated to practical classroom considerations: any video document, authentic or not, may be considered for use with learners, and while the principle remains valid that the principal input to communicative video classes should be naturally-occurring, contextualised speech, teachers in the real world are eclectic, glad to *faire flèche de tout bois*. To convert the input to 'intake', the classroom focus needs to be primarily on an activity or task, rather than the language itself, although foreign language acquisition is enhanced by a focus on form as part of the exploitation of authentic inputs, to ensure that learners notice how meaning is encoded in target language form.

3   Video advantages. Why video?

So why has video come to be regarded as an essential part of language teaching at university?

3.1 Firstly, as input it is cheap, inexhaustible, topical, lively, and professionally made with all the technical and aesthetic qualities which experienced audiences demand.

3.2 Secondly, it provides authentic foreign language input in a controllable form: speech without ephemerality.

3.3 Video provides a variety of input which no teacher, even the most talented thespian, can offer: a variety of speakers (old/young, child/adult, male/female, urban/rural, educated/uneducated, speaking standard/sociolectal/dialectal language), of topic, of location, of situation, of level of formality, of language function. The expression of emotion through language, especially extreme emotions such as anger or grief, which are especially difficult for non-native speakers, cannot be authentically portrayed through any other medium.

3.4 With video, the verbal communication is not stripped of the paralinguistic signs – facial expression, gesture, posture, etc – which accompany all natural speech.

3.5 The visual context provided by video but not by audio-only recordings offers clues to the communicative situation, including speakers' identity and level of formality, which is essential to grasping the pragmatic and other variables which determine the exact language used. It may also incorporate aspects of the L2land (target language community) culture in landscape, dress, interpersonal behaviour and so on, some of which the learner may wish to imitate, others merely to comprehend. (The many uses of video in area/cultural studies courses are beyond the scope of this chapter.)

3.6 Video input, appropriately selected, can offer more clues to comprehension than other media, since students are viewing the speakers in context, with full paralinguistic information, and often lip movements to help them. The redundancy of verbal and non-verbal content in much broadcast material helps less proficient learners.

3.7 Video is infinitely flexible, with its different document types some of which are reviewed below. It is adaptable to all levels of learner, with many users stressing that while you can choose simpler natural dialogue or even action without dialogue in the Mr Bean mode, what matters is that the *task* is adapted to the learners' competence, rather than the video material. It can be suited to all teaching styles, particularly the conception in which the teacher is facilitator or *animateur*, not a focus of attention and dispenser of wisdom but a guide and resource, structuring and supporting students' learning. As we have seen, it corresponds well to a communicative methodology but allows the teacher to adopt an eclectic approach. Video is to the spoken language what the printed word is to the written language. In both cases there is no single *mode d'emploi*, and very much depends on the tutor's judgment, matching the material and the activity to the class's level of proficiency, and to the balance of skills defined in the class objectives. Video is also easily adapted to independent and autonomous learning.

3.8 Video can enhance motivation and reduce anxiety. In SLA research, motivation was for many years defined, in the context of research by Gardner and his colleagues in Canada (e.g. Gardner & Lambert, 1972; for a summary see Coleman, 1997), as trait motivation, i.e. a more or less unchanging attitude. Key articles by Crookes and Schmidt (1991), Dörnyei (1990) and Oxford and her colleagues (Oxford & Shearin, 1994; Ehrman & Oxford, 1995) extended the theoretical context to embrace educational and industrial notions of far more transient motivations, and this broader definition is reflected in more recent surveys of motivational research (Dörnyei, 1998; Ushioda, 1996) and a new process model of language learner motivation (Dörnyei & Ottó, 1998; cf 'Ten Commandments for motivating L2 learners' in Dörnyei & Csizér, 1998). Video and video-based activities which are matched to the interests, needs, cognitive capacity and linguistic proficiency of the learner can be highly motivating. Additionally, it is not difficult with judicious use of video to demonstrate to learners that they are making progress in aural comprehension, thus triggering the virtuous circle in which perceived success generates self-esteem which in turn motivates to greater success.

In the language classroom, of course, teachers have long been aware that happy learners are more effective learners, and that involvement with the task can reduce the classroom anxiety and language anxiety (Horwitz, Horwitz & Cope, 1986; MacIntyre & Gardner, 1994; summary in Coleman, 1997), or in Krashen's term the affective filter (Krashen, 1985), which can otherwise be an obstacle to participation and thus to language acquisition. A relaxed and confident learner will exploit available input most effectively. As an MA student recently put it to me, communicative language teaching should be fun. The fact that our students watch television, on average, for three hours each day and feel comfortable with it should contribute to this motivation. If properly introduced, video is unthreatening – although it is necessary to provide active tasks which overcome viewers' natural passivity, and may be necessary with some students to counter the intuitive belief that enjoyment and serious learning are incompatible.

3.9 Video is by definition a *visual* medium, and humanity has evolved as a primarily *visual* species. The majority of our interpersonal communications take place through the medium of sight. Although humankind, uniquely among the great apes, has developed language, sophisticated auditory communication is a recent add-on, without which our near relatives (evolutionarily speaking) cope very satisfactorily. In any individual communication between two people, the contribution of language is a mere supplement to more fundamental messages which continue to be conveyed visually – by proximity, posture, gesture, facial expression and so on. In evolutionary terms, verbal communication without concomitant visual

29

communication is an extremely recent and unsettling phenomenon. While passive listening has a long history, and listening to the radio or to music can be relaxing, most of us have anecdotal experience of problems raised by audio-only communication. Whether we think of students who never attend language lab classes, of friends who will do anything to avoid making telephone calls – or other friends who have to doodle – of the incompetent driving of reps on mobile phones, it certainly seems (although if there has been empirical research, I am not aware of it) that the human brain has difficulty in processing spoken interaction at the same time as disparate visual input. Most recently, I have observed the phenomenon in web-based videoconferencing, where participants seem relaxed by the visual presence of the interlocutor, even if they almost never actually look at the screen.

Teachers who use video will have observed precisely this behaviour in class: even if learners are not watching the screen, the speakers' presence seems reassuring, reducing any anxiety occasioned by the unnatural presence of disembodied voices on audio cassette. The visual reinforcement of a spoken message, especially if viewed attentively, purposefully and repeatedly, must also assist memory retention: seen and heard is better than heard alone.

4   Video: disadvantages. Why is video not more widely used?

The principal reason given for not using video is inadequate facilities: old or insufficient VCRs, restrictions imposed by falling budgets. There is no alternative to proper video facilities, with remote control and real-time counter, in all language teaching rooms. This in turn requires adequate technical support and security measures – which in turn can become a further bureaucratic obstacle to free and spontaneous use. As video equipment with moving parts is phased out over the next few years, perhaps access to equipment will become easier.

The other main drawback to using video is the time required, firstly to locate useful material (unlike reading, the process cannot be accelerated by skimming, since the sound is lost), secondly to transcribe the material, and thirdly to prepare exercises and activities. There are ways of reducing the time taken: sharing the workload, pre-processing only good videos which will not date, devising self-access exercises, using templates for regular classroom activities. And of course, since video is a primarily spoken medium, it is not always necessary, and indeed may be undesirable, to undertake full transcription.

Tutor lack of confidence, or unfamiliarity with equipment, needs to be addressed through staff development: training is usefully followed by micro-teaching, with colleagues teaching each other on the basis of a very short off-air extract. Having role-played the teacher, each explains their choice of video sequence and of activity.

One of the most frequently cited arguments against video use is student passivity: this particular danger is countered by an appropriate choice of activity: video viewing should always be *active*. If, despite training, colleagues are still wary of using off-air video recordings, there are alternative approaches which retain many of video's virtues: they may be summarised as make it, buy it, share the work, or get the students to do it (see below, section 7).

A final disadvantage of video use is its limited shelf-life. Even if the topic is not one which dates rapidly, visual details give away the age of a recording, and students are easily put off by an out-of-date clip. Fashions in clothes and shoes change with particular rapidity – this is why publishers prefer cartoons in language coursebooks – and once a campaign is over, even ads look old-fashioned. This is perhaps the strongest argument for developing techniques for using off-air video with minimum preparation, so that last night's viewing can become tomorrow's class with least effort.

5   Using video in language teaching and learning

5.1 Basic rules

Video is not a panacea, and will not compensate for poor planning, poor syllabus design, or poor classroom technique. Rules of use dictate, firstly, that teachers should avoid overkill. Video is one type of input, one approach among many, and perhaps no more than one class in four should be video-based. Within the class, it is a mistake to try to cram in too much video: a three-minute segment is adequate for an hour's learning activity. The tutor should always re-establish the group dynamic and the exclusive use of the target language in each class before touching the equipment.

The tutor must know the equipment thoroughly, practising privately if necessary. Nor should s/he be hesitant about using all the buttons, not just play, rewind and replay: freeze-frame, sound-off vision-off and fast replay all have a place in classroom activities. It is vital to vary these activities, especially at the comprehension stage. And it should always be borne in mind that video is essentially for *spoken* language: during teacher preparation a transcript can mislead on audibility and comprehensibility, while during student activities the transcript should be used sparingly and late, if at all. It can be healthy to undermine adult learners' over-dependence on written props, and prepare them better for real target language use. Finally, one should beware of equating intellectuality of content with usability as authentic input for language classes. The recent French literary magazine *Apostrophes* – effectively a talking book watched by a forgivably somnolent cameraman – epitomises broadcasts with high intellectual snob-value but few of the qualities which make television motivating to students. Banal soaps or silly quiz shows can be far more useful in language learning.

5.2 Approaches

There exists an academic approach to video use: one begins by analysing a document into its genre, categorising the nature of the images, the nature of the sound, the degree of redundancy between the two, the communicative functions encountered, etc. While this may be good discipline for those unfamiliar with video use, I find it unrealistic unless the aim is to develop materials for publication or long-time use – at which point the question of ephemerality arises. Others prefer to separate the language skills, reserving video for a 'listening' class, perhaps with a sheet of comprehension questions. It is true that watching and listening to a video provides plenty of interaction *with* the target language, interaction which is enhanced by the authenticity of the input document. Personally, I prefer to mix skills in a non-linear way, alternating listening with interaction *in* the target language, and leaving aural comprehension for independent learning outside the class. This is not to say that the class should not be carefully structured: indeed, in what follows, I assume for convenience a rather old-fashioned sequence of Presentation > Practice > Production, where initial exposure to new material is followed by work on the detail of the video, and then by activities further removed from it. In this format, stage 1 incorporates presentation and gist comprehension, stage 2 analysis and listening activities, stage 3 practice in the form of close imitation and repetition, and stage 4 production (communicative activities and freer re-use).

5.3 Pre-processing

Prior to showing the video, some pre-processing may be necessary, especially with lower-level learners. This may take the form of revision or presentation of vocabulary, of introduction of the topic and its key terms, of an outline description of what learners are about to see. Such preparatory work can reduce the spontaneity of students' reactions to the material. More imaginative might be to give L1 phrases of which an L2 version is in the video text; students translate, then watch the video to spot the actual expression used. Alternatively, the tutor provides a series of near-synonyms; after discussion, students watch out for the phrase actually used.

5.4 Presentation

As a matter of principle, students should never be asked to write during the first viewing of the video extract. Also, the first viewing should normally be complete, unless the activity involves deduction from incomplete information (as in prediction, sound-off or vision-off).

5.5 Comprehension

The available options for comprehension activities give more or less emphasis to the gist or the detail of the extract, and more or less emphasis to the visual content. As with all activities, a balance needs to be struck between individual work, pair work and small group work. Some teachers like to introduce a fun element of competition, with teams striving to produce the most complete or most accurate answers. Learning will obviously be enhanced if students need not only note down answers, but also have to restate them to each other, to the teacher, or to the class, thus activating structures and lexis which were previously acquired, helping the memorisation of what is new or unfamiliar, moving learnt elements from recognition to active use, and contributing to the slow process of automatisation or the proceduralisation of declarative knowledge.

Turning the sound off obliges students to concentrate on the visual aspect – which is, as I have said, the principal reason for using video in the first place. On a second or third viewing, they note what they see, then in small groups (and in the target language) reconstitute the sequence of pictures and imagine what the missing dialogue relates. Such an activity embodies, as well as purposeful interaction within the class, two further widely applicable principles: the use of students' own imaginations, and the enhanced attention to the spoken text which arises from student prediction of what it will be. An alternative vision-only approach to comprehension consists of handing out a list of descriptions of successive scenes: students tick the images they have actually seen and number them in the correct order, later checking with a partner. This provides a way of feeding in new or uncertain vocabulary, and/or the metalanguage of television – *gros plan, travelling, fondu enchaîné*, etc.

Comprehension options with sound on are multiple, and need to be used in combination to avoid boredom. If the teacher has time to prepare worksheets, then these may take several forms. Gapped texts can help in the earlier stages of learning: to allow time for filling in, at least ten words must be left between gaps, which should normally focus on reusable structures and very common words, rather than technical terms, although gapping can also help to deal unobtrusively with hard passages (very rapid delivery, dialogue drowned by music, unusual structures and vocabulary). Gapped texts do, however, encourage reliance on the written word, while the essence of video is a concentration on the spoken word: the majority of learners will need to speak and listen far more than to read and write, and other techniques will probably be more appropriate to developing written skills. On the other hand, adult learners sometimes feel insecure without something in writing, and a gapped text may help wean them from over-reliance on written language towards feeling more comfortable with the spoken.

Comprehension grids or lists of questions are easily devised, and can move from general questions to the more particular – though without, at this stage, focussing on single expressions. (My examples are given below in English, but would normally be in the L2.) True/false questions can encourage students to distinguish between similar sounds, or expressions which are similar in form but different in meaning. If issued in advance, they can encourage comparison of synonymous phrases. They motivate careful listening and focus attention on details of expression, so are probably better at the stage of detailed, rather than gist, comprehension. An alternative is a vocabulary list: only 60% of the words listed are actually in the clip. Like comprehension questions, they may be issued in advance, after the first showing, or afterwards. In advance, questions draw attention to particular elements of the sequence – which may often be undesirable, if students seek to answer the questions rather than understand the whole piece. Issued afterwards, they encourage students to focus hard in order to memorise, which can be demanding but have a greater linguistic pay-off. Asking students to take notes to answer questions to be issued afterwards ensures they concentrate on the whole sequence. Putting questions on the overhead projector rather than individual sheets reduces tutor preparation time. If students, in turn, write their answers on the whiteboard or OHP for class discussion, there is less danger of reinforcing inaccurate interlanguage by leaving errors uncorrected.

By now, the sequence may well have been played four or five times, but since student attention will have been focussed on completing a task, repetition which would otherwise be unacceptable passes unnoticed, and students unconsciously absorb the words, the structures, the pronunciation, intonation and emphases of the speakers. This repetition of a short piece of language is one of the strong points of video as model for internalisation and imitation. Sometimes, I deliberately rewind too far.

There are further options: after viewing and note-taking, students devise five comprehension questions for each other, and ask them in pairs or teams. Students produce a summary, alone or in small groups, with or without guidance or a skeleton, such as the statistics or proper names appearing in the text. Multiple choice questions require a lot of preparation; their difficulty varies according to the closeness of the wrong answers; they can be used at the detailed comprehension stage to shade attitudes or emotions, draw attention to exactly how a question was asked, or the wording of descriptions, or matters of register; they can also concentrate on areas of L1 interference, or metaphorical/symbolic usage, or cultural allusions and so on.

The options for comprehension are still not exhausted. 'Who said what?' lists statements for students to allocate to speakers. The dialogue can be scrambled for pairs to put back in the right order; in a news report, the pictures are listed in a column in the correct order, but the voice-over column is jumbled. Or a slightly inaccurate summary can be provided for students to correct. Whatever the initial comprehension activity, checking and feedback should be immediate. They may include reviewing difficult sequences.

In each case, students should be encouraged to reformulate first the gist and later the detail of sections of the video document, so as to re-use structures and lexis as well as demonstrating comprehension. However, the temptation to exploit every word should be resisted. 100% comprehension is not needed: better to avoid saturation and over-working the material.

From the tutor's point of view, if working with the whole class, comprehension options requiring least preparation are to dictate questions (before/after first showing/after several showings with note-taking) or to require small-group reconstitutions from individual note-taking on a short section of video.

Occasionally, ask students to note roughly what percentage they have understood on a first viewing. After working on the text for a whole lesson, play it through in its entirety and ask them again to note what they understand: the message that working at a video improves their listening skills is both useful and motivating.

5.6 Splitting the group

Separating the group into two, where the classroom configuration permits, introduces one of the staple elements of the communicative approach – the information gap. If A knows something which B needs to find out, and vice versa, then there is a real communicative need to be met, one which makes learners concentrate on the sense rather than the form of their language, and at the same time can stretch them to use all their L2 resources, including re-use of material contained in the video input. If, additionally, the two have to accomplish a joint task with the data each brings, then negotiation is added to the linguistic functions employed, and the re-use of lexis and structures is intensified.

A simple example of such activities, sometimes called video split, is to let Group A hear the soundtrack without vision, Group B to see the pictures without the soundtrack, make pairs of one A and one B, and ask them to reconstitute the whole in the target language. To save making an audio copy of the video, one television may be turned to the wall, or a sheet of card stuck on with masking tape. In a variant appropriate to a news report with a voice-over, A's have a numbered sequence of images, only half of which have an accompanying description, B's have a jumbled soundtrack transcript. After a couple of viewings, they complete and compare: the activity provides help both with the soundtrack and with description.

5.7 Sound-off activities

Vision-only activities may move beyond mere comprehension. Students may practise inferencing by being asked to construct the dialogue using non-verbal clues contained in the images. Separate groups might be asked to concentrate on different features (e.g. characters, setting) before discussion in pairs. Extracts from feature films can thus provide a basis for work on the realisation of functions (e.g. phatic, suasion) and of notions (e.g. personal emotion), or on register, with learners discussing and testing out their intuitions in a safe environment. They can be asked to describe the scene, the decor, the characters, the action, the mood – an activity well suited to work on particular lexical fields. They might have to select music to accompany the scene – and to justify their choice.

5.8 Picture-off activities

Many scenes from feature films, documentaries or advertisements have a purely musical soundtrack, and great fun can be had in trying to guess from the music, in small groups, what the pictures might be. What is the setting? The situation? The story? Groups have to justify their choice. Even scenes with dialogue can be hard to identify accurately in the absence of pictures: the puzzle element and the anticipation of comparing one's guess with the actual video are very motivating. Attention may be drawn to non-verbal communication if students imagine and act out dialogue they have heard several times (or have the script of) before comparing their efforts with professional actors: such activity develops close attention to the nuances of language.

5.9 Imaginative activities: prediction, post-prediction

Motivation can be heightened where students are called upon to use their imagination. The first question and answer of a televised interview are shown a few times. Students in pairs or small groups, perhaps with some working on the whiteboard and/or OHP, devise five more questions, then work out answers for each other's questions (which may be intended to be accurate, or deliberately fantastic/comic): this helps sharpen concentration and comprehension, and sensitises learners to both the questions and the answers in the actual broadcast.

Prediction is of course an essential part of language proficiency in the native as well as the foreign tongue: it accelerates real-time language processing, even if it can be irritating when your interlocutor completes your sentence for you. So 'what happens next?' is a valuable lesson in inferencing which matches the fun of checking your own guess against the reality with enhanced attention and retention when hearing the actual version. After playing a short piece to give context, the tutor pauses the video and asks the class, in pairs or groups, to predict what happens next/what they're talking about/what it's advertising/what the news item is about. After hearing a representative sample of guesses, the rest of the piece is played. What is sometimes called retro-prediction is a variant on this activity: students invent the previous story-line in a drama, or the characters in a news story.

5.10 Description, lexical and syntactical work

Learners may be asked to describe the mood, the action, the music, the type of décor/scenery/landscape, the characters, the costumes, the qualities of the scene. This can lead to drawing up a list of several words/structures expressing a particular function/notion (futurity, positive qualities, approval, etc). Learning new vocabulary may be helped by translating from foreign to native language of phrases whose precise meaning is not known but is deducible from the context. More attention is drawn to the language itself if transcription or translation are used, or for example if students have to note how often particular words were used. At this level of detailed analysis, students may write a short transcription of part of the text, or correct the tutor's inaccurate transcription. Activities working on the detail of expression are similar to those found in written coursebooks: find a synonym, define in the target language, use in a new sentence, deduce the rule, what is the English equivalent, why the subjunctive, explain the use of tense, how does the level of formality influence the expression, etc.

But to these are added exercises on intonation and pronunciation, using the video as a model for phonological analysis and imitation to develop accuracy and fluency. The video is paused at the end of an appropriate sentence, which a student repeats verbatim. Repeating whole sentences at real speed not only develops *fluidité verbale*, but also, like so many classroom activities, shows students what they can usefully be doing when using video in self-access mode. The fun is increased when a couple of students, at the end of a lesson in which a piece of film dialogue has been studied, deliver the dialogue to match the speakers' lip-movements.

Personal involvement may mean better retention, so activities eliciting a personal response to issues can be used: what are the first five words you think of when seeing this? What is your response to the presentation? Was it well done? Was it fair?

Rather than giving a short passage to be translated in writing, it can be more fun and more authentic to work on subtitles. Once students have studied some and defined their characteristics (notably concision), a strip of cardboard and some sticky tape allows groups to write their own, then compare them with the – often inadequate – professional version.

5.11 Extension work

Initial study of a video can give rise to a number of wider activities, in which newly learned language can be incorporated into the learners' repertoire. The topic of the extract may lead to a role play, a discussion or formal debate, a pastiche or parody. The location of matched written documents (statistics, a multi-strand advertising campaign, a newspaper report – particularly easy with news items) allows comparisons of style and register, and other information-gap activities, for example where the position adopted by a newspaper and by a television reporter on a recent film or event are opposed to one another. Where production and editing facilities are available, groups of students may prepare a reportage, news broadcast, mini-documentary or TV advert.

6 Types of authentic video document

Certain types of video document lend themselves to particular forms of exploitation. The next section considers the specific characteristics of news, adverts, films, quizzes, documentaries, soaps, etc and offers some self-access templates for their use.

Any programme may be of value in independent language learning: a simple grid (normally in the L2) is enough to make viewing into an active task. A 'comments' box is included to encourage the learner to become more involved, and thus more likely to concentrate on the programme and to retain elements of it.

What kind of programme?	
Duration	
Target audience	
Comparison with similar programmes in UK	
Aspects of language – what register(s)? – what lexical field(s)?	
Presentation: studio? Location? Report? Interview? Discussion? Feature film? Voice-over? Scripted?	
New language learnt	
Comments	

6.1 News

Television news is more often used in the language classroom than any other type of broadcast. It is not hard to see why, even if we set aside the intellectual snobbery which equates weight of content with value as language input, and if we discount the obvious dual purpose of area/cultural studies content – learning *about* the country through its language. Newscasts are topical, cut into discrete short sequences, with a high speech:image ratio. They offer clear speech, often to camera, in a standard variety little marked by dialect or sociolect. Students' pre-knowledge of recent events of global importance – whether American politics, natural disasters or sporting events – helps their comprehension. The content keeps teacher and student alike in touch with a country's cultural and linguistic development, including the spread of neologisms.

On the other hand, from a teacher's viewpoint, news is ephemeral so there is little point in investing time and effort to prepare classroom materials around a news broadcast. Students are bored by old news, and can easily be saturated by over-exposure to this single type of television. The range of topics is narrow, and mostly depressing, especially cumulatively. A single language function, that of exposition, is privileged, even where the broadcasting channel has revised the format, introducing two presenters to break the monotony, or inserting semi-scripted 'live' question-and-answer sessions between studio presenter and on-the-spot reporter.

From a linguistic point of view, the newsreader's delivery is fast, while in film reports the reporter uses voice-over and cannot be seen, and there is often competing noise to convey local colour. Both studio and location reports are scripted, so the natural redundancy of speech, with its multiple aids to comprehension, is missing. The existence of a script can also mean unnatural delivery which is a poor model. The counterbalance to student familiarity with international news stories is that interviewees are often non-native speakers with bizarre grammar and pronunciation, or else interviews are in English or a third language with a faded-in voice-over. Where stories are local rather than international, they may demand impossibly high cultural knowledge, and topics may be of little interest to foreign students.

Although its content dates back at least to Quintilian's *Institutio Oratoria* of the late first century A.D., the standard listening grid for news recalls the poem of news reporter R. Kipling:

> *I keep six honest serving-men*
> *(they taught me all they knew);*
> *Their names are What and Why and When*
> *And How and Where and Who.*

News item	where?	who?	when?	what?	why?	comment
1						
2						
3						
4						
5						
6						

It is possible to exploit the fact that news broadcasts of whatever origin follow a similar format: Headlines, main story, second main story, other stories in order of importance, sport, optional silly story, recall of headlines, and sometimes weather forecast. One activity is to issue a list of headlines, and invite students to put them in order: this motivates subsequent viewing. Another is to view the items and ask students to write the initial headline, or *vice versa*. In this context, discussion of the relative importance of national and international stories (a) in general (b) in the target country's media (c) in one's own media can introduce a cultural element. Sadly, foreign students are unanimous in finding British television news parochial.

6.2 Adverts

6.2.1 Why use television adverts?

Ads are scripted but contain a high level of repetition and redundancy which aid comprehension. They are expensive to make, so every word, angle and shot is deliberate, precise, purposeful, and contributes to the message. They are short and self-contained, offering natural pauses for reflection and discussion. The usual verbal and visual redundancy, as well as being very helpful to less advanced learners, makes them suitable for a wide range of exercises (sound-off, vision-off, video split, etc), although, interestingly, more recent adverts dispense with such duplication and increasingly seek to be intriguing and amusing – hence suitable for prediction. They are professionally produced, authentic, attractive and stimulating. The topic is often motivating, and the language idiomatic. They have the immediate impact of news, but are less ephemeral, so re-usable for longer. The behavioural conventions and cultural allusions in advertisements help build sociocultural competence, while the message highlights the functions of description and suasion. They offer a good basis for self-access work, and it is frequently easy to find matched press ads which form part of the same campaign.

The drawbacks of adverts are equally numerous. Air time is expensive to buy, so the verbal content may be delivered too fast – and any video is demotivating if too difficult. Puns and word-plays can be tricky and not very productive, and the inevitable accompanying music may damage comprehension.

6.2.2   Using television adverts

Adverts are suitable for most types of comprehension task, with grids (see below) highly suitable for self-access work. Repetition exercises and sound-off dubbing develop phonetic and intonational accuracy. Transcription ensures students listen several times (thus internalising the model) and provides a basis for commentary on particular features, and for lexical and structural work, such as the study of synonyms and antonyms, or of collocations, especially noun + adjective.

Frame-by-frame description can be at first factual, later interpretative – students are often surprised by the number of cuts in a typical advert, and the number of details identified in freeze-frame which are not consciously observed at normal speed. What are the characteristics of the setting, decor, characters (sex, age, dress, socio-economic group, activity, etc), music, voice-over (what kind of voice?), and why has the maker chosen these? What is the mood? What is the structure – a sequence of images, actions (verbs), a mini-soap, a series of contrasts? For many subsequent exercises it is important that students become familiar with the resources and strategies available to a video director.

If the ad is stopped before the product is identified, prediction can embrace the product, the clues to its identity and 'what happens next?'. After watching a whole advert with sound-off, students can write the dialogue or voice-over and choose the music before comparing their efforts with the original. Vision-off can be taken one step further if small groups of students are simply given a transcript of the advert and have to invent the characters, setting, music, etc, themselves.

Analysing similarities and differences in comparison with L2 magazine ads for the same product, or with adverts for similar products in the UK, can be stimulating, as can analysis of students' own reactions to the ad. A corpus of adverts lends itself to analysis on several levels:

- *linguistic* – written vs. spoken registers, short sentences and slogans, repetitions and synonyms, weasel words and modals, verbless statements, abstract nouns; choice of person: je/tu/nous/vous/impersonal/imperative

- *attitudes* – portrayal of women, men, children, business life, ecology, fast cars, sex, childcare, etc.

- *strategies and techniques* – the combination of voice/text/image /music/ sounds; the voice-over (male or female, young or old, standard or dialectal, intimate, authoritative, etc.); contrasts and repetitions

Following which, a productive exercise works well, with students demonstrating their understanding of the medium and their ability in the target language by producing a videotaped advert, which may be serious, spoof or politically correct. Such an activity builds in a number of transferable as well as linguistic skills, and is probably best assessed as a group exercise, with a shared mark for the overall production and an individual mark for individual *journaux de bord* which include a diary, story board, and analysis of roles, problems and solutions. Based on my own experience, I would advocate banning adverts for the home town or university or any alcoholic product.

6.2.3 Sample listening template for adverts

Product/service
- Name
- Type
- Highlighted features

Target
- Buyer
- User

Technique/appeal
• Greed/Laziness/Vanity/Sexuality/Fantasy/Dream/Ecology/Snobbery/
Pseudo-science/Logic/etc.

Presentation
• Humorous/innovative/traditional/striking/visual/surreal/sexist/stereo-
typed/soap/etc.

Language
• Key or repeated words (positive/negative)
• Slogan
• What else?

Effectiveness: would it convince *you*?

6.3 Feature films and other genres

Available on video as well as off-air, films are too long for classroom viewing
in extenso, but are excellent for independent work, alone or in small groups.
The viewing grid which ensures active viewing might be as follows, once
again with scope for expressing personal views:

Title
Genre
Date
Period set
Summary of story
Comments on attitudes, characters, narrative techniques, actors, acting, visuals, camera work, etc
I liked
I did not like

As mentioned above, a strip of cardboard with two pieces of masking tape allows a range of activities based on sub-titles. Students may listen to L2 dialogue and write L1 sub-titles, or watch without sound and reconstruct the L2 dialogue from the L1 sub-titles. Such activities can lead, for example, to transcription and analysis of the dialogue and of cognate expressions, and then to L2 dubbing, with students watching the silent screen and trying to coordinate their lines with the on-screen lip-movements – great fun and excellent practice in developing *fluidité verbale* (near-native speed of delivery).

Quiz shows and **game shows** often share formats familiar to British viewers – each nation has its own version of *The Price is Right, Wheel of Fortune*, or *Countdown*. The predictability and repetitiveness of the language helps understanding, and they offer huge scope for imitative role-plays. **Soaps** are good for conventional and phatic language – greetings, apologies, invitations, condolence, telephone formulae – and for emotional terms. **Cartoons** offer an impoverished visual environment, and may well have been dubbed from an American or Japanese original, but they provide a skeleton structure for dialogue writing in the same way as a guided essay can support original L2 writing, and allow L2 dubbing as described above. Programmes with videotext support make possible a range of activities based on comparison of written and spoken registers.

7   Self-access viewing

It is perfectly possible to make unprepared satellite viewing purposeful, especially after student familiarisation in class. Simple grids give a purpose to one-off viewing, regular news watching can be recorded in folders or on-line diaries, while thematic dossiers can be built up over a term or semester, providing the basis for a class presentation or written summary and analysis of news treatment of a particular theme (finance, defence, European Union affairs). Open access viewing can be integrated in many ways into regular coursework. Task-based projects developing transferable skills, including the skills of video production, are now quite widespread (see e.g. Coleman, 1992). In many cases, video is the output.

Typically, a five-minute video is accompanied by a written dossier on the theme, incorporating a diary of the project. Within a set field such as contemporary France, self-selected groups of 3–6 students negotiate a topic with the tutor – the negotiation helping student motivation. In-class familiarisation with the camera, pre-production, filming, and post-production (editing) de-demonises it. Three or four weeks are allowed – any less and the task is impossible, any more and it dominates all other work and colleagues complain. To ensure proper planning, equipment use is limited to four hours' use of a domestic camera, and four hours in the editing studio. All four language skills can be developed, though it is very hard to encourage L2 spoken interactions outside the class or the videotaping itself. Exchange students can usefully be involved. Assessment criteria include transferable skills, since language students are seen as experts in communication – information research, retrieval and selection, information management, information structuring and presentation, teamwork, realistic objective-setting, assessing and utilising resources, organising selves and time, meeting deadlines, imagination and creativity, word processing and other IT skills, analytical skills, video production, written and spoken presentation skills. Questionnaire feedback suggests that students appreciate such a learning opportunity. Indeed, for not a few it is the only part of the course they remember after graduation!

References

1 Publications specifically on the use of video in language teaching

Several practical manuals on the use of video in the language classroom have been published. They frequently offer little or no theoretical back-up, although Jane Willis (in McGovern (ed.), pp.29–42) does look at the role of the visual element in spoken discourse. A full survey article on the use of educational technology in language teaching and learning was written by Jack Lonergan for *Language Teaching* (1990).

Allan, M. (1985) *Teaching English with Video*, London, Longman.

Birks, R., Udris, R. and O'Neil, C. (1998) *Le Français en gros plans*, Paris, Didier.

Blane, S. (1996) 'Interlingual Subtitling in the Languages Degree', in P. Sewell & I. Higgins (eds), *Teaching Translation*, AFLS/CILT: 183–208.

Bouman, L. (1996) 'Video, an extra dimension to the study of literature', *Language Learning Journal* 13: 29–31.

British Journal of Language Teaching, no. 28, 2/3, (1980): 59–226.

Broady, E. and Le Duc, D. (1995) 'Learner autonomy and the video camera: A wider role for video recording activities?' *Language Learning Journal* 11: 74–77.

Brown, Eric, (ed.) (1988) *Learning Languages with Technology*, London: NCET.

Buttjes, D. (1980) 'Schulfernsehen im Englischunterricht: fach- und medien-spezifische Leistungen am Beispiel des Westdeutschen Schulfernsehen', *Die Neueren Sprachen* 79: 378–95.

Candlin, J., Charles D. and Willis J. (1982) *Video in English Language Teaching*, University of Aston in Birmingham Languages Studies Unit Research Report.

Charge, N.J. and Giblin, K. (1988) 'Learning English in a Video Studio', *English Language Teaching Journal*, 42, 4: 282–7.

Coleman, J.A. (1987a) 'Putting Communicative Theory into Practice: The Pilot-testing of Lyon à la Une', in J.A. Coleman and R.J. Towell (eds), *The Advanced Language Learner: Papers of the Joint AFLS/SUFLRA Conference held in London in April 1986*, London: AFLS/SUFLRA in association with CILT: 213–54.

Coleman, J.A. (ed.) (1987b) *The Interactive Videodisc in Language Teaching*, Dundee, Lochee Publications.

Coleman, J.A. (1990) 'Starting with Satellite: A basic guide to using off-air video recordings in the language classroom', *Language Learning Journal*, 2: 16–18.

Coleman, J.A. (1992) 'Project-based learning, transferable skills, information technology and video', *Language Learning Journal*, 5: 43–5.

Cooper, R., Lavery, M. and Rinvolucri, M. (1991) *Video*, Oxford: Oxford University Press.

Fernández-Toro, M. (1997) 'Subject-specific video projects for beginners', *Language Learning Journal* 16: 40–45.

Fisher, B. (1993) 'CALL and Video in the University Sector – the Bangor Experience', in J.A. Coleman & A. Rouxeville (eds), *Integrating New Approaches: The teaching of French in higher education*, London, AFLS/CILT: 52–65.

Fisher, B. (1995) *Satellite Television in the Classroom. A Practical Guide for Language teachers*, CILT/National Comenius Centre of Wales.

Gardner, D (1995) 'Student-produced video documentary provides a real reason for using the target language', *Language Learning Journal*, 12: 54–56.

Geddes, M. and Sturtridge, G. (1982) *Video in the Language Classroom*, London, Heinemann.

Greaves, C. (1998) 'Language learning and multimedia on the Internet: defining a strategy for a virtual language centre', *The Hong Kong Linguist*, 18, 1: 18–26.

Hill, B. (1981) 'Some Applications of Media Technology to the Teaching and Learning of Languages', *Language Teaching and Linguistics: Abstracts* 14: 147–61.

Hill, B. (1989) *Making the Most of Video*, London, CILT.

Hill, B. (1991) *Making the Most of Satellites and Interactive Video,* London, CILT.

Hill, B. (1996) 'Moving Text – TV, Video and Satellite', in E. Hawkins (ed.), *30 Years of Language Teaching*, London, CILT: 223–8.

Jancewicz, Z. (1987) *Film and Television in Optimising Teaching and Learning English*, Warsaw University Press.

Lancien, T. (1986) *Le document vidéo dans la classe de langue*, Clé International.

Le français dans le monde, numéro spécial, 157 (1980).

Lonergan, J. (1984) *Video in Language Teaching*, Cambridge: Cambridge University Press.

Lonergan, J. (1990) *Making the Most of your video camera*, London: CILT.

McGovern, John (ed.) (1983) *Video Applications in English Language Teaching*, Oxford: Pergamon (ELT Documents, 114).

MacWilliam, I. (1986) ,Video and language comprehension', *English Language Teaching Journal*, 40, 2: 131–5.

Marsh, C. (1989) 'Some observations on the use of video in the teaching of modern languages', *British Journal of Language Teaching*, 27, 1: 13.

Meinhof, U. (1998) *Language Learning in the Age of Satellite Television*, Oxford: Oxford University Press.

Powrie, P. (1993) 'Interpreting from a video source', in J.A. Coleman & A. Rouxeville (eds), *Integrating New Approaches: the teaching of French in higher education*, London, AFLS/CILT: 79–94.

Price, Karen (1987) 'The use of technology: varying the medium in language teaching', in Wilga M. Rivers (ed.), *Interactive Language Teaching*, Cambridge University Press: 155–69.

Reader, K. (1990) *The Uses of Film in the Teaching of French*. Kingston-upon-Thames: Kingston Polytechnic.

Schilder, H. (1977) *Medien im neusprachlichen Unterricht seit 1880*, Kronberg/Ts.

Schilder, H. (1980) 'Stationen des neusprachlichen Mediendidaktik seit 1945. Versuch einer Ortsbestimmung', *Die Neueren Sprachen* 79: 330–48.

Secules, T., Herron, C. and Tomasello, M. (1992) 'The Effect of Video Context on Language Learning', *Modern Language Journal* 76, IV.

Stempleski, S. and Tomalin, Barry (1990) *Video in Action. Recipes for using video in language teaching*, New York: Prentice Hall.

Tomalin, Barry (1986) *Video, TV and Radio in the English Class*, London: Macmillan.

van Els, Theo, *et al* (1984) *Applied Linguistics and the Learning and Teaching of Foreign Languages*, London: Arnold: 280–97.

Walker, A. *et al* (1986) *Lyon à la Une. Livre de l'animateur*. Edinburgh: University of Edinburgh.

Zettersten, A. (1986) *New Technologies in Language Learning*, Oxford: Pergamon.

2 Other publications mentioned in the chapter

Bachman, L.F. (1990) *Fundamental Considerations in Language Testing*, Oxford: Oxford University Press, chapter 4.

Brumfit, C. (1984) *Communicative Methodology in Language Teaching*, Cambridge: Cambridge University Press.

Canale, M. (1983) 'From communicative competence to language pedagogy', in J. Richards and J. Schmidt (eds), *Language and Communication*, London: Longman.

Canale, M. and Swain, M. (1980) ,Theoretical Bases of Communicative Approaches to Second Language Teaching and Testing', *Applied Linguistics*, 1, 1: 1–47.

Coleman, J.A. (1996a) *Studying Languages: a survey of British and European students. The proficiency, background, attitudes and motivations of students of foreign languages in the United Kingdom and Europe*, London: CILT.

Coleman, J.A. (1996b) 'University Courses for Non-Specialists', in Eric Hawkins (ed.), *Thirty Years of Language Teaching: challenge and response*, London: CILT, 70–78.

Coleman, J.A. (1997) 'Residence abroad within language study', *Language Teaching*, 30, 1: 1–20.

Coleman, J.A. and Rollet, B. (1997) 'Television in Europe: issues and developments', in J.A. Coleman and B. Rollet (eds), *Television in Europe*, Exeter: Intellect Books: 5–20.

Coleman, J.A. and Rouxeville, A. (eds) (1993) *Integrating New Approaches: the teaching of French in higher education*, London: AFLS/CILT, 1993.

Crookes, G. and Schmidt, R.W. (1991) 'Motivation: reopening the research agenda', *Language Learning*, 41, 1: 469–512.

Dörnyei, Z. (1990) 'Conceptualizing motivation in foreign language learning', *Language Learning*, 40, 1, 45–78.

Dörnyei Z, (1998) 'Motivation in second and foreign language learning', *Language Teaching*, 31: 117–135.

Dörnyei, Z. and Ottó, I. (1998) Motivation in action: a process model of L2 motivation. *Working Papers in Applied Linguistics*, Thames Valley University, 4: 43–69.

Dörnyei, Z. and Csizér, K.(1998) 'Ten commandments for motivating language learners: results of an empirical study', *Language Teaching Research*, 2: 203–229.

Ehrman, M.E. and Oxford, R. L. (1995) 'Cognition plus: correlates of language learning success', *Modern Language Journal*, 79, 1: 67–89.

Ellis, R. (1994) *The Study of Second Language Acquisition*, Oxford: Oxford University Press.

Horwitz, E.K., Horwitz, M.B. and Cope, J. (1986) 'Foreign Language Classroom Anxiety', *Modern Language Journal*, 70, 2: 125–132.

Kelly, L.G. (1969) *25 Centuries of Language Teaching*, Rowley, Mass.: Newbury House.

Krashen, S. (1985) *The Input Hypothesis: Issues and Implications*, London: Longman.

Little, D., Devitt, S. and Singleton, D. (1989) *Learning Languages from Authentic texts: Theory and Practice*, Dublin: Authentik in association with CILT.

MacIntyre, P.D. and Gardner, R.C. (1994) 'The Effects of Induced Anxiety on Three Stages of Cognitive Processing in Computerized Vocabulary Learning', *Studies in Second Language Acquisition*, 16: 1–17.

McLaughlin, B. (1987) *Theories of Second-Language Learning*, London: Edward Arnold.

Mitchell, R. and Myles, F. (1998) *Second Language Learning Theories*, London: Arnold.

Oxford, R.L. and Shearin, J. (1994) 'Language learning motivation: expanding the theoretical framework', *Modern Language Journal*, 78, 1: 12–20.

Stern, H.H. (1983) *Fundamental Concepts of Language Teaching*, Oxford: Oxford University Press.

Ushioda, E. (1996) *Learner Autonomy 5: The Role of Motivation*, Dublin: Authentik Language Learning Resources.

Exploring television as an exponent of pragmatic and sociocultural information in foreign language learning

Anne M. O'Keeffe
Mary Immaculate College, University of Limerick

1 Introduction

It is increasingly recognised that being both fluent and accurate in a foreign language will not always guarantee successful communication between speakers. According to Hyde (1998: 10), in his discussion on intercultural competence in English language education, even if someone has perfected standard grammar and pronunciation, 'there is no guarantee that they will be effective intercultural communicators... Successful communication is not simply about acquiring a linguistic code: it is about dealing with different cultural values reflected in language use'. Communication is coded differently across languages and cultures, and unfortunately this dimension is not often explored in language learning. This paper will focus on the potential of using television material in language learning within the context of English as a Foreign Language (EFL), for the purpose of raising students' awareness of how certain aspects of communicating in their first language might differ in their target language. Crystal (2000: 3) tells us that over the past one hundred years, English has become spoken by more people in more places than ever before and that current estimates suggest that 1.5 billion use it as a first, or second foreign language – one in four of the world's population. This statistic is indicative of socio-economic change amid vast development in the way we communicate on a global scale. Communicating across cultures brings new challenges for foreign language teaching and learning; language course designers and textbook writers increasingly have to grapple with the cultural diversity of their 'customers'. In appealing to a global audience, course materials published internationally can easily become culturally diluted.

Burns, Gollin and Joyce (1997: 72–3) point out that 'if we believe that language learners need to be able to deal with the unpredictability of spoken language outside the classroom, then we need to introduce them to authentic texts in the security of the classroom'. Television and video have enormous potential for classroom use in this respect. Vanderplank (1996: 32) asserts that no teacher, no textbook, no classroom can provide the richness and variety of language, content, accent and culture that television can. Apart from providing a rich source of material for language development, the audio-visual medium also carries pragmatic richness, as to how a language is used as well as sociocultural information. This paper will examine the potential of television and video material as an exponent of pragmatics and sociocultural information in language learning. It is the contention of this paper that some of the pragmatic, social and situational norms of a language can be highlighted in the language classroom by using authentic television extracts from the target language as supplementary material. In so doing, learners can ultimately develop their awareness of *difference* across cultures.

1.1 Pragmatic information

Pragmatics is about distinguishing between what a speaker's words literally mean and what the speaker might mean by his words (Grundy 1995: 5) in that it deals with intended meaning. Within the framework of pragmatics, we can look beyond language at the level of grammar (syntax, semantics and phonology) and deal with how language users make sense of each other linguistically. By looking at language in this way, one can talk about speakers' intended meanings, their assumptions, their purposes and the kinds of actions they are performing when they speak (Yule 1996: 4). It is worth noting that the study of language in use and its users is normally carried out in the context of native speakers (for an interesting discussion of this, see Thomas 1983: 104). These speakers have, from an early age, become accustomed to the norms of using a language within a particular society. Take as an example the function of *thanking*, in Western English-speaking societies, children are normally taught to say *thank you* when they have been given something (see Aijmer 1996: 33–79). Yet this example would not be valid in the context of every language environment. In many societies, politeness can be expressed in ways other than saying thank you. For instance, the norm of politeness in English tells us that the utterance: *Could I have a cup of coffee, please* is more appropriate in a café than the utterance *I want a cup of coffee*, which would be interpreted as rude. However, in many languages, the latter, more direct, form of request would be much more common and indeed, the polite English equivalent, when transferred into some languages, could even sound obsequious.

Tomas (1983: 106) asserts that cross-culturally two things may occur which appear to involve a fundamental conflict of values, but in fact stem from socio-pragmatic mismatches: (1) in different cultures, different pragmatic 'ground rules' may be invoked and (2) relative values such as 'politeness', perspicuousness, and so on may be ranked in different order by different cultures. Along the same lines, Aijmer (1996: 33) notes that even advanced learners of English have problems with *thanking* due in part to the idiomatic nature of the phrases used and 'the socio-pragmatic constraints on their use...when one compares English with other languages, there are differences in whom one says *thank you* to, when one says *thank you*, the setting in which thanking is expected, etc.' Communication can break down between a speaker and a hearer from two different discourse cultures just as it can sometimes break down between native speakers. Thomas (1983: 93) provides the following example where a native speaker misinterprets the pragmatic information:

A: *Is this coffee sugared? [intended as a complaint]*
B: *I don't think so. Does it taste as if it is?*
    [misinterpreted as a genuine request for information]

In face-to-face interaction, native speakers can normally *read* the signals as to what is required pragmatically. Take as an example the utterance: *Is that right?*, as native speakers of English, we can usually infer from a given context whether the utterance is being used to query the validity of new information or if it is simply facilitating the flow of a conversation (as a backchannel, an utterance used to show speakers' interest or surprise, etc and which does not seek to take over the speaking turn – see Yngve 1970). Knowing which act is being performed by an utterance normally comes naturally to native speakers because they have acquired pragmatic competence as they acquired the language itself. In other words, they

55

intuitively know the ground rules. Pragmatic failure on the part of a non-native speaker can lead to more than communication failure according to Thomas (1983: 97): 'while grammatical errors may reveal a [non-native] speaker to be a less than proficient language user, pragmatic failure reflects badly on him/her as a person'.

Moving into a new language 'territory' turns up a pragmatic minefield for learners and dialogues that are found in foreign language course books cannot plausibly cover the vastness of pragmatic meaning which utterances can carry. For instance, most language courses begin with the function of introducing oneself to someone new, using, among other exponents: *Hello. How are you?*. However, in everyday usage, the same utterance often functions as a greeting rather than as a genuine request for health information. Indeed, in the absence of such pragmatic knowledge, a non-native speaker of English might reasonably infer that the speaker is being grossly insincere in asking the question *how are you?* without entertaining a reply. For language learners who wish to engage in face-to-face interaction with native speakers, it is essential that they have attained pragmatic competence in the target language. Gunn (1999: 17) refers to pragmatic competence as 'the art of consistently using both an appropriate meaning and form in given social situations'. It will be argued that television clips can be used as a means of sensitising language learners to pragmatic information.

1.2 Sociocultural information

Within any discourse culture, speakers follow a large number of social rules. As in the case of pragmatic information, these conventions are nurtured from an early age in children, for instance, knowing when to use *tu* and *vous* in French, knowing not to blow your nose in public in Japan and so on. The factors governing our choice of language and our behaviour in social interaction are culture bound and problems arise when these norms are transferred to a new language environment. It is not difficult to see how cultural misunderstandings occur. Cohen (1996: 254) talks about socio-cultural choices which he defines as the speaker's ability to determine whether it is acceptable to perform a speech act in a given situation and, if so, to select a semantic formula that would be appropriate in the realisation of a given speech act. He provides the example of when a professor is given a small gift in a university setting: an American person would choose to thank the giver whereas a Japanese person would normally apologise for being unworthy. On a broader level, when this idea is extended to social behaviour, an error can cause great offence and compound negative stereotyping. In some cultures, for example, it is possible, in certain situations of 'service encounter' (see Aston, 1988) such as a bar or café, to attract the attention of the person serving by whistling or hissing, while in other cultures, eye contact is the sole means of engagement. Obviously, to suggest that sociocultural components of a language can or should be taught is to enter the territory of linguistic imperialism. It is important, however, that foreign language learners gain an awareness of the sociocultural aspects of the language they are learning.

1.3 Audio visual material in language teaching

Tatsuki (1997: 13) describes video as an endless source of models of grammar structures, vocabulary, authentic discourse sequences and variety in pronunciation, conversational register and dialects. Pearson (1988: 143) states that television offers an open window on the landscape and culture of the foreign country bringing the land alive and enabling the learner to see as well as hear the speaker. Further to this, one can add the 'total situational matrix' (Rivers, 1964: 44): the external non-verbal context comprising facial expressions, gestures and associated objects and activities. Effective and systematic exploitation of selected video sequences could focus students' awareness of these aspects of the target language beyond the literal verbal message. On this point, Willis (1983: 36) warns that if this is to be achieved, teachers need to have a clear understanding of the visual medium and how it interrelates with the aural medium of communication. The most comprehensive attempt to analyse this area systematically in terms of how it relates to language teaching can be found in Riley (1981). Riley sets out to examine how video can be used in the teaching of comprehension. In order to use video effectively, Riley believes the role of the audio-visual channel of communication in interaction must first be explored. Riley (1981) identifies six communicative functions of visually perceived aspects of interaction. These features are extremely useful categorisations when applied to television material. In terms of adapting television material for the language classroom, Riley's work offers great insights into the non-verbal aspects of meaning.

2   Riley's model

At this point, Riley's communicative functions of the visually perceived aspects of interaction will be outlined and a suggestion will be made with each one as to how the function might be explored within a lesson so as to highlight the particular function for language learners. These suggestions do not constitute full lessons, in many cases they are basic strategies that can be incorporated into any lesson where video material is being used:

The deictic function

This refers to the way we point to people, physical places and objects in our conversational environment, e.g. Could you ask *him* to pass *that* book *there…* Language learners need to be exposed to language in an audio-visual context so as to prepare for the reality of face-to-face encounter. Language in interaction is not always explicit and it is often very allusive, especially when compared with the language used on language learning cassettes.

Classroom focus on deixis

One way of bringing overt focus to this area in the language classroom is to create a 'deictic void'. This can be achieved by viewing a television clip without its visual component, simply by covering the screen. A clip involving speakers whose relationship is close, where the shared knowledge is high and where some goal, for example, cooking, putting up shelves and so on is involved, will yield a high level of deictic items (see McCarthy, 1998: 3–47). As a follow up to explaining the concept of deixis to the class, a transcribed extract of the audio visual text could be explored. Students could be asked to identify deictic references and to consider the differences, if any, between deixis in their target language and their first language.

The interactional function

One of the main features of face-to-face interaction is the process by which speaking turns are negotiated. Riley reminds us that this is 'almost exclusively regulated by visually perceived non-verbal communication' (Riley, 1981: 148). Gaze, posture, orientation and gesture are used in this negotiation of who speaks when and to whom. Duncan and Niedereche (1974: 234) refer to *turn yielding signals* (TYS) which are displayed at points where the person who is listening might want to begin to speak. In their analysis of two-person face-to-face conversations, they found that in 92 per cent of cases where the TYS existed, the turn passed smoothly. The subtle differences in the way turns are negotiated across languages can be explored through television material.

Classroom focus on the interactional function

The exponents of the interactional function, the non-verbal process of negotiating speaker turns, may be examined in terms of how gaze, posture, orientation and gesture operate in a scene containing a business meeting, a political debate or a group discussion, etc. This could be compared with less formal settings where friends are chatting or where a family is gathered. Speakers could be numbered on a grid and students could be asked to note how speakers signal that they want to speak next. Looking at the speaker-relationships of the participants could be fruitful here since it may have a bearing not only on who speaks when and to whom, but also on how turns are negotiated in terms of level of formality. In comparative terms, it may be discussed how in some languages the non-verbal processes of turn-taking can be more aggressive than in other languages. Hierarchical aspects of turn-taking may be relevant to some language learners, where power and status strongly influence the process (some of the verbal aspects of turn-taking will be addressed in a subsequent section).

The modal function

This involves the non-verbal means by which we show commitment to the literal meaning of an utterance: a cynical smirk, a sympathetic smile or a dismissive shrug. This area can be highly problematic as one crosses from one discourse culture to another. In some societies, for example, a smile is used to accompany profuse apology while, in other cultures, smiling while apologising negates the sincerity of the verbal message. It is also interesting to consider the area of 'deadpan' humour where facial expression, or lack of it, is an essential part of the genre. In this case, when the subtle facial expression is missed and the sentence is taken literally, it can be highly confusing for the non-native participant in a conversation.

Classroom focus on the modal function

Examining the non-verbal means by which speakers show their commitment to the literal meaning of what they say involves looking at a video clip in micro-detail and so it is wise to select one or two utterances within a longer stretch of discourse. Subtle facial expressions and gestures serve as exponents in what Riley terms the Modal Function. The nuance carried by such facial expressions is closely tied to intended meaning and so students can focus on what particular facial expressions might mean, based on the non-verbal information as an extra dimension to the literal meaning of an utterance. Choose a suitable utterance and show it initially without the sound. Encourage students to guess what the facial expression might mean based on the non-verbal information, then introduce what the speaker actually says and explore the intended meaning. Obviously, this strategy is best suited to material which highlights the ambiguity between the literal meaning of the utterance and the visual message signalled by non-verbal exponents such as facial expression, shoulder shrugging and smiling, etc. Instances of sarcasm and humour could be chosen, especially with advanced levels. It is often only possible to gauge sarcasm, humour and irony from facial expression. Checking predictions encourages language learners to develop very subtle awareness of the nuances of non-verbal communication which can often be missed, even at very advanced levels.

The indexical function

This refers to the information communicated about a speaker's emotional state, age, social class, ethnic group, nationality and so on. The function communicates clues about the identity and frame of mind of the speaker in an interaction. These signals are very often misinterpreted from one culture to another, for example, the significance in some cultures of having a particular hairstyle or wearing certain clothing.

Classroom focus on the indexical function

The Indexical Function can be explored with most video material simply by asking students to make predictions about speakers' ages, emotional states, occupations, social classes, nationalities, ethnic groups and so on. In doing this, students will quite naturally draw on their own cultural framework when they try to create a character profile. Through focused discussion in the classroom, their 'judgements' about characters may reveal some interesting cultural differences since the indices on which we form our opinions may be coded quite differently across cultures.

The linguistic function

Here Riley classifies systematic gestures into four categories:

- Emblems (verbal substitutes, e.g., *OK* sign, *V* sign, thumbs up, etc);
- Illustrators (used to show the propositional content of the message, e.g., *It was at least this wide*);
- Enactions (gestures which add to the illocutionary force of the message, e.g., beckoning gesture which could accompany the utterance *Come here at once*) and
- Batons (usually head and hand movements in time with the stress, rhythm and tempo of the utterance).

Classroom focus on gestures

When using video in the language classroom, opportunities to focus on the meaning of different gestures should not be missed. Take, for example, the simple act of shrugging one's shoulders: in English, this functions either on its own as an *emblem* or verbal surrogate for *I don't know* or as an *enaction* adding to the illocutionary force of the verbal message *I don't know*. However, its use may differ in other languages, and as a classroom task, it is very interesting to explore gestures in this comparative way.

The situational function

The Situational Function refers to a macro-category encompassing everything from signs and buildings to behaviour in a given setting, for example, the setting and behaviour in a bank, an examination hall, at a bus stop or a supermarket – all of which are culturally coded. A sign saying *No Standing Anytime* on a New York sidewalk to mark an area where a driver cannot stop even temporarily in a car can be as confusing as an *L* plate on a car to signify a learner driver. Our expectation of what happens in public or institutional settings in our own society is not universally transferable. Riley (1981: 153) remarks:

> *Banks, churches and examination halls are all places where an English-man's behaviour becomes formal, reverential and hushed: but when one looks at, say, banks in the Middle East, churches in Italy or examination halls in France, it soon becomes obvious that this is not an immutable law of nature, merely a cultural choice.*

Classroom focus on situational functions

The situational function of most television material can be highlighted by overt comparison to the first language equivalent. The signs, symbols and behaviours associated with a situation can be compared and discussed with a view to sensitising language learners to the notion of difference.

3   Face-to-face interaction

Within the framework thus elaborated, the question remains as to how television and video can be exploited in language teaching and learning so as to raise awareness of the pragmatic and sociocultural pitfalls of verbal face-to-face interaction that might await a language learner. In this section, two areas will be examined. The procedures outlined do not necessarily correspond to complete language lessons; they are offered as prototypes, which can either be built upon, or which can be integrated into existing lessons. In reality, any class will be guided by the actual video or television clip chosen by the learner or the teacher, based on 'local' needs and learning conditions. It is hoped, however, that these suggestions are flexible enough to be adaptable to different languages, learning situations and different television material.

In each case, the teacher needs to focus the task by providing explanations or background as appropriate. This raises issues in terms of native versus non-native teachers of a foreign language which I will return to in the discussion that follows this section. The two areas that will be explored are (1) the verbal aspects of turn negotiation and (2) speech acts and sociocultural choices. These areas are seen as fundamental to successful face-to-face interaction in that they are the most likely sources of sociopragmatic failure as defined by Thomas (1983: 103).

3.1 Verbal aspects of turn negotiation

Duncan and Niederehe (1974: 234) cite Goffman's (1955) insight that in any society whenever the physical possibility of spoken interaction arises, it seems that a system of practices, conventions and procedural rules come into play which guides and organises the flow of messages. So while turn taking might be universal, the system within which it is manifested may be culturally-specific. In its broadest sense, turn-taking could also include turn-avoiding, that is, when a speaker wishes to maintain the flow of the conversation without taking over the turn. This is often achieved verbally through backchannels. Tottie (1991: 255) explains backchannels as 'the sounds (and gestures) made in conversation by the current non-speaker, which grease the wheels of the conversation but constitute no claim to take over the turn'. Backchannels can included such items as *yeah, oh, right, mm hm* and so on. Gardner (1998: 204–24) argues strongly for the importance of addressing backchannels (also referred to as minimal response or receipt tokens) in the teaching of conversational skills. He says that 'if language teaching is to prepare learners to talk in the real world, then part of that preparation would need to take into account participation in interactive talk that involves these very common vocalisations' (Gardner, 1998: 204). Research has shown that each response has at least one distinct function; they provide important feedback to the speaker about how their message is received and so influence the path of the conversation (see Schegloff, 1981). By using video clips, backchannels can be examined in both verbal and non-verbal forms. Potential for pragmatic errors at this level is high, especially when substituting a token from one's first language could have the wrong effect on the course of the conversation. Take, for example, news marking items such as *Really* and *You're not serious*, if translated, they run the risk of being interpreted as challenges to the validity of the message rather than as backchannels.

To focus on backchannelling in the classroom, isolate a suitable clip involving informal conversation, for example two friends chatting. Transcribe the dialogue leaving out the backchannels. The items that have been omitted from the transcript are placed on the whiteboard. Having introduced and developed the notion of backchannelling and having supplied different examples to the class, divide the class into groups and ask students to categorise these backchannels in terms of how they function (as agreers, continuers, news markers, evaluators, clarification seekers, etc). Monitor the progress of the groups and gather whole class feedback. Eventually, distribute the transcript and ask students to predict where each of the tokens will be used in the dialogue. Play the clip at least twice so that students can check and alter their predictions if necessary.

It is important to examine backchannels in the context of equivalent forms in the learner's first language. Through this reflective and comparative process, pragmatic problems can be unearthed. Thomas (1983: 101) offers an interesting discussion of the 'pragmatically inappropriate transfer of semantically/syntactically equivalent structures'. She gives the example of *of course,* which in Russian is often used to mean *yes* to convey an enthusiastic affirmative similar to *yes indeed.* In English *of course* is often used when something is self-evident, so the following inappropriate transfer might result between Russian and English:

> *A: It's so cold today, isn't it?*
> *B: Of course.*

Without pragmatic competence in this area, non-native speakers of a language may be compromised in face-to-face interaction with a native speaker. The potential for misunderstanding or misrepresentation in a real time conversation is enormous as Thomas' example from Russian clearly illustrates.

3.2 Focusing on speech acts and sociocultural choices

As mentioned earlier, Cohen (1996: 254) defines sociocultural choices as the speaker's ability to figure out whether it is acceptable to perform a speech act in a given situation and, if so, to choose an utterance that is appropriate in the realisation of a given speech act. Television and video can help greatly in preparing students in this respect. By isolating clips containing speech acts, transcribing them and then taking out certain lines of the segment that contain the speech act or part of it, one can set as a task: predicting what is said next. Take, for example, a scene where someone answers the phone; the generic sequence of what happens when the telephone is answered varies from culture to culture. In some cultures, rigorous self-identification is the normal response to a ringing telephone, for example, in Dutch, *This is Tom* is typical of an answerer's immediate response on picking up the phone (see Houtkoop-

Steenstra (1991) for a comparison between American and Dutch opening sequences in telephone conversations).

Other areas that can be explored here are complimenting and apologising. Find a sequence where, for example, complimenting takes place, transcribe it and leave out the utterance that comes immediately after the compliment. Ask students, in pairs or in groups, to write some possible utterances which might follow the compliment. This activity should reveal what the students expect will happen next based on their native language pragmatic norms. For some, an apology should follow a compliment while for others, an utterance giving thanks will sound more appropriate (this idea is based on Cohen, 1996).

Mey (1993: 153) points to intercultural difference that can arise in relation to the force of a speech act verb. He gives the example of when Americans want to draw their interlocutor's attention to the fact that they have been misunderstood, they may try to clear up the misunderstanding using a speech act of 'self-correcting': *I'm afraid I didn't express myself too clearly.* Mey compares this with what French speakers might say in a similar situation: *Mais vous ne comprenez pas!* (literally, 'But you don't understand'). Though both utterances represent the same underlying intention of setting a misunderstanding straight, they differ in how they approach it. In (American) English, speakers pre-empt causing face threat by blaming themselves whereas the Frenchman 'goes 'bald on record' as stating the fact of mis-understanding' (Mey 1993: 154). Cohen's strategy of exploring speech acts could be adapted and extended here also. Not only could television excerpts be used to focus on sequencing aspects of speech acts, but also to unearth how similar intended meanings manifest differently across languages and cultures.

4 Problems and issues

Having explored some of the applications of television material for awareness raising in the area of pragmatic and sociocultural difference, we cannot ignore the validity of the criticism that not all language students will need to use a foreign language in face-to-face interaction with a native speaker. This is especially relevant in the case of English as a foreign language as the potential for 'linguistic' and, by extension, 'cultural imperialism' is a plausible one. Even though English is so widely spoken globally, it does not give it a *de jure* position among languages and we cannot assume that all learners, or indeed any learner, would wish to reject their first language pragmatic and sociocultural norms when they speak a foreign language. This paper is not advocating this notion. Nor is it attempting to undermine non-native teachers of foreign languages. Television material is relatively easy for language teachers to attain and offers native and non-native teachers access to language in use outside of a native speaking environment. Such pragmatically and socioculturally rich and diverse material cannot be conjured up from textbooks.

Albeit a vicarious experience, 'seeing' language in use on television, gives language students a view of what native speakers *do* when they speak. They get an opportunity to see face-to-face interaction *in situ*, and they are thus in a position to see how their first language and their target language differ pragmatically and socioculturally. Television is pervasive in our lives and it is my contention that for teachers and learners it has vast potential for bringing issues of language and culture into the classroom. Pragmatic and sociocultural aspects of a language as discussed in this paper are not discrete items, which can be packaged, taught and evaluated. A teacher cannot readily measure what has been 'learnt' as in the case of grammatical items and we must accept that learners have every right to reject certain norms which they observe in the foreign language. But what is important is that we acknowledge that different norms exist in the pursuit of intercultural understanding. Byram (1999: 18) describes the 'intercultural speaker' as someone who needs 'multilingual competence' sensitivity to the identities present in intercultural and cross-frontier interaction; an ability to mediate/relate own and other cultures with 'intercultural competence' i.e. a communicative competence … complemented by 'intercultural competence'. As pre-conditions to intercultural competence, Byram lists the following: *Attitude*: the ability to relativise self and value other; *Knowledge*: of one's own and other behaviours, beliefs and values, of how intercultural interaction works.

5   Conclusion

Television is by no means the panacea for modern language teaching, but it has great potential. It is hoped that this paper has provided some insights into how this type of material can be used beyond the level of listening comprehension.

Television and video material originally designed for native speakers can offer foreign language students an authentic language experience on many levels. It will put the learner into a situation that demands native-speaker-like comprehension. Dealing with the pragmatic and sociocultural content of the material brings many challenges for both language teachers and language students. Overall, the material can provide an instructive bridge between viewing interaction in a foreign language environment and actual interaction in a foreign language environment. At a minimum, television is extremely motivating and not only provides visual information and stimuli to make learning more memorable, it brings foreign language interaction in context into the classroom allowing it to be examined at levels which go beyond language into conversational, pragmatic and sociocultural norms.

References

Aijmer, K. (1996) *Conversational Routines in English – Convention and Creativity*, London: Longman.

Aston, G. (1988) *Negotiating Service: Studies in the Discourse of Bookshop Encounters*, Bologna: Editrice CLUEB.

Burns, A, Gollin, S and H. Joyce (1997). 'Authentic Spoken Texts in the Language Classroom', *Prospect* 12/2: 72–86.

Byram, M. (1999) 'Developing the Intercultural Speaker for International Communication' in A. Chambers and D. P. Ó Baoill (eds), *Intercultural Communication and Language Learning*, 17–36, Dublin: Irish Association of Applied Linguistics.

Cohen, A. (1996) 'Developing the Ability to Perform Speech Acts', *Studies in Second Language Acquisition*, 18: 253–67.

Crystal, D. (2000) 'Emerging Englishes' *English Teaching Professional*, 14: 3–6.

Duncan, S. and G. Niederehe, (1974) 'On Signalling That It's Your Turn to Speak', *Journal of Experimental Social Psychology*, 10: 234–47.

Gardner, R. (1998) 'Between Speaking and Listening: the Vocalisation of Understandings', *Applied Linguistics*, 19/2: 204–24.

Grundy, P. (1995) *Doing Pragmatics*, London: Edward Arnold.

Gunn, C. (1999) 'An attempt to Test Sociolinguistic Competence in a Grade 6 ESL Classroom', *IATEFL Issues*, 146: 17–8.

Houtkoop-Steenstra, H. (1991) 'Opening Sequences in Dutch Telephone Conversations', in D. Boden and D. Zimmerman (eds) *Talk and Social Structure: Studies in Ethnomethodology and Conversation Analysis*, 232–50, Oxford: Polity Press.

Hyde, M. (1998) 'Intercultural Competence in English Language Education', *Modern English Teacher,* 7/2: 7–11.

McCarthy, M.J. (1998) *Spoken Language and Applied Linguistics*, Cambridge: Cambridge University Press.

Mey J.L. (1993) *Pragmatics – An introduction*, Oxford: Blackwell.

Pearson, J.A. (1988) 'Satellite Dish Well Worth the Cost', *The British Journal of Language Teaching*, 26/3: 143–4.

Riley, P. (1981) 'Viewing Comprehension 'L'oeil écoute' ', in *The Teaching of Listening Comprehension*, 143–55, London: The British Council.

Rivers, W. (1964) *The Psychologist and the Foreign Language Teacher*, Chicago: Chicago University Press.

Schegloff, E. A. (1981) 'Discourse as an Interactional Achievement: Some Uses of 'Uh Huh' and Other Things that Come between Sentences', in D. Tannen (ed.) *Analysing Discourse: Text and Talk*, 71–93, Washington: Georgetown University Press.

Tatsuki, D. (1997) 'Video in Curriculum Design', IATEFL Newsletter, 138: 13.

Tomas, J. (1983) 'Cross-Cultural Pragmatic Failure', *Applied Linguistics*, 4/2: 91–112

Tottie, G. (1991) 'Conversational Style in British and American English: the Case of Backchannels', in K. Aijmer and B. Altenberg (eds) *English Corpus Linguistics*, 254–71, London: Longman.

Vanderplank (1996) 'Really Active Viewing with Teletext Subtitles and Closed Captions', *Modern English Teacher*, 5/2: 32–7.

Willis, J. (1983) 'The Role of the Visual Element in Spoken Discourse: Implications for the Exploitation Of Video in The EFL Classroom', in J. McGovern (ed.), *Video Applications in Language Teaching*, 29–42, Oxford: Pergamon Press Ltd.

Yngve, V. H. (1970) 'On Getting a Word in Edgeways', *Papers in the 6th Regional Meeting of the Chicago Linguistic Society*, 16–18 April: 567–77, Chicago: Chicago Linguistic Society.

Yule, G. (1996) *Pragmatics*, Oxford: Oxford University Press.

Learning from jumble

Catherine Pope
Goldsmiths College, University of London

This paper will examine the pedagogical implications of the use of text-jumbling software as a type of text manipulation package. It will first present the context of the study, providing background information on text jumbling and the cohort of students observed. The methodology used is then introduced, followed by considerations on learner strategies and human-computer interaction insofar as it is relevant to the study. Finally, the move towards learner independence is outlined to highlight how a change in strategies can help to improve competence.

1   Context of the study

1.1 Student cohort

16 students in the first year of their degree course in French were asked to reconstruct text that had been cut up and jumbled within *DJSJUMBL* text-jumbling software (Shaw, 1995–97). There were initially 3 native and 13 non-native speakers. Another 3 native speakers were included in the project subsequently as will be explained under learner evaluation.

1.2 Text-jumbling software

Text-jumbling software is a type of text manipulation. According to Hewer 'TM essentially encompasses a range of computer-based activities during which students make changes to a previously written text… TM provides students with linguistic problem-solving activities which, if well set up, motivate and promote lasting language learning' (Hewer, 1997: 2). *DJSJUMBL* is a text-jumbling authoring package which allows the tutor to observe students reconstruct jumbled text. The tutor selects a text and breaks it up at strategic points to focus the students' attention on grammatical dependencies or other linguistic concerns. The text needs to be selected for its qualities of cohesion and coherence as these highlight a network of syntactic and semantic links (Halliday and Hasan, 1976; de Beaugrande and Dressler, 1981) which remain once the text has been broken up. These connections form clues which can help to rebuild the original text.

The linguistic and pedagogic value of text reconstruction can be established in terms of raising the students' grammatical awareness and level of accuracy as well as developing the ability to identify their own learning styles and to evolve strategies which are most appropriate to their needs. But while it may be argued that text jumbling can equally be carried out on paper, this study aims to highlight the differences in outcomes between text reconstruction on paper and text reconstruction within text-jumbling software. In this study, the students were all asked to keep a diary of the reconstructed phrases in the order of their initial reconstruction. Any subsequent re-ordering was recorded as well. The diaries were also used to note down any thoughts the student may have had about the reconstruction. As native and non-native speakers were observed in their reconstruction of jumbled text both on paper and in the computer version, this paper looks at the differing learning strategies used by native and non-native speakers in the two environments. The diaries where the students recorded the various stages of their text reconstruction and their observations are analysed in relation to the strategies used.

This study aims to offer an insight into text-jumbling software as a good example of how CALL is perceived by learners to be both motivating and conducive to learning. Rebuilding jumbled text on screen can help students to generate accurate and appropriate language which can be negotiated with their peers and the teacher. Beyond word grammar, this paper will give an account of how the technology allows students to explore text grammar and become more independent learners.

2 Methodology

Methodological problems need to be considered as they affect the way data is collected and processed. The methodology used in this study can be described as what Levi-Strauss calls *bricolage*. As Denzin and Lincoln (1998: 3) observe after many other researchers, *bricolage* involves the use of a variety of strategies, methods or empirical materials depending on the context or the object of the study. The following methods of data collection were used:

1 *direct observation* of students by the tutor;

2 *notes*:

    a) written record of the sequence of phrases offered as reconstructed text;

    b) student notes on the different steps they took in their reconstruction of the text, *thinking aloud, concurrent verbalization* (Ericsson and Simon, 1980)

3 *evaluation*:

    a) reflective comments by students (*retrospective verbalization*);

    b) interviewing the students (open-ended questions by the tutor inviting the students to develop their comments/evaluation of the process;

    c) whole class discussion.

2.1 Observation

If the ideal of observing 'the way that people use language when they are not being observed' (Labov, 1975) is difficult to meet – Labov himself notes the difficulties involved in implementing this method and judges that one-to-one interviews are suitable substitutes – it may be more practical, as suggested by Kellerman (1986: 35), 'to settle for (quasi-) spontaneous data deriving from observed interaction between learners and between learners and native speakers.'

The data was thus collected from the interactions between learners (non-native and native speakers) paired in front of computer screens. The pairings allowed the students to suggest and discuss possible ways of reconstructing the text. Students chose their own partners and the language of the interaction

(English/French) as they need to feel comfortable if they are to contribute to and benefit from the interaction. The tutor observed pairs of students at work and made notes on the interactions. The negotiated outcomes (which phrases are selected in which order) resulted from choices made by the students after considering the implications of those choices with their partners. It appears that the decision that the tutor/researcher should be present when data is collected may have an impact on the data gathered; the presence of the tutor seemed to improve the students' awareness of their learning as they mentioned that they would probably not have asked such searching questions of themselves and their partners if the teacher had not been there. The alternative of the tutor leaving the room to minimise the risk of interference with the students' thinking and questioning may have lead to misinterpretation by the tutor/researcher of what the students meant and how their thinking developed. It was thus considered that the non-intrusive presence of the researcher would offer the best chances to monitor the process and enhance the integrity of interpretation of the reports kept by the students themselves.

2.2 Written records and verbal reports

Observing learner interactions clearly bypasses the difficulty of tapping into the minds of learners to access the source of their metalinguistic reflections. A written record of all the attempts at connecting phrases provides the student with a ready reference of all the possibilities already explored. It also offers the student and tutor material for subsequent reflection/analysis.

Bull (1997) mentions how in *Meta Text* (Gillespie and Gray, 1992) note-taking can contribute to making language learners more autonomous and by extension better learners. It should also be noted that, like *Meta Text*, *DJSJUMBL* is not an *intelligent* system which can evaluate student competence at note-taking. Another method is to record learner's *thoughts*, preferably as they occur, rather than at a later stage when the thoughts not only lose spontaneity but also integrity as they are affected by the capacity of the learner to recall data and report accurately.

Concurrent written reports may be preferred as they provide direct reliable evidence of the student's attempts at reconstruction. And yet, contrary to many researchers and in particular Nisbett and Wilson (1977), Ericsson and Simon (1980) consider that verbal reports are of value. They agree with

Nisbett and Wilson that retrospective verbalizations can make it difficult for the information to remain in *short term memory*. But the defects of the method seem to be largely due to the way verbal reports are elicited or a significant delay in retrieving information. This does not occur with *concurrent verbalizations*. These have the added advantage of speeding up the retrieving of information.

2.3 Interviewing

The interviews conducted were largely unstructured to allow the students to voice thoughts that may not have emerged at the *thinking aloud* stage. Tutor sensitivity in interviewing students is paramount. This is especially important in the case of classes made up of students from different language and culture backgrounds as observed by Denzin and Lincoln (1998). Success of the interactions is indeed dependent on the ability of the tutor to gain the students' trust which in turn relies on the tutor understanding problems that the students may encounter with meaning and cross-cultural issues.

The interviewing stage in the project was said by the students to be facilitated by the positive relationship between tutor and students. As a result, the students were forthcoming with their comments as they did not feel they were being judged. Class discussion occurred towards the end of the cycle and the issues related to it will be dealt with in the evaluation.

3 Learner strategies

Cognitive, metacognitive and social strategies are clearly at work in the students' reconstruction of the text but it is important to take a step back first and reflect more generally on the use of learning strategies. As Bull (1997) shows in her review of the literature, learning strategies are closely related to the issue of effectiveness. While language learners do not seem to have exclusive rights to learning strategies, it appears that the more effective learners are those who are better at using appropriate strategies Chamot (1987) reminds us how good language learners can help less able students by sharing their more effective learning strategies with them. Pairing students in front of computers as in this study and encouraging them to think aloud can help all students to benefit from this learning opportunity. It should in any case be remembered that not all strategies are as effective and this is where O'Malley and Chamot's (1990) categories are helpful.

In the overview which follows, I have largely adopted the categories used by Bull (1997) as they are particularly suitable to appraise the strategies used by learners attempting text reconstruction. The categories retained here and the comments made all apply to this study.

3.1 Cognitive strategies

Resourcing in this study is minimal. The students do not use reference materials such as dictionaries and grammar books. They do not use the tutor as a source of reference either. There is no formal help provided as part of the software and any questions the students may have tend to result from their own *concurrent verbalization* or be addressed to their partners. This stimulates problem-solving with an interactive approach.

Note-taking, as was previously mentioned, forms an important part of the process. The notes are here again generated by the students themselves and are available for future reference. The students do make use of the notes which tend to speed up the reconstruction process where a student has already encountered – and solved – a similar difficulty. The information may be *summarized*, *grouped* (*re-ordered*, *classified* or *labelled*) to facilitate retrieval.

Deduction does not tend to be mentioned as a strategy used by the learners even though accurate reconstruction of text does suggest that it has played some part. *Inferencing* is acknowledged by native speakers of French who tend to *rediscover* rules of grammar.

3.2 Metacognitive strategies

Metacognitive strategies help students become more independent learners:

Strategy planning: students tend to select strategies that suit them once they have become more familiar with the task.

Self-monitoring: French native speakers check that their reconstruction is 'logical'; non-native speakers ensure that it 'makes sense'. A score is available at each stage of the text-reconstruction to monitor progress.

Self-evaluation: students can check their performance with the help of the score displayed on the screen. It is printed at the bottom of the page reconstructed text.

3.3 Social strategies

Questioning takes place between partners who may wish to verify examples.

Cooperation is at the basis of pair work. The students work with their partners to clarify their thoughts, formulate hypotheses and discuss possible outcomes.

The strategies mentioned above appear to promote autonomous learning. Evaluation of the process will show whether it has been effective. But other perspectives need to be considered.

Wenden (1991: 1) reminds us for instance that humanist and cognitive psychology, while stressing the importance of developing leaner-centred teaching methods, do so from two different perspectives. She cites Dubin and Olshtain (1986) for whom a humanist focus on 'self-concept and affective factors' will be reflected in language teaching objectives in the following way:

1   Emphasize meaningful communication.

2   Place high respect and value on the learner.

3   View learning as a form of self-realization.

4   Give learners considerable say in the decision-making process.

5   Place teachers in the role of facilitator whose task is to develop and maintain a supportive class atmosphere

6   Stress the role of other learners as a support group.

These objectives are outwardly different from the mental processes highlighted by cognitive psychologists who 'have observed that learners are actively involved in the process of learning – selectively attending to incoming data, hypothesizing, comparing, elaborating, reconstructing its meaning and integrating it with previously stored information for future use'. The learners are thus given the opportunity to:

1   Test their hypotheses.

2   Draw upon their prior knowledge.

3   Take risks.

4   Use the language to communicate.

While humanist psychology focuses on the conditions of learning, cognitive psychology is more interested in the learning process itself. In any case, the objectives of both humanist and cognitive psychology appear to be satisfied in the study. Some of these will be considered now.

1   Emphasis is clearly on communication for both humanist and cognitive psychology.

2   The learners are at the centre of the learning experience, whether making decisions about their learning, formulating or testing hypotheses or supporting each other...

We shall now see how these objectives may be met in human-computer interaction.

4   Human-computer interaction

Computers are no longer regarded as *electronic brains* built and understood only by experts. The wide spread of computers with a user interface which allows human-computer interaction has implications for the way computers are perceived. This is particularly important in the case of users who are not IT specialists and require a system to do the jobs that they need to do. They have little time and patience for a system which seems to make their task more arduous, is difficult to understand or use and does not seem to respond to their needs.

This is why a well-designed user interface will go a long way towards making the experience of using computers a rewarding and enjoyable one for non-specialists. In the case of language learners, it seems that any system will only meet with student approval if it is 'easy to understand and /fun/ to use' and it appears to 'help [the student] to learn and improve'. This requires, as Baecker et al (1995: XI) observe, 'new specialists trained to understand and improve the ways in which humans interact with computers and broad enough in their outlook to work successfully on multidisciplinary teams'.

In the case of *DJSJUMBL*, Shaw's experience of French language teaching and software design have helped him to produce a text-manipulation package which constitutes a useful teaching, learning and researching tool .

With Computer Assisted Language Learning software, and in particular text manipulation packages, it is important to satisfy the requirement that:

> *a technical system should be designed in every detail so as to be comprehensible to the humans operating it*

and

> *the way information is presented [should fit] in with the way human eyes and minds work ...* (Michie and Johnston, 1985: 58).

When working in an educational context, it is important that users/students should understand and adhere to the way the system in use is supposed to help them to learn. If there is resistance or reluctance to use the system (as in the case of one student who took part in the project), the system clearly does not help the student to learn anything. The student who was paired with the reluctant learner was also prevented – by the reluctant student – from exploring the possibilities of the software and hence of the text. Not only did the reluctant student give up, but she also made it difficult for her partner to use the system effectively.

It appears that unless the learners can understand how to use a computer system and why it will help them, the system will not be used to its full potential. The software should be introduced to the students in advance so they are familiar with the way it works – the keys or buttons to be pressed, the effect of pressing them – so the students feel happy using the technology. If and when things go wrong, the student who is happy to use the system will accept that, whatever the difficulties, it is worth persevering.

Traditionally, knowledge is represented in a machine in a way which is very different from human representations of knowledge. In the case of

DJSJUMBL, it is not knowledge which is represented but forms which require processing by applying systemic and schematic knowledge. (Widdowson: 1990). What are the implications for text-reconstruction?

DJSJUMBL has the capability to recognize competent attempts at reconstructing chunks of text. It credits possible phrases by increasing the score while giving full credit to the full reconstruction of the text (there only appears to be one possible full reconstruction). The program does not provide answers; it encourages students to ask – and answer – questions raised by the points at which sentences are cut-up. The students' questions and answers therefore appear to be at least as important to them as their ability to reconstruct the text successfully. The students themselves note that they learn more from the questions elicited by their attempts than from a simple restitution of the original passage. As the students work in pairs, they elaborate their own answers, exploring together what they know of the grammar and the topic in the process.

Should the computer attempt to answer the students' questions? Although a *View Text* BUTTON is available, all students refrained from using this facility which, in their words, 'would not teach [them] anything'. Similarly, it is understandable that, once the students understand the purpose of the task, they prefer to negotiate answers to their own questions with their partners.

Pre-written notes offered by the system would, it appears, oppose what is sought in the task, not least by the students themselves: to allow the students to develop their ability to process text through observation and, if required, analysis of the phrases provided. Providing the students with ready-made answers would go counter to this aim while asking them pre-written questions would look a poor substitute for the questions learners actually ask. Learners ask questions that are relevant to their needs and their experience of learning and processing language. Ready-made questions asked indiscriminately can, on the other hand, restrict a learner's view of a particular utterance by directing the said learner in a direction which may have general syntactic or semantic value rather than the more unpredictable avenues which a learner may wish to explore.

5 Learner autonomy

In *Autonomy and Foreign Language Learning*, Holec reminds us after B. Schwartz that autonomy is associated with responsibility. Autonomy is defined further in *L'éducation demain* as 'the ability to assume responsibility for one's own affairs'. In the context of language learning, Holec himself defines autonomy as 'the ability to take charge of one's own learning' (Holec, 1981: 3). This ability, according to Holec, must be acquired as it is not inborn. The autonomous learners take charge of their own learning which is said to be *self-directed*.

Learners who are responsible for their learning may determine their objectives, define the contents and progressions, select methods and techniques to be used, monitor the process of acquisition and/or evaluate what has been acquired (see Holec, 1981: 3–20). Learners do not need to make all these decisions to be called *autonomous*. In the study, the students themselves selected the methods and techniques used whether *trial and error*, *reconstruction by meaning* or *analysis of form*. The variety of learner experiences and learning styles accounts for the range of methods and techniques used.

5.1 Trial and error

Some students opted for the *trial and error* method to experiment with and produce language. They tended to be native speakers. Two (additional) native speakers mentioned 'trial and error' as the main technique they used to reconstruct text. Four native speakers recorded 'moving the words about' to 'see possible connections'(two students). One student mentioned using trial and error 'to see the score rise'!

Where *trial and error* is used, it appears at the beginning of the text reconstruction process and is then followed by reflection and evaluation. This is consistent with Licklider's (1960) view that:

> *many problems that can be thought through in advance are very difficult to think through in advance. They would be easier to solve, and they would be solved faster through an intuitively guided trial-and error procedure in which the computer co-operates [...]*

The *feasibility* argument seems to be a powerful one in the case of students led to reconstruct the text *by meaning*. What makes sense appears *feasible* and therefore does not seem to make undue demands on the learners.

5.2 Towards learner independence: monitoring and evaluation

The learners monitor their language activity at various stages of their reconstruction of the text and evaluate what they have acquired by means of the notes in their diaries. The score also helps them with monitoring and evaluation by providing a focus as well as an instrument of measure. but monitoring and evaluation are two distinct procedures.

5.3 Student diaries

The students first produce a record of the phrases selected. Each selected phrase appears where it occurred in the reconstructed sequence even if the order of phrases was subsequently reworked. (Any subsequent alterations also features in the diary notes.) The students are then encouraged to reflect on their text reconstruction, comment on the strategies they have used to re-write the text and describe what they have learned and how they had come to learn it.

After Cazden, Birdsong (1989: 1) observes that human beings 'not only learn and use language but treat it as an object of analysis and observation in its own right'. Learners who make utterances often monitor the language they produce and are therefore engaged in metalinguistic activity. Birdsong (1989: 1) defines 'metalinguistic performance' as 'attention to linguistic form rather than content' which may or may not be conscious. It appears that non-native learners of French reconstruct text analytically on paper (by analysing the form), but tend to be led *by meaning* when they attempt to reconstruct the text within text-jumbling software. This was observed by the learners in their diary notes and discussed with the tutor.

In discussion, the students reported not being so much interested in 'what is grammatically correct' as 'what looks right', 'what makes sense'. The students' attention appeared to have shifted from an anxiety with words to the production of meaning. As a result, they moved from paying attention to word grammar to a wider interest in producing meaningful text. Their preoccupation was therefore less with individual words or even sentences than with the expression of meaning. It would appear that *making sense* thus resulted from the ability to relax about the form. This ability, commonly found in native speakers, seems to be helped by the use of computer software. The computer screen, by taking learners away from specific linguistic features, encourages them to look at text in its entirety (Van Dijk, 1972).

5.4 From learner evaluation to independent learning

Nunan (1992: 118–24) acknowledges the value of diaries for the insights they provide into language development. He also views them as useful research tools into learning strategies. It appears that students who reflect on their learning strategies are already engaged in autonomous learning.

Wenden (1991: 54) observes that knowledge which leads into action has value for the learner. With learner evaluation, learners produce value for themselves. How can this be achieved?

While the different stages in the students' reconstruction of the text are useful for the students concerned and the teacher to review (*formative* for the students and *informative* for the tutor), there are also instances of reconstruction which would not 'make sense' or be useful to the group at large. Not everything can be shared and it is not necessarily desirable or useful for students to share with the whole class every piece of language they produced in the form of notes. For notes to function efficiently as genuine records of a student's activity and reflections, they need to remain private should the student choose not to communicate the content (or form) of a given note to his/her peers. The students have mentioned that 'It's all right for [the tutor] to see the notes' but they are worried they might appear 'silly' in front of their friends if they write down everything that comes into their minds and then communicate it to the class. It seems that if that were to be the requirement, the students would not be happy writing everything down but they confess that they would instead be tempted to censure their notes.

The students, paradoxically perhaps, were anxious for the tutor to see their notes – all their notes – once the principle of note-taking was established. In fact, they all expected the tutor to monitor their notes and to offer *corrections* as and when needed. It was established that the notes were neither *right* nor *wrong* but were only useful if they represented a true reflection of their thoughts and the various stages in the process of reconstructing text. This was understood by all students except for one, the student who incidentally had found it impossible to reconstruct text.

With *trial and error*, the personal nature of the experience from which *trial and error* phrases proceed may get in the way of that experience being shared. Many of the hesitations encountered by the students in their *trial and error* attempts at reconstruction do not constitute findings as such but rather blind alleys down which students go. Without a reflection on the nature and implications of their *choices*, the students find it difficult to have anything to share of their experiences.

One native speaker mentioned using trial and error to see 'the score rise' [sic]. In the latter case, a combination of 'trial and error' and score-led reconstruction helped the student to achieve a perfect score of 100. This native-speaking student took significantly less time than the average (15 minutes against 1 hour allocated for all students (French native speakers included) to complete his text reconstruction. The score-checking facility was used by this student to re-order complete sentences in order to form text rather than reconstitute individual sentences from jumbled phrases.

The same was observed of all students who watched the score as a means to improve their performance. (It is worth noting that only the 3 pairs of students who noticed the score-checking facility on their own achieved 100%). It also appears that the students who realised the presence of a score-checking facility on their own did so after scoring over 50%. Those students who at the end of the session still scored below 50% were still oblivious to the score button.

Those students who used the score-checking facility to improve their performance reported finding the score 'motivating'. The *Score* display allows the learners to monitor their reconstruction of the text at each stage. The score is updated every time phrases are connected.

The scoring facility was seen as motivating by the students as the score remains level if no positive suggestion is made while it improves if the suggested reconstruction is syntactically possible. The learners are therefore credited for what they can do – whether their suggestions correspond to the final reconstruction of the text as known to the system or not – rather than penalised for what they do not know/cannot do. Given that extensive research has shown since Gardner and Lambert (1972) that motivation is the chief factor involved in what engages language learners, positive attitudes to the score-checking facility are to be welcomed.

The presence of the *Score* display was reported by students as 'an incentive to carry on'. One group did, with significant success, after overhearing their neighbours' comments about their rising score. A high score which was just short of 100% encouraged the students to review the text as a whole rather than as individual sentences. The students concerned then turned their attention away from word or phrase grammar to look at what constitutes a text. They showed concern for the way the text was structured, looked for a way into the text, a general fact that would introduce the subject matter and devices that would ensure the cohesion and progression of the text.

Here are the 3 most popular ways demonstrated by students to reconstruct the beginning of the text in order of popularity:

Une couche d'ozone
entoure la terre. (1)

Certains gaz,
Comme le CO2
Ou les CFC,
Détruisent la couche d'ozone
De notre planète. (2)

Les rayons du soleil
ne touchent pas
tous la terre. (3)

Incidentally, the *correct* start (3) was the least popular!

Non-native speakers produced meaning by connecting phrases that '[made] sense together'. Their reconstructed text showed linguistic knowledge which allowed them to produce 'une couche d'ozone/entoure…' with the verb in the singular as opposed to 'les rayons du soleil/ne touchent pas…'. And yet the students perceived that they were led by meaning. Their schematic knowledge or knowledge of the world seemed to form the basis for their reconstruction of the text. What they knew of the subject helped them to establish meaning. Skehan (1998) similarly finds that foreign language learners tend to use their schematic knowledge to compensate for a lack of systemic knowledge.

In the study, the topic was familiar to the students as it formed part of a five-week cycle of work on the environment. 11 non-native students recorded that familiarity with the subject helped them to reconstruct the text. This is consistent with recent research findings. Roller and Matambo (1992), for instance, observe after Swaffar (1988) that L2 learners who use schemata and top-down processing like L1 readers improve their reading comprehension. The link between reading comprehension and the ability to reconstruct previously written text is clear as can be seen in Carrell's (1983) study of background knowledge in reading comprehension.

Strategies clearly differed between non-native and native speakers. Where non-native speakers of French tried to write something that made sense when working with a computer, the objective of native speakers was to restore the 'logical' progression of the text by paying attention to linguistic devices. This was an unexpected finding and one that prompted the (small) sample of 3 native speakers to be doubled. The results remained the same.

It therefore appeared that when moving from a manual reconstruction of cut-up text on paper to reconstructing the text within text-jumbling software, the native speakers stopped being led by meaning to concentrate instead on form. They would typically reconstruct chunks of the text which identify grammatical dependencies rather than attempt to restore the text sequentially.

Here are some examples of text reconstructed by 4 native speakers. (They variously started with one or the other phrase but strikingly showed no concern for writing full sentences. They recorded wanting to explore grammar instead!):

Certains gaz/
Certains sont absorbés

Si rien n'est fait/
on assistera à/
qui affecteront notre vie

The text-jumbling software seemed to be used as a laboratory where experiments could be conducted to 'see what happens' between words. The repetition of *Certains* prompted a reflection on its different functions in different contexts (*Certains gaz*/*Certains sont*) while the selection of a condition expressed in the present tense (*Si rien n'est fait*) called for the future tense which only occurred in two verbs. As meaning was not a priority, the antecedent of *qui* was not required at this stage.

Text reconstruction by non-native speakers also differed on paper from its computer version. While non-native speakers of French were anxious about 'getting the grammar right' when presented with text cut up on paper, they reported being more relaxed about the form when working with the computer. When they worked with the software, they adopted strategies which are generally expected of native speakers or the most competent learners.

There was one exception. One pair of English native speakers was unable to offer any form of reconstruction of the text. Their difficulties seemed to reflect the problems one of the two students had understanding the purpose of the exercise, problems that were considered personal to that student by the rest of the class. That her difficulty might have sprung from a nervousness with using the technology was disproved by the fact that she did not seem to cope any better with text cut up on paper or many other tasks which form part of her first year course. Her experience was felt to be (highly) individual and therefore impossible for the group to share and learn from.

When asked what they had found useful in their reconstruction work with the software, native speakers and non-native speakers alike mentioned that it made them think about grammar! Grammar had clearly taken a new meaning for them as they considered it related to text more than to individual words and phrases.

6   Conclusion

DJSJUMBL has proved a useful and popular tool in the development of students' writing. By encouraging learners to process language as they understand it rather than as they analyse it, it helps them to set aside their anxiety with the form and behave in ways that are generally more familiar to native speakers. As a result, their level of communicative competence has improved beyond the screen as they negotiate ways of reconstructing the text with their partners, discuss outcomes with the tutor or their peers and evaluate their performance.

The learners' response was very positive. The technology may have caused nervousness when it was first introduced (some students were afraid of being marked down for their lack of competence in IT). But it has been the instrument of the students' newly gained confidence in their ability to carry out the task successfully. It appears that a more intelligent system might have discouraged students. Instead, the computerised text-manipulation was reported to be interesting and motivating. The learners wanted to go further both in their attempts at reconstructing text and in the discussions they initiated outside the computer room. This is an example of how CALL can be used to improve competence and promote learner autonomy. Beyond this study also lies an on-going project which intends to look more closely at the relationship between score and motivation. Motivation is defined according to what students themselves perceive as motivating. As they find the presence of a score motivating, their scores are put in relation with the strategies they use and their performance. This is one way to find out to what extent there is a relationship between a high(er) level of motivation and higher achievement; and this is why the new version of *DJSJUMBL* with improved scoring facilities should be even more useful.

References

Baecker, R.M. and Buxton, W.A.S. (eds) (1987) *Readings in Human-computer interaction*, San Mateo, CA: Morgan Kaufmann Publishers.

Baecker, R.M., Grudin, J., Buxton, W.A.S. and Greenberg, S. (eds) (1995: 2nd ed.) *Readings in Human-computer interaction: Toward the Year 2000*, San Francisco, CA: Morgan Kaufmann Publishers.

Birdsong, D. (1989) *Metalinguistic Performance and Interlinguistic competence*, Berlin: Springer-Verlag.

Broady, E. and Kenning, M-M. (eds) (1996) *Promoting Learner Autonomy in University Language Teaching*, London: AFLS with CILT.

Bull, S. (1997) 'Promoting effective learning strategy use in CALL', *CALL*, 10(4): 3–39.

Carrell, P.L. (1983) 'Three components of background knowledge in reading comprehension', *Language Learning* 33, 183–205.

Chamot, A.U. 'The learning strategies of ESL students', in A. Wenden and J. Rubin (eds) (1987) *Learner strategies in language learning*, London, Prentice Hall.

Crombie, W. (1985) *Process and Relation in Discourse and Language Learning*, Oxford: Oxford University Press.

De Beaugrande, R. and Dressler, W. (1981) *Introduction to Text Linguistics*, New York: Longman.

Denzin, N.K and Lincoln Y.S. (1998) *Collecting and Interpreting Qualitative Materials*, Thousand Oaks: Sage.

Ericsson, K. A., and Simon, H.A. (1980) 'Verbal Reports as Data', *Psychological Review*, 87 (3): 215–51.

Gardner, R.C. and Lambert, W.E. (1972) *Attitudes and Motivation in Second Language Learning*, Rowley, Mass.: Newbury House.

Gillespie, J.H. and Gray, B. (1992) 'Hypercard and the Development of Translation and Vocabulary Skills', *CALL* 5 (1-2) 3–11.

Halliday, M. and Hasan, R. (1976) *Cohesion in English*, London: Longman.

Hewer, S. (1997) *Text manipulation*, London: CILT.

Holec, H. (1981) *Autonomy and Foreign Language Learning*, Oxford: Pergamon Press.

Kellerman, E. 'An Eye for an Eye: Crosslinguistic Constraints on the Development of the L2 Lexicon' in E. Kellerman and M. Sharwood Smith (eds) (1986) *Crosslinguistic influence in Second Language Acquisition*, Oxford: Pergamon Press, pp.35–48.

Labov, W. (1975) 'What is a linguistic fact?' in Lisse N.L. The Peter de Ridder Press.

Lewis, C. and Norman, A. 'Designing for Error' in R.M. Baecker and W.A.S. Buxton (eds) (1987) *Readings in Human-computer interaction*, San Mateo, CA: Morgan Kaufmann Publishers, pp.627–38.

Licklider, J.C.R. (1960) 'Man-computer symbiosis', *IRE Transactions on Human Factors in Electronics* HFE 1(1), 4–11.

Michie, D. and Johnston, R. (1985) *The creative computer: Machine intelligence and human knowledge*, Harmondworth: Penguin.

Nisbett, R.E. and Wilson, T. D. (1977) 'Telling more than we can know: verbal reports on mental processes', *Psychological Review*, 84(3), 231–59.

Nunan, D. (1992) *Research Methods in Language Learning*, Cambridge: Cambridge University Press.

O'Malley, J.M. and Chamot, A.U. (1990) *Learning strategies in second language acquisition*, Cambridge: Cambridge University Press.

Oxford R. (1990) *Language Learning Strategies: What every teacher should know*, New York: Newbury House.

Preece, J. and Keller, L. (1990) *Human-computer interaction*, Hemel Hempstead: Prentice Hall.

Roller, C.M. and Matambo, A.R. (1992) 'Bilingual readers' use of background knowledge in learning from text', *TESOL Quarterly*, 26(1), 129–39.

Shaw, D.J., *DJSJUMBL* version 1.5, 1995–1997 (Licenced for use with CKS TLTP software), Not yet published.

Skehan, S. (1998) *A Cognitive Approach to Language Learning*, Oxford: Oxford University Press.

Schwartz, B. (1977) *L'éducation demain*, Paris: Aubier Montaigne.

Swaffar, J.K. (1988) 'Readers, texts, and second languages: The interactive process', *Modern Languages Journal*, 72, 123–49.

Van Dijk, T.A. (1972) *Some Aspects of Text Grammars*, The Hague: Mouton.

Wenden, A. and Rubin, J. (1987) *Learner strategies in language learning*, London, Prentice Hall.

Wenden, A. (1991) *Learner strategies for learner autonomy*, London, Prentice Hall.

Widdowson, H.G. (1990) *Aspects of Language Teaching*, Oxford: Oxford University Press.

The changing perceptions and expectations of undergraduates and postgraduates learning with multimedia and text-based French CALL packages

Liam Murray
University of Warwick

1 Introduction

After a relatively long period of development and evaluation, certain CALL (Computer-Assisted Language Learning) programs can now be seen as having established themselves as a valuable language learning resource at some tertiary level colleges and institutions in the U.K (see for example Hewer, 1998: 39). Other evaluators and researchers have gone further in stating that there can no longer exist any argument against integrating CALL into our teaching practices. The essential point is to use CALL software to make a significant and effective difference (Barnett: 1993; Higgins: 1998; Cooper and Selfe: 1990; Van den Burg and Watt: 1991: 123). Others have been more cautious yet ultimately positive in their assessments. Peterson, in a summative paper on the advantages and disadvantages of target language autonomous and observed e-mailing, notes that such activities do facilitate heuristic learning but he also relates the dangers of educational technology in creating: 'greater regimentation and homogenization of classroom learning experiences', (1997, 34). Against this, Jamieson and Chapelle (1988: 152) in describing five 'learner variables' that should be borne in mind when assessing CALL effectiveness, emphasise the importance of teachers being aware of a student's individual learning or cognitive style if the CALL activities are to make a difference. The message is that CALL programs should aim to help in localising learning against teaching regimentation. The remaining four variables would also impinge upon the influence of the CALL learning situations and these include the learner's age, background, ability and affect (i.e. motivation and attitudes towards the target culture). Unfortunately for language tutors using CALL programs, no one single variable can claim primacy over the others so each must be considered in its own right because: 'Teachers cannot expect all students to have positive attitudes toward all lessons. Instead, attitude toward various CALL materials may be a function of students' objectives for language study, cognitive style and other personal factors' (Jamieson and Chapelle: 1988, 158).

These types of perennial pedagogical difficulties are also known in general L2 teaching research and Garrett has written much on overcoming these localised problems for CALL practitioners in emphasising the need for constructing a proper learning situation either within the classroom or in our materials where learner variables in language acquisition can be successfully addressed (1991: 92). It is one of our goals here to contribute to this growing awareness. We may also respond, in part, to the demands led by Warschauer and Healey (1998: 62) and more locally by Gillespie and McKee (1999: 45) for exploiting students' enjoyment in using computers and for additional research into uncovering the major factors involved in utilising CALL effectively and appropriately especially in overcoming problems of student opposition to CALL. Such factors must include those of the learner's perceptions and expectations.

1.1 Purpose of the study

One of the purposes of the present study was to perform an illuminative, integrative and summative evaluation of three pieces of CALL software by recording and interpreting the changing attitudes and expectations of students using the software over an academic year. In Hewer's (1998: 5) accepted definition of evaluation types, we would be attempting to discover the most important factors in a given situation of use (illuminative); helping learners to make the most efficacious use of the software (integrative) and ultimately providing learners with the proper skills to assess their current and any future examples of CALL software (extended summative). In addition, because of this author's desire to improve the main undergraduate language course on which the software is used and also extend the possible uses of the software to other courses, the results have been interpreted in the context of: linguistic and cultural gains; users' changing attitudes to CALL and the development of transferable skills such as critical evaluation, language learning strategies and study skills. When profiling the two groups in our study there appears to be some similarity in their backgrounds: the vast majority of the members remain native speakers of English born in the U.K. with an increasing number of students being non-native English speakers from other European countries. This increase is becoming especially marked in recent years among the PGCE students. By involving postgraduates in the study it was hoped to develop their critical faculties for CALL for their future teaching needs and offer them the opportunities to practise and evaluate their own language skills. By involving both groups it was hoped to map any crossover of needs and to collate experiences and opinions for future uses of the software in different situations and to find any possible areas for improvement. For everyone concerned it was intended to enhance the language learning process and practices.

Hewer (*op. cit*) has provided a helpful evaluation template and questionnaire for reporting on student uses of two of the three pieces of software in our study, namely *GramEx French* (GEF) and *GramDef French* (GDF). However, her report findings are concentrated on the use of the software over a four week period in the middle of one academic year. Our study, as well as including an additional piece of software, Télé-Textes Author 2 *(TT2), covers* the entire year, from pre-registration to pre-Summer examination. Further differences with our study include the length of time in gathering the data: four years for GEF, GDF and TT2; and the number of students involved: 70 undergraduates (the total for all four years) and 103 postgraduates (for three years only).

1.2 Agents and instruments

Agentive CALL programs are those that offer target language text or multimedia, often with a small amount of context and always with variations of rote practice via gapfills, cloze exercises and text reconstruction. Two of the three CALL packages in our study, GEF and GDF may be defined as being of this kind. The third package TT2 although containing several agentive uses, also provides some instrumental open-ended exercises and we have chosen to extend this and exploit its greater communicative and creative potential as a proper project-based language learning tool beyond the original intentions of the software developers. TT2 is also an authoring package and is similar to other types of instrumental tools which include those that can make real communicative demands on the user in the target language. Examples of such tools include: e-mail software; spreadsheets; concordancers; web editors and word-processing packages. Many CALL practitioners (including Debski: 1997, Levy: 1998, Barson: 1997) wish to build upon the limited use and success of agentive CALL and extend the practice of instrumental use to project-based classes. However, none could seriously dismiss the continued use of agentive programs because of their proven potential as a resource for revision and reinforcement and because they may suit certain learners' cognitive styles and expectations and thus help to maintain motivation. For Debski, the social action facilitated through the instrumental use of electronic communication media is highly important as a resource in language learning. However, it brings with it certain questions that he has already identified and these include establishing and supporting appropriate levels of student creativity and co-operation on projects of mutual interest (1997: 48).

One possible method for measuring the creativity and collaboration is through the recording of student preconceptions, expectations and attitudes as they experience learning within the CALL type of teaching paradigm. Accompanied by later analysis, this is what we have attempted to do in this paper.

1.3 Structure, context and autonomous learning needs

In the last few years there has been a growing pressure on tutors to increase the already existent amount of learner autonomy within language courses and to encourage students to take more responsibility for their own learning (see for example Wenden: 1991). Several CALL programs claim to be highly suited to autonomous learning needs. Few programs, if any, may satisfy this claim adequately because of the complexity of the already discussed learner variables and of the language learning process. Even within project-based classes which can offer an excellent motivating context for language practice, students still expect to learn a language structure and this expectation is (literally) more pronounced on advanced level courses. To this end, they tend to look to their grammar knowledge as a way of forming their own language structure and fulfilling their individual needs.

Interestingly, members from both groups of students in our study shared this desire for knowledge about grammar and language structures. For the undergraduates it was a question of extending and deepening their knowledge through formal *and* communicative techniques in class as prescribed by Rogers (1996, 37–8). In and outside class these techniques were encouraged and supported by individual and group use of the agentive CALL grammar program GEF. Among the most common student grammatical needs covered quite adequately and successfully by GEF were: the subjunctive; the passive; pronouns and pronominal agreements; the article (definite, indefinite and partitive); prepositions; conjunctions; verbs and the appropriate use of tenses. For the postgraduate teacher trainees the other agentive grammar program GDF was initially believed to be more appropriate to their personal needs in helping to revise, confirm and maintain their grammar and communicative competences. The historical reasons for the lack of deep grammatical competence among undergraduates have been extensively discussed elsewhere (e.g. Metcalfe, 1992 and Rogers, 1996). However, less widely investigated have been the reasons for the small yet significant number of grammatical deficiencies and uncertainties observed in PGCE students' oral and written work.

Such deficiencies have been noted both by PGCE lecturers and by students themselves. Our own repeated findings indicate that these 'knowledge gaps', although by no means widespread varied greatly in both type and seriousness and were discovered to be particularly prevalent among those students possessing degrees with major and minor language components when measured against those who had completed joint language degrees (Barnes and Murray, 2000). Again, among the most frequent were the following: grammatical terminology; idiosyncratic comprehension of certain rules governing verb tenses; 'fluidic' genders; superficial understanding and in some cases a re-learning of the subjunctive; erratic spelling; pronominal verbs in the perfect tense where '*se*' is an indirect object; and the use of *en/au* with countries. The steps that are taken to resolve these difficulties are discussed later in this paper, but the point here is that even PGCE students need to have their L2 language awareness tested and reinforced. To this end the use of existing agentive CALL grammar programs must be employed for those who aim to learn with them, for those who wish to teach with them and for those who need to do both.

2 Methodology: materials description and elicitation of data

2.1 Materials description

The undergraduates following our advanced level post-18 French language course are non-specialist language learners coming from a wide variety of disciplines which use traditional methods of program delivery (lectures and seminars) and in some cases use a computer-based delivery e.g. the Law Courseware Consortium's materials (for more information see: http://www.law.warwick.ac.uk/lcc/). Our learners have two hours per week class contact time over a 25-week period. The project-based part of the course involves students producing multimedia documents for TT2 (for a more detailed description of the practical integration of TT2 see Murray: 1998). TT2 is aimed at advanced learners and is a CALL multimedia authoring package using original French videoclips on a wide range of topics with transcriptions and a variety of linguistic exercises ranging from cloze exercises to more open ended questions, discovery and debate topics. It offers a word-processing facility and authoring studio for students to prepare their own audio and typed versions of reports based on the supplied videoclip subjects. This is an example of the program's instrumental uses.

GDF is a text-based largely agentive grammar definition program and like GEF is aimed at intermediate to advanced learners. It includes five short texts for grammatical analysis in the explore mode and in the test mode the user is asked to complete grammatical definitions on the same texts by clicking in a list that is shown in a drop-down box or by typing. A menu-driven hypertext grammar help is also available. GEF uses the same grammar help but is this time linked to jump to one of the thirteen grammar exercises that are offered on the main menu screen. The exercises here are randomly produced and the user is prompted for a suitable number of examples to attempt. Like GDF, the user must supply the correct answer before they can continue to the next example. Unlike GDF, if a user gains a less than ninety per cent success rate at the first attempt of each example, they are given the incorrect responses to attempt again. Both use a simple scoring facility. As with TT2, both programs' instructions, layout, and descriptions are in the target language. (More detailed descriptions of GDF and GEF are available at the following address: http://www.law.warwick.ac.uk/lcc/

Given the limited exposure time in class, TT2 is introduced during the first term and used in groups for short induction periods with GDF and GEF during the class. All the materials are also made available for general student use in the Open Access Area of the Language Centre throughout the whole of the year. GDF and GEF are also available on the University network and so may be accessed from over five hundred campus-wide PCs. Currently, TT2 may only be used outside class in the Open Access Area. In the second term, the students are divided into workgroups and the project work begins in earnest with the projects being submitted at the end of this term. In producing their own materials and exercises with other students on a final project, we are employing what Plowman (1988: 291) calls 'cognitive enhancers', in which the user is given the tools to 'repurpose' existing materials. In this way the project activities force the students to think carefully about what they are compiling and what they are offering to future users of TT2 as they are informed that their materials will be authored into future editions of the program.

The course itself is conducted, for the most part, in the target language environment. A noted major adjustment for several students was in learning to participate and contribute to a working project group. With a maximum of three students per project group, the 'division of labour' choices were left entirely to the individual students. There were no major problems reported in this respect but there were a few minor problems caused by personality clashes and disagreements over the choice of video subject matter. To iron out these problems we are now using Gibbs' (1994) short but very useful student guide to working in groups using: team action sheets; division and planning of labour sheets; responsibilities for scheduling work deadlines and dynamics of teamwork descriptions. This has been translated into French for our particular use.

2.2 Elicitation of data

Data from undergraduate students during the four years of the study was collected in the following ways:

- interviews were conducted on an individual basis prior to enrolment on the course regarding attitudes to and previous use of CALL software;
- observation in a natural language-learning setting;

- reactions to the software were recorded on anonymous questionnaires based on Hewer's (*op. cit.*) template, three times during the year (this has been used for two years while another similar type of questionnaire was used during the previous two years);

- individual work 'diaries' or log books were required to be kept up to date and in French and submitted with the finished project;

- use of the Language Centre's general questionnaire on CALL software use (based on a template available from the CTI Centre at Hull University) was encouraged;

- an end-of-year group interview on all aspects of CALL use and multimedia projects was set up and audiorecorded.

Data from postgraduate students during the three years of the study was collected in the following ways:

- copies of the Language Centre's general questionnaire on CALL software use were distributed to all students at the start of their PGCE course;

- the same copies were distributed again to targeted users mid-way through the year;

- copies of the ICT competence questionnaire from the PGCE course handbook;

- individual interviews with several PGCE students;

- observation in a natural language-learning setting.

3   Analysis of results

3.1 Context

In an early attempt to glean student attitudes to CALL, Hart (1988) describes some problems in convincing students to use CALL programs outside classroom time despite the general response in his questionnaire being quite favourable to CALL. One possible solution to this problem of usage is for selected CALL programs to be appropriately and strongly integrated into language courses. However, there are many pitfalls on the road to integration.

For example, in our study we had to be wary of what might be termed 'multimedia overload' and remain mindful of Englesberg's (1997) experience where, after achieving some success in using courseware intensively during the first five weeks of the course, student interest then tailed off. This was because they had exhausted the uses of their chosen courseware and the language tasks therein had become unchallenging. Reading this confirmed our decision in choosing CALL programs of sufficiently high task difficulty and quality that would allow us to structure their integration by staging the introduction of grammar topics (with GDF and GEF) and news topics (with TT2) until at least the end of the second term of the course. From this time on all three programs were and are reportedly being used quite heavily by students for revision and reinforcement and also as part of their multimedia projects.

Finding appropriate programs proved to be not too difficult. Englesberg (*op. cit*: 19) attributes their early success with their courseware to: 'the humanistic orientation of the courseware, which afforded the learners control over the learning process'. Such programs are rare. Watts (1997: 3) is rightly critical of the dearth of appropriate and useful CALL software especially at advanced level and much software that already exists has been created by developers who have not adopted a learner-based approach in their design principles. They do not accommodate different student learning styles and after all: 'the needs of the learner are paramount in software development'.

In our analysis we must remember where the two groups' needs and interests crossed. Apart from the grammatical and linguistic needs of both groups that have been described earlier, undergraduates needed to be able to evaluate current CALL programs in order to create and produce useful teaching materials for TT2. For postgraduates it was a necessity to be competent enough to evaluate all types of CALL programs for possible integration and use in their own teaching and learning situations.

3.2 Changing attitudes and expectations

Due to the fact that most students had limited previous exposure to CALL, they had to be introduced in a planned and careful way to the software. For the undergraduates, this occurred from the beginning of the first term when they were interviewed prior to the course enrolment for their opinions and any possible concerns about producing the multimedia project as a learning resource. It can be reported that student opposition was for the most part minimal and this may be attributed perhaps to early enthusiasm and a positive approach to the course as a whole. Each year for the past four years there have always appeared several cases of technophobia, but the large majority of the students have already used computers to some degree in their learning. There is a growing general expectation among students that they will use pedagogical software in some form (and forum) during their university careers as these types of software steadily become the norm within our teaching institutions. The major questions and concerns from our particular learners were related to receiving adequate tutoring in the use of the software and gaining sufficient access to the materials. To combat these problems, students are introduced to the software during short inductions both during the class and outside the class where required. They are also supplied with a general ICT and CALL student guide booklet that was produced jointly by members of our Modern Languages Departments and the Language Centre.

PGCE students also received copies of this booklet in their tailored induction classes. During and outside the classes, the students are introduced to a wide range of CALL materials both agentive and instrumental. After approximately two months and again after six months, the PGCE students must attend CALL evaluation seminars where their experiences and opinions of CALL programs are sought. A definite change in attitudes can be charted between these periods. A typical early response to a lot of CALL programs was favourable in the main, however by the time of the final session attitudes have hardened and become quite critical. This is a reflection of the students' different priorities in using the software. At this stage they are more interested in making appropriate use of programs in their own teaching environments and assessing the software against other learning materials. They are less interested in making personal use of the programs to cover their linguistic and grammatical gaps (which were described earlier), feeling at this time more confident in their comprehension of the grammatical complexities and terminology used in their chosen target language(s). Written comments from students included: 'Gramex/Gramdef – tested my grammar – good but quite academic. Looking at grammar books is quicker sometimes than running to the computer' and 'Télé-Textes – useful for independent pupil work to practise reading, comprehension and listening skills and vocabulary concerning particular topics. Fairly easy to read and follow but quite good standard of French required'. Others said: 'GramEx can be more stimulating and interesting than reading a grammar book but it is not easy to plan its use in a classroom context' and: 'The grammar programs helped to reinforce my grammar competencies but I would need to be very careful when including it in my lessons'. Nervousness in using the programs in their own teaching situations is understandable among PGCE students (and is by no means confined to them alone because of their limited experience of teaching). Jones (1986: 171), in an influential paper, has underlined the importance of engendering a positive teacher attitude when using CALL materials: 'because there is no better way to ensure a flop than to go into class expecting one'. Whereas such an attitude is applicable when using all types of learning resources, it must however be particularly underlined to PGCE students and this is mainly because CALL programs are only just beginning to establish their rightful place in the language tutor's pedagogical armoury. One telling comment from a student concluded: 'The CALL materials are different, I don't know if they are better than all the many other materials that I can use with pupils but the kids love to use the computers and if it keeps them interested in the grammar topics that we're studying, then I would keep using it'.

Maintaining the interest of undergraduate students in the grammar programs was less of a challenge for us than had been envisaged. By establishing a pattern of extended program use on the course, it was easier for students to appreciate the role and place of CALL within the course. In preparing for each week's lesson, students were expected to consult and use those grammar topics from GDF and GEF that would be relevant. This involved the tutor following closely those topics that the programs offered and matching them with identified student grammar problems such as those mentioned earlier in this paper. The benefits were clear in that students were soon forming their own pattern and practices in using the software. For some undergraduates there were early worries and difficulties because for them it was a new learning method. One comment recorded at the end of the course was revealing: 'At the start I couldn't really see the point of using them and I felt terrified of doing the project. After a few weeks, it was ok, it was good to feel my grammar improving and testing it on the program. Yes, it was good fun and really nice to work in a group'.

Further consolidation of the pattern occurred when students began working on their projects, as one said: 'It was good to be able to check some grammar points in the program when we were putting together our exercises for the project.' For some students the learning method and group work were not altogether unfamiliar. This was especially true for those students from the Engineering School: 'In Engineering we're always working together on projects but working with students from other departments was sometimes difficult and frustrating'. These types of students needed peer-support during the group work and guided help from the tutor as it was a totally new educational experience for them and a period of adjustment was required. Debski (*op. cit.*, 59) has also reported similar findings and goes on to emphasise the importance of setting long-term linguistic goals when employing project-based learning techniques.

At the end of the course, the undergraduates summarised their feelings and attitudes to the CALL programs and the multimedia project. The following comments represent the most salient points for our study:

- Too much autonomy? Some students continue to ask for more information and structure especially with regard to their project, i.e. they want to know 'the limits' or 'the absolute minimum' that is required of them in respect of background reading and time management of the project. It is tempting to conclude that some learning styles never change. However, the point is accepted that some learners require more assistance and guidance than others in spite of the already mentioned guides and inductions that are supplied to students.

- Freedom to learn. Many students welcomed the opportunity to spend time during their project work concentrating on a particular subject that interested them and that they had chosen. This sometimes reflected interests from their main degree course e.g. engineering students tackling slightly technical subjects, politics students covering local elections and sociology students examining homelessness issues. In the majority of cases, however, because the students come from different disciplines the subject must be chosen by mutual agreement with all members of the group. No comments have yet been made regarding difficulties in agreeing a suitable subject.

- Pride in work. Learner's pride in their finished project is clear both during the presentations and from recorded comments. A definite satisfaction among students was discernible when they knew that future learners would be using their projects and this also provided extra motivation during the production phase.

- TT2, GDF and GEF work well together. Several students noticed that they made greater use of the grammar programs during the final write-up of their projects. Others reported on the 'physical setting' when using the software. When they had completed their grammar preparations of GDF and GEF, they would often switch to using TT2, 'because it was there and easy to use'.

- Importance of early inductions. Students generally accepted using all three pieces of software once they had been convinced of their potential and overcome their own fears in some cases and had established a study rhythm for using them.

For PGCE students, the relevant comments included points on:

- Less importance on early inductions. For these students the changing attitude was one of: 'Show what it can do and later convince me why I should use it'. They will use a piece of software until they have mastered it and then move on to analysing how they can make use of the software in their future teaching.

- Extended evaluation skills. The greatest appreciation was for developing a critical attitude for evaluating other possible teaching resources such as the Web. They grew to appreciate the various 'learner variables' (*op. cit.* Jamieson and Chapelle 152) and to extend their understanding of their own 'teacher variables' (i.e. a teacher's cognitive style, age, background, ability and motivation) when using CALL and ICT materials both for their personal learning (what certain students referred to as 'revision') and also for their teaching classes.

- Appropriateness. 'The Government tells us that we have to use ICT 'where appropriate', I feel now that I am in a more 'appropriate position' to decide what, where and when to exploit ICT materials', said one teacher trainee.

The main transferable skills developed to a greater or lesser degree by both groups of students included the following:

- critical evaluation;

- language learning strategies, (especially relevant to PGCE students);

- accepting and adding other tools to the repertoire of learning styles which would not exclude other styles learned and exploited earlier in the student's life;

- working with and 'reading' news images and analysing news presentation styles and contents (most pertinent to undergraduates);

- personal study skills (e.g. précis writing, see Murray and Barnes, *in press*)

- autonomous learning (with some limitations as described earlier, for undergraduates);

- general ICT skills and

- project organisation and delivery (several undergraduate students reported that they had used their experiences with the projects on their job applications and added them to their CV).

3.3 Linguistic and cultural gains

Further long-term definitive research involving many different types of evaluation variables would be needed in order to judge whether the undergraduate students learn more or learn less from the use of the grammar programs and the project than they would do if they had not made any use of the materials. However, one might question the ultimate utility of such research as the findings may prove to be limited, slightly redundant and somewhat anachronistic. It may be limited because, for example, Jamieson and Chapelle (*op. cit*, 158) have noted how difficult it is to measure the effectiveness of CALL quantitatively and concluded that this obstacle is not confined to research in CALL but is common in many areas of L2 research. It may be slightly redundant because over the four years of our study there has been no appreciable nor discernible decrease in the quality of students' linguistic output as evidenced from standard evaluation methods such as class and Summer examinations. Even with students achieving higher marks for their projects in the third and fourth years of the study over other groups of students in the preceding two years, it would be unwise to attribute this to the benefits of a single resource. This is due to the fact that there are so many resources used both on the projects and on the course in general. As well as that, there are several complex and composite variables to consider such as student abilities, motivation and project time-management skills. It may be slightly anachronistic because during the course of the year these CALL programs become established as part of their normal language learning strategy. Outside of the course students are expecting and in some cases demanding to have more and more on-line and Web-based resources available to them. Such demands can hardly be surprising nor can they be ignored as the use and influence of pedagogical software in pre-18 education continues to grow and become the norm. It is not, of course, our intention to advocate a blind acceptance of each CALL program new or otherwise but we are proposing the proper and supported integration of proven software to meet students' changing expectations and needs.

The undergraduate students in our study are motivated by the software and they are also deeply interested in their projects and benefit from peer-learning thus leading to linguistic gains in the following areas. They receive extensive practice in and testing of the intralingual skills: listening (through the video search and in using and imitating TT2); speaking (during the presentations and 'justification' of their projects); reading (when performing their background research on the subject matter of their project and also in using the grammar programs); and writing (for the production of the multimedia materials including a video transcription, a video summary, the creation of language exercises, a work diary, a strategy for using their project and some grammar-checking with GEF and GDF). Based on questionnaires carried out periodically over a four year period with different cohorts of students, it can be reported that on average over fifty per cent believed that their writing skills had improved because of the project and all students believed that their listening skills in general had improved. Many students, while enjoying the opportunity to form a deeper appreciation of their chosen aspect of French *civilisation*, did come to realise that their choice of news footage: 'forces you to see beyond the clip and not just accept their [the television reporter's] version of the events'. Thus students are motivated enough to perform additional background research on their chosen topic and gain a deeper awareness of French culture and society. An interesting change in student perception that may be noted is that when students have gone through the whole process of project work with TT2, many of them make the recommendation that the choice of video for the projects should be enlarged to include a film or documentary extract. This demand has been reiterated each year and when asked if they would repeat the project at a higher level of French to include these possible topics, the responses have been invariably positive. The conclusion here is obvious but it should not be ignored, we believe.

One of the most persistent criticisms of GDF by both sets of students in the study is that all of the grammatical explanations are in the target language. This can result in resistance to using it outside the class inductions. Such opposition may be tackled by repeated immersion in the context of study that uses GDF. However, it cannot be claimed that a final 'cure' was found to combat all learner reluctance to using it. Many students at this level of French still appear to want their grammar definitions in L1 for as long as possible. Short-term research to explain this continuing phenomenon may perhaps provide fruitful results and would be greatly welcomed. When our students were questioned on the subject some undergraduates said that they: 'didn't like GDF and found the program difficult to follow and it took a lot of effort and practice to get used to it'. Perhaps the most revealing comment was: 'GEF was easier to use and understand, so we tended to use that a lot more'. This begs the question as to whether these two programs should continue to be used together or if greater emphasis should be placed on GEF with GDF left as a background support resource for desirous learners.

PGCE students from joint language degree programs tended to make the greatest use of the grammar software to 'revise' and perfect their grammatical competencies during the early stages of the course. They later used their timetabled language refresher courses with tutors to cover any remaining and serious gaps without giving up total use of GEF and GDF for some personal revision. While appreciating the value of the programs for their own uses, again the overriding final attitude was one of integrating their use in their own future language classes. TT2 was used and evaluated by all French-specific trainees and they appreciated its strong potential for classroom use and revealed more interest in the language exercises than in the cultural subjects of the newsclips.

4   Conclusion

The software programs used in our study have become established and valued resources on undergraduate and postgraduate courses and similar studies must be conducted to extend their (and other CALL software's) possible use on other courses. It may be concluded that the induction phase in CALL usage is important for introducing both sets of students to a clear context of study. PGCE students need the skills to assess CALL software and once acquired, they will readily employ them in evaluating all types of educational media as well as their own language learning and teaching processes and strategies. As one trainee commented: 'I find myself thinking increasingly about the very nature of language and how it is learnt, interpreted and generated'. For the vast majority of these students, their attitudes and expectations change and develop rapidly during their teaching placements in secondary schools where they must apply their skills in classrooms. It is therefore essential that they hone their skills during several final CALL sessions involving their peers back at the university setting before the end of the course. For undergraduates, the staggered and 'rationed' integrative use of the software is critical. Agentive software such as GEF and especially GDF must be introduced and used in a structured and direct way both inside and outside the class environment. In our case, it proved to be beneficial to use them in conjunction with the instrumental software TT2 as this helped to bring about a definite pattern of use. This is where undergraduate attitudes and expectations change. As one student said: 'In term one I didn't use GDF and GEF outside the class much as I thought they were really there for revision but in term two I came to see the software more as part of the course or 'courseware' as somebody here called it'.

Given that in the future students at all levels of education will be making greater use of ICT for many of their (life-long) learning needs, it is incumbent upon us in our current CALL practice to possess the necessary critical acumen and experiences before we can pass them on to both future language teachers and students. Undergraduates must be shown the reasons for using and the methods for evaluating putative CALL software for their own language needs. This is equally true for PGCE students during their training. They also have to consider the differentiated needs and abilities of younger learners before integrating educational software into their lesson planning. These teachers have an even greater responsibility in that the effectiveness of their approach will undoubtedly influence in no small way the attitudes, expectations and learning styles of future generations of language undergraduates.

References

Barnes A. and Murray L. (2000) 'Diverse and Reverse Management in ICT to Support Knowledge of Language', in E. Brown (ed.), *CALL REPORT 15: Improving student performance in language learning through ICT*, London: CILT.

Barnett, L. (1993) 'Teacher Off: Computer Technology, Guidance and Self-Access', *System*, 21/3, pp.295–304.

Barson, J. (1997) 'Space, Time and Form in the Project-Based Foreign Language Classroom', *Language Learning Through Social Computing*, Occasional Papers Number 16, ALAA and The Horwood Language Centre, Univ. of Melbourne, Australia, pp.1–37.

Cooper, M.M. and Selfe, C.L. (1990) 'Computer Conferencing and Learning; Authority, Resistance and Internally Persuasive Discourse', *College English*, 52/8, pp.847–69.

Debski, R. (1997) 'Support of Creativity and Collaboration in the Language Classroom: a New Role for Technology', *Language Learning Through Social Computing*, Occasional Papers Number 16, ALAA and The Horwood Language Centre, Univ. of Melbourne, Australia, pp.41–65.

Englesberg, R. (1997) 'An Evaluation Study of a Multimedia Package for Learning English', *CAELL Journal*, 8/1, pp.15–20.

Garrett, N. (1991) 'Technology in the Service of Language Learning: Trends and Issues', *Modern Language Journal*, 75/1, pp.71–101.

Gibbs, G. (1994) *Learning in Teams: a Student Guide*, Oxford: Oxford Centre for Staff Development, Oxford Brookes University.

Gillespie, J. and McKee, J. (1999) 'Resistance to CALL: degrees of student reluctance to use CALL and ICT', *ReCALL*, 11/1, pp.38–46.

Hart, S. (1988) 'What University Students Think of CALL in Language Courses', *Modern Languages*, 69/3, pp.174–8.

Hewer, S. (1998) 'Optimising the Use of TELL products: an Evaluative Investigation into TELL Products in Use', copies are available from the TELL Consortium, University of Hull, Hull HU6 7RX, UK or can be downloaded from their Website at this address: http://www.hull.ac.uk/cti/eval.htm

Higgins, J. (1988) *Language Learners and Computers*, London: Longman.

Jamieson, J. and Chapelle, C. (1988) 'Using CALL Effectively: What Do We Need To Know About Students? ' *System*, 16/2, pp.151–62.

Jones, C. (1986) 'It's Not So Much The Program, More What You Do With It: The Importance Of Methodology in CALL', *System*, 14/2, pp.171–8.

Levy, M (1998) 'Two Conceptions of Learning and Their Implications for CALL at the Tertiary Level', *ReCALL*, 10/1, pp.86–94

Metcalfe, P. (1992) 'CALL, The Foreign-Language Undergraduate And The Teaching of Grammar: A Linguistic And Political Battlefield', *ReCALL*, 7, pp.3–5.

Murray, L. (1998) 'Why Integrate? Reactions to Télé-Textes Author 2, a CALL Multimedia Package', *ReCALL*, 10/1, pp.102-8.

Murray, L. and Barnes, A., 'Précis Writing in a Multimedia Environment', in E. Broady (ed.) *Second Language Writing in a Computer Environment* (*in press*) London: CILT/AFLS.

Peterson, M. (1997) 'Language Teaching and Networking', *System*, 25/1, pp.29–37.

Plowman, L. (1988) 'Active Learning and Interactive Video: A Contradiction In Terms ?', *Programmed Learning and Educational Technology*, 25, pp.289–93.

Rogers, M. (1996) 'What's Theory Got To Do With It?', in D. Engel and F. Myles (eds) *Teaching Grammar: Perspective in Higher Education*, London: CILT/AFLS, pp.21–43.

Warschauer, M. and Healey, D. (1998) 'State of the Art: Computers and Language Learning: an Overview', *Language Teaching*, 31, pp.57–71.

Watts, N. (1997) 'A Learner-Based Design Model for Interactive Multimedia Language Learning Packages', *System*, 25/1, pp.1–8.

Wenden, A. (1991) *Learner Strategies for Learner Autonomy: Planning and Implementing Learner Training for Language Learners*, Englewood Cliffs, NJ: Prentice Hall.

Van den Berg, S. and Watt, J. H. (1991) 'Effects of Educational Setting on Student Responses to Structured Hypertext', *Journal of Computer-Based Instruction*, 18/4, pp.118–124.

Designing a community learning environment using a Bulletin Board System: A trial with advanced French written communication

Caroline Sheaffer-Jones
University of New South Wales

1   Introduction

Foreign language learning, particularly in the classroom, has often appeared to be lacking any real communicative purpose. Meaningless practice has been pursued with the deferred goal of realising this expertise one day in a foreign country. Certainly, computer technology can fall into the trap of perpetuating such meaningless practice if it becomes merely another tool for drill, continuing what Sherry Turkle has called the 'modernist computational aesthetic' (1995: 18–20). However the advent of computer technology has also signalled an approach to foreign language learning in which real communication can empower the learner (Moran, 1990; Nunan and Lamb, 1996: 195–6).

With the increased use of technology such as e-mail, writing is assuming greater importance. Writing skills can now be developed in a new and meaningful way through authentic written communication. This paper describes synchronous classroom writing on a Bulletin Board System (BBS), during an intensive French course, to illustrate the significance of this interactive learning environment. Some similarities between this closed system of group writing on the BBS and Seymour Papert's concept of a *microworld* (Papert, 1980) will be outlined.

2 A selective review of relevant studies of computer-mediated communication

There is a gradually accumulating literature exploring the educational worth of computer-assisted communication in language learning. For example, Chun (1994) collected data over a two semester period from first-year German students using a real-time networking program on the Macintosh and analysed it for the number and length of each student's entries, the syntactic complexity of those entries and the type and number of different discourse structures. She concluded that by exploiting this computer-assisted class discussion, learners were able to develop their discourse skills and interactive competence. They took the initiative in asking and answering each other's questions, initiated questions, constructed and expanded on topics and took 'a more active role in discourse management than is typically found in normal classroom discussion. In addition, learners [exhibited] the ability to give feedback to others, as well as socio-linguistic competence in greeting and leave-taking, requesting confirmation or clarification and apologizing' (Chun, 1994: 28). Moreover, Chun inferred from her findings that students' comprehension of discourse, their coherent thinking and use of cohesive linguistic references and expressions had actually been enhanced by computer-assisted classroom discussion. Her belief in the authenticity of this medium also provoked optimism as to the beneficial effects on students' oral competencies.

Such beneficial effects on the quantity and characteristics of students' language and the diminution of teachers' central roles are echoed in other studies of classroom interaction with networked computers (for example, Debski & Gruba, 1998; Kern, 1995). Some researchers attribute these effects to the existence of authentic communicative purposes in language learning (for example, Peyton, 1990); others implicate characteristics of the medium itself, such as its flexibility to provide fast-paced interaction as well as time for critical reflection, whether individually or collaboratively (Evard, 1996; Kroonenberg, 1994/5). For these reasons, researchers are beginning to advocate the pedagogical benefits of designing particular forms of computer-based environments for language learning (Eldred, 1991; Warschauer 1996). The present study was designed to explore the effects of using a BBS to mediate experienced language teachers' communication and their critical reflection on the worth of the medium itself for their own teaching practices.

By analysing the nature of these learners' contributions to the BBS (learners who were themselves teachers, as has already been noted), I set out to investigate in particular such features as:

- their participation and motivation;
- their development of fluency;
- the variety of communicative functions which they demonstrated;
- aspects of their extended vocabulary;
- the accuracy, revision and structure of their writing;
- the nature of their descriptions;
- the feedback provided to each other.

3 The design and context of the present study

An intensive professional development course was held at the University of New South Wales in 1997. The class consisted of fifteen secondary school teachers, aged from twenty to sixty. The participants were employed at private and public schools, for the most part in metropolitan Sydney, but some in rural New South Wales.

The teaching took place in a laboratory of Power Mac 7600 computers networked to the World Wide Web. The BBS was accessed on a Macintosh or an IBM computer through a Web browser such as *Netscape Navigator* or *Internet Explorer*; my preparatory work of posting the tasks on to the BBS was done remotely using an IBM computer. The equipment and networking in the laboratory must allow fairly rapid use of the Web on all of the class terminals concurrently, so that BBS communications can be posted promptly. My laboratory terminal was also equipped with data projection, which was particularly useful in the initial phases for demonstrations.

Before giving details on the specific tasks involved in the present study, it is necessary to describe, in general terms, the way in which this BBS functioned. Prior to the course, a new address for our class BBS had been set up on the server for the participants to access. There was also a special administration page address, which was available only to me, but not to the students, in order to post information. These notices appeared at the top of the main page of the BBS. This noticeboard section was entitled *Affiches* and the tasks appeared here as links. By clicking on the name of each task, students could access the detailed requirements for each one. This part of the BBS was not interactive and so students could only read this section.

Our discussions were held in the interactive chat section entitled Chez Esmé which appeared just below the noticeboard section on the main page. On the main page, the number of comments on a particular item was entered automatically. Names or pseudonyms, as entered by the participants, were also shown underneath the comments. For a representation of the main page of the BBS please see Appendix, Figure 1.

A representation of the linked page is also to be found in the Appendix, as Figure 2. Comments which directly responded to the tasks outlined in the noticeboard section were typed into the box at the bottom of the main page and then the button 'Start New Chat' needed to be clicked (Figure 1). The full comment would not appear on the main page, but rather a title in the form of a link would be shown. All of the participants entered their work in this way on the main page.

At any time when participants wished to read or comment on each other's work, they would click on a particular title on the main page. A linked page would appear (Figure 2) showing the original comment at the top of the page. In order for participants to contribute subsequent remarks on those initial comments already submitted, they needed to write into the box which appeared at the foot of the linked page, and not into the one on the main page. These remarks would then be shown underneath the original comment on the linked page. The remarks appeared on the BBS in the order in which they were submitted.

Since many members of the group were unfamiliar with the keyboard layout for typing French on Macintosh computers, it was first necessary to practise typing with the diacritical marks. This was done with the aid of *Key Caps*, located in the menu under the Apple icon.

One of the most important objectives of the whole course was to target the improvement of fluency in oral and written skills, however at the same time, participants wished to gain new pedagogical ideas. The computer-mediated communication provided an interesting approach for targeting the development of written skills, which will be discussed in this paper, nevertheless it should be noted that speaking and listening skills were also used, in particular in group work, to negotiate the tasks. All communications were in French in this learning environment.

Until recently, circulating written work among class members was a slow and disjointed process which generally operated on a one to one basis. The technology of the BBS enables members of a group to interact collectively, either at a distance or in the classroom. In synchronous classroom exchanges, writing is submitted on to the BBS by the members of the class and can be viewed almost instantaneously and discussed by the whole group. Various types of Bulletin Board Systems are currently available. The BBS which I used was created by Mr Chris Hughes of the Professional Development Centre at the University of New South Wales, Sydney, although in this trial I did not exploit all of the possibilities which it offers. Prior to the present investigation, I had already incorporated the BBS into several intermediate and advanced subjects over the past two years in ways which were consistent with Laurillard's student-driven philosophy of technologically-mediated learning (Laurillard, 1980: 213). In this report, I focus on some classroom exchanges in the intensive course to illustrate the close productive interaction which this computer-mediated communication established.

3.1 Using the BBS in this intensive teacher professional development course

As experienced language teachers, these participants had enrolled in this course with the expectation that they would enhance their professional expertise as well as their linguistic competencies. For these reasons, tasks were designed which would incorporate opportunities for both of these developments. Therefore, various types of interactions took place on the BBS, some making extensive use of Francophone sites on the World Wide Web. I will use, as an example, the following initial set of activities and then discuss the results of this BBS communication, the limitations of the study, as well as some theoretical implications of learning using a BBS. This example utilised a particular question drawn from the NSW matriculation examination (Higher School Certificate) in which students were asked to construct a dialogue between an eighteen-year old and one parent. The subject of the dialogue was to be a birthday party and there was to be conflict between the two interlocutors. In the present study, I instigated for participants a three phase activity as follows:

1   *Conseils pour répondre au dialogue de l'examen écrit.* In pairs and in one group of three, participants presented advice and discussed, on the BBS, the best ways of approaching the dialogue question in the Writing Section of the final New South Wales secondary school French examination.

2   *Dialogue: comment bien préparer une boum.* With the same partners, they wrote dialogues on the BBS in answer to the question. Individually or with partners, these were then discussed on the BBS, in particular in the light of the initial advice which they had offered each other.

3   *Remarques.* Individually, they provided feedback on the value of using the BBS for such writing activities.

4   Results and discussion

In general, the members of the group shared many useful suggestions about tackling the dialogue question, for example, concerning register, the importance of varying grammatical structures and the need for careful editing. By using the BBS, they were able to brainstorm their ideas and to pool advice for the benefit of the group. The dialogues and ensuing discussions were both lively and amusing, and some of the suggested advice had clearly been taken into account in the dialogue writing. It was also evident that by working in groups in these initial activities, participants were able to offer each other some technical support. However, a number returned to their own terminals periodically, in order to make further contributions individually. In the following remarks, I will examine the ways in which the BBS interaction extended written communication.

Sustained participation and motivation. The BBS enabled ongoing work and discussion by everyone contemporaneously. The class was a hive of activity throughout the BBS writing and everyone was visibly motivated; a couple of people even added a few remarks in the evening from their home computers. All members of the group submitted comments frequently. They all commented on the work done by nearly all of the other members, as well as replying to remarks on their own work. A close interaction and camaraderie developed on the BBS among class members who were brought together by a common purpose. Some goaded others into submitting their work more rapidly, when they felt that the interactive pace was too slow:

> *Où sont les commentaires du reste du groupe? Vous vous êtes endormis, ou quoi? Vous avez besoin de café?? Nous, aussi! Vous prenez trop de temps pour réfléchir, ou bien, vous tapez... plus lentement que nous, et c'est pas possible! Dépêchez-vous! On vous attend!*

The first group to finish submitted this remark, with some irony, under the pseudonym 'les profs extraordinaires'. This option of not giving one's name made it possible to assume a different role, and perhaps to write more freely, although it did not always guarantee anonymity in the classroom. Generally, however, participants elected to give their own names.

The development of fluency. By enabling continuous interaction, the environment promoted the acquisition of greater fluency by all class members. The comments, questions and replies on the BBS were always an impetus for further discussions. The length of the contributions and the rate at which they were submitted increased markedly during the trial. Through the sustained interaction, it seemed that most members of the class were indeed also thinking in French. Some used puns or language games, for example, with the word '*boîte*', or by juxtaposing '*bonbon*' with '*bon, bon*'.

Utilising of a variety of communicative functions. Participants were immediately able to utilise language previously acquired, as well as to extend their skills. They used many different grammatical structures, as well as functions, of which I will provide a few brief examples:

- *Giving advice/instructions* (frequently coupled with the imperative or the subjunctive): 'Il faut que vous utilisiez la forme 'tu' et n'oubliez pas de l'utiliser tout le temps.'

- *Agreeing/disagreeing*: 'A notre avis, ce n'est pas du tout le cas parce que …'

- *Requesting information*: 'Vous pouvez expliquer ce que vous voulez dire dans le deuxième paragraphe?'

- *Praising/Encouraging*: 'C'est un dialogue fantastique. Plein de vocabulaire, de structures variées, d'idées intéressantes. Dix sur dix.'

- *Thanking*: 'On vous remercie de vos remarques mais il nous semble que vous venez de l'école du troisième âge.'

- *Expressing conditions*: 'S'il y a des dégâts à la maison, c'est toi qui paieras.'

Extending vocabulary and using a colloquial register. Participants learnt new vocabulary from each other and by consulting on-line reference tools, such as *Cyberdico*. They focused on colloquial French in the written dialogue, for example: '*Quoi? Une boum chez nous! Tu blagues, hein? Alors, qui va préparer la bouffe? Moi, j'n sais pas cuisiner.*' As well, their own interactions became increasingly informal, such as in the following example: '*Bravo, les deux mecs, vous avez très bien réussi.*'

Improving accuracy and revising. While participants attempted to write accurately and to edit their writing competently, the emphasis in this environment was on communication, rather than on absolute correctness. This helped to encourage participation and to free up discussion. When comprehension was impeded, an explanation was usually requested. This interaction forced the writers to review their French and to clarify passages. Sometimes corrections were made by modelling the correct form, sometimes the discrepancy between two juxtaposed forms was enough to lead participants to verify their usage. For example, when one group commented on a dialogue: '*Votre français est vachement impressif!*', and another added: '*Oui, votre utilisation du français est très impressionnante*', the first group in fact consulted a dictionary and corrected the Anglicism. Some self-corrections were also made on the BBS by resubmissions.

Structuring written communication. Apart from refining their competencies in French, participants learnt to structure their writing. By reading another piece of work, they were often able to understand how to improve their approach. For example, some of the advice submitted lacked clarity. However, when one group presented a particularly well developed piece of work, a number of positive comments were offered about the clearly defined structure of the paragraphs and the use of markers such as '*d'abord*', '*puis*', '*ensuite*', '*enfin*'. Sharing work by posting it to the group was productive and correction often took place by the example of a good response, rather than by negative comments. Participants were engaged in thinking explicitly about language together and about how to improve their French communication. A metalanguage developed, for example: '*Pensez aux mots charnières qui peuvent mieux lier vos idées.*'

Describing a real world context: Francophone culture in Australia. Aspects of Francophone culture were incorporated into the writings, in particular cuisine such as *pâté*, *escargots*, *vol-au-vent*, *camembert* and *calvados*. However, what resulted on the BBS was not just a window on the French-speaking world, but rather a new hybrid environment in which Francophone culture coexisted with elements of the immediately relevant Australian scene, as illustrated in the following dialogue:

Mère: Écoute, Lulu! Ton père et moi, nous avons décidé d'aller au restaurant du Club RSL [Return Servicemen's League] pour ton anniversaire, avec les grands-parents, les oncles, les tantes…

Lulu: Non, je voudrais bien préparer des plats à la maison pour mes invités. Tu sais bien que j'aime beaucoup faire la cuisine.

Mère: Mais qui aime les quiches, les cuisses de grenouilles, les escargots, le coq au vin, les tartes aux pommes et la crème caramel? Moi, je préfère le steak-frites, et ton père, lui, il aime bien les hamburgers du club. Alors, c'est décidé. On mange au club!

References to the Australian popular culture were an important part of this communication in French which could take account of and satirise that which was closest to home and of immediate relevance.

Feedback. Participants provided feedback, in the final task, about learning and improving written communication by means of the BBS. Without exception, every member of the group evaluated the work as an extremely worthwhile learning experience. A few reservations were expressed about the need for some technical knowledge; others noted that this was fast becoming indispensable. Several people raised the possibility of technical difficulties: '*On peut 'tomber sur un os' avec la technologie*'.

Some of the positive remarks made included the following:

> Ça va mieux avec cette méthode, parce qu'on a plus de temps de penser à une réponse. C'est aussi une façon de partager nos idées, on s'est amusé beaucoup.

> Tout le monde y participe, même les timides à l'oral.

> C'est beaucoup plus intéressant d'écrire ensemble. Les élèves peuvent enseigner et s'instruire dans le groupe.

A number of participants said that conceptualising, as a group, the makings of a good response facilitated the dialogue writing. This conceptualisation was also important for the final discussions. They also said that the BBS had enabled them to consolidate their skills and to begin writing with greater ease and confidence. They considered that it was a very effective and enjoyable means of learning and teaching, in which they could interact, yet also have more time to think.

Limitations of the trial. It must be noted that while this trial gives some insight into the use of a method of teaching and learning with advanced learners, it focuses on a relatively short interaction with a select group of people. A decision was also made to report qualitative evidence of learning, although it would have been possible to make quantitative analyses, in particular in relation to sharp improvements in fluency and accuracy.

A question which needs to be raised about this style of learning concerns the ways in which the interaction might change at elementary levels. In the discussions among advanced learners, interaction was dynamic, profound and covered a range of issues, as has been the case in other courses.

In terms of the practical use of the BBS, there were some difficulties, mainly at the beginning, for example the members of the group occasionally failed to indicate whether they were discussing the original comment or interacting with a subsequent remark on that initial comment. This information needed to be specified because the object of their discussion did not necessarily directly precede their remarks on the BBS where postings are in chronological order.

4.2 Implications of this BBS teaching

The findings of this short study appear to fit comfortably with those reported in the selective review of research in computer-mediated communication at the start of this paper. However, they also suggest the worth of such learning environments for teaching professionals. How then did the group communication on the BBS not only improve written communication, but indeed establish a new notion of learning?

Networked writing has been found to offer more opportunities for frequent and active participation, when compared with oral discussions (Kern, 1995: 470). As has been suggested in other analyses of BBS writing (Kroonenberg, 1994/95: 25), the fact that all writing was posted for the whole class to read was an added incentive to improve accuracy and quality. Due to interactive communication, many participants became much more attuned to the fundamental need for detailed revision. The development of a metalanguage was an important tool for thinking about their own learning.

In some ways, the type of learning environment which I have described has parallels with Seymour Papert's concept of a *microworld*, an incubator where innovative ideas could flourish (Papert, 1980: 125). The notion was developed to combat a model of irrelevant rote learning or 'dissociated' learning identified by Papert, not simply in the study of mathematics, but also in the wider learning culture (Papert, 1980: 47). Papert's invention of 'Mathland', a province of this microworld in which children could experience creative, hands-on computer programming, established a completely different relationship to learning via the computer. It also helped to eliminate 'mathophobia', namely the fear of mathematics or the fear of learning, in the etymological sense of the term (Papert, 1980: 38–40).

Writing interactively in French on the BBS within a group was indeed a type of 'Mathland', where learning could take place through purposeful communication. A sense of community developed in this interaction, as has been highlighted in other research (Evard, 1996: 238). Participants were able to discuss their own cultural context within this relatively unthreatening, limited environment and to gain confidence. As in the concept of a microworld, this was not a practice ground, but already authentic interaction, in which the BBS provided a tangible, cultural milieu through which to think, what Papert called an 'object-to-think-with', 'objects in which there is an intersection of cultural presence, embedded knowledge, and the possibility for personal identification' (Papert, 1980: 11). Writing was generated out of the very process of network interaction (Barker and Kemp, 1990); technology had created a new form of plural communication in which all members were drawn together to write a text concurrently.

This computer-mediated communication implies a radically different model of instruction from that of a teacher-centred classroom in which information is imparted to students. There is a more collaborative relationship between teacher and learner. It has been found that network writing can clearly undermine teacher-centred communication (DiMatteo, 1991: 14; Peyton, 1990). After my initial demonstrations and opening questions, my role became much less prominent. In the myriad of concurrent discussions, my comments were simply offered, alongside many other remarks, via a terminal in the network. As one participant realised somewhat nostalgically: '*on n'a plus le contrôle de nos élèves!*'. Most importantly, the BBS fosters peer instruction, rather than competition, and participants interact more realistically as both teachers and learners.

As in the environment proposed by Papert, learners could become 'the active, constructing architects of their own learning' (Papert, 1980: 122). In this perspective, learning is not the assimilation of established facts, but rather a process of knowledge construction. Such a process was first made explicit in computer-mediated learning by Papert in 1980 in his seminal work, *Mindstorms*, and now others have been exploring the value of similar strategies in the area of computer-mediated language learning (for example Debski and Gruba, 1998). Learning on the BBS is clearly a process and editing, or 'debugging' (Papert, 1980: 23) is a fundamental part of it. This became evident to members of the group who constantly needed to refine communications which had been misunderstood. Moreover, without delay, participants were able to build upon each other's work and they often rethought their own positions. For example, the simple acquiescent words of a mother to her teenage daughter were substituted, in one rewriting, for a much more militantly feminist ethic. Learning was team-based and took place through interactive communication, across a range of areas, such as ethics, education, music, film, art, cooking and fashion. This is in keeping with a

119

fundamentally new type of transdisciplinary knowledge, emerging today from collaborations among various researchers, and identified by Gibbons as 'Mode 2 knowledge production' (Gibbons *et al*, 1994). In contrast with Mode 1 knowledge production where knowledge is generated in academies and later applied in the field, Mode 2 knowledge generation occurs as a result of interdisciplinary collaborations in the places in which it is to be used.

Writing on the BBS within a small group made it possible for the participants to improve their written communication in a meaningful interaction. Warschauer's research demonstrates the motivational role of computers in written communication (1996). The BBS generated enthusiasm; participants actively took charge of their learning. They reflected on the work together, a critical part of the learning process. This interactive communication constituted a new type of writing which fostered community learning. Many realised the unfinished nature of this project and that the learning would continue, in different contexts, as a work-in-progress. With reference to Lévi-Strauss, Papert and Turkle write about the notion of *bricolage* in relation to learning and underline the importance of working and reworking materials (Papert, 1980: 173; Turkle and Papert, 1991: 168–75). This 'tinkering' needs to be understood not as an activity which exists for want of a better one, but as the foundation of a positive, constructive community learning environment.

Acknowledgements

I thank Mr C. Hughes (Professional Development Centre, University of New South Wales) for the use the BBS software which he developed and I would like to acknowledge his technical assistance as well as that of Mr P. Sluis, Mr R. Hilder and Mr B. Johnston. I would also like to thank Dr Lynette Schaverien for her useful comments on this work.

References

Barker, T. and Kemp, F. (1990) 'Network theory: A postmodern pedagogy for the written classroom' in C. Handa (ed.) *Computers and Community: Teaching Composition in the Twenty-first Century*, Portsmouth, NH: Boynton/Cook: 1–27.

Chun, D.M. (1994) 'Using Computer Networking to Facilitate the Acquisition of Interactive Competence', *System*, 22(1): 17–31.

Debski, R., and Gruba, P. (1998) 'Attitudes towards Language Learning through Social and Creative Computing', in K. Cameron (ed.) *Multimedia CALL: Theory and Practice*, Exeter: Elm Bank Publications, 1998.

DiMatteo, A. (1991) 'Communication, Writing, Learning: An Anti-Instrumentalist View of Network Writing', *Computers and Composition*, 8(3): 5–19.

Eldred, J.M. (1991) 'Pedagogy in the Computer-Networked Classroom', *Computers and Composition*, 8(2): 47–61.

Evard, M. (1996) 'A Community of Designers: Learning Through Exchanging Questions and Answers', in Y. Kafai and M. Resnick (eds) *Constructionism in Practice: Designing, Thinking, and Learning in a Digital World*, Mahwah, New Jersey: Lawrence Erlbaum Associates.

Gibbons, M., Limoges, C., Nowotny, H., Schwartzman, S., Scott, P. and Trow, M. (1994) *The New Production of Knowledge: The Dynamics of Science and Research in Contemporary Societies*, London: SAGE.

Kern, R.G. (1995) 'Restructuring Classroom Interaction with Networked Computers: Effects on Quantity and Characteristics of Language Production', *The Modern Language Journal*, 79(4): 457–76.

Kroonenberg, N. (1994/95) 'Developing Communicative and Thinking Skills Via Electronic Mail', *TESOL Journal*, 4(2): 24–7.

Laurillard, D. (1993) *Rethinking University Teaching: A Framework for the Effective Use of Educational Technology*, London and New York: Routledge.

Moran, C. (1990) 'The Computer-Writing Room: Authority and Control', *Computers and Composition*, 7(2): 61–9.

Nunan, D., and Lamb, C. (1996) The Self-directed Teacher: Managing the learning process, Cambridge and New York: Cambridge University Press.

Papert, S. (1980) *Mindstorms: Children, Computers and Powerful Ideas*, New York: Basic.

Peyton, J.K. (1990) 'Technological Innovation Meets Institution: Birth of Creativity or Murder of a Great Idea?', *Computers and Composition*, 7(Special Issue): 15–32.

Turkle, S., and Papert, S. (1991) 'Epistemological Pluralism and the Revaluation of the Concrete', in I. Harel and S. Papert (eds) *Constructionism*, Norwood, N.J.: Ablex: 161–91.

Turkle, S. (1995) *Life on the Screen: Identity in the Age of the Internet*, New York: Simon & Schuster.

Warschauer, M. (1996) 'Motivational Aspects of using Computers for Writing and Communication', in M. Warschauer (ed.) *Telecollaboration in foreign language learning*, Honolulu, HI: Second Language Learning & Curriculum Center: University of Hawaii Press: 26–46.

Appendix
Figure 1: Section of Main Page of BBS

Affiches

- Conseils pour répondre au dialogue de l'examen écrit
  (Original post by Caroline…)

- Dialogue: comment bien préparer une boum
  (Original post by Caroline …)

- Remarques
  (Original post by Caroline …)

Chez Esmé

- Conseils pour répondre au dialogue de l'examen écrit
  x Comments…
  (Original post by Simone and George…)

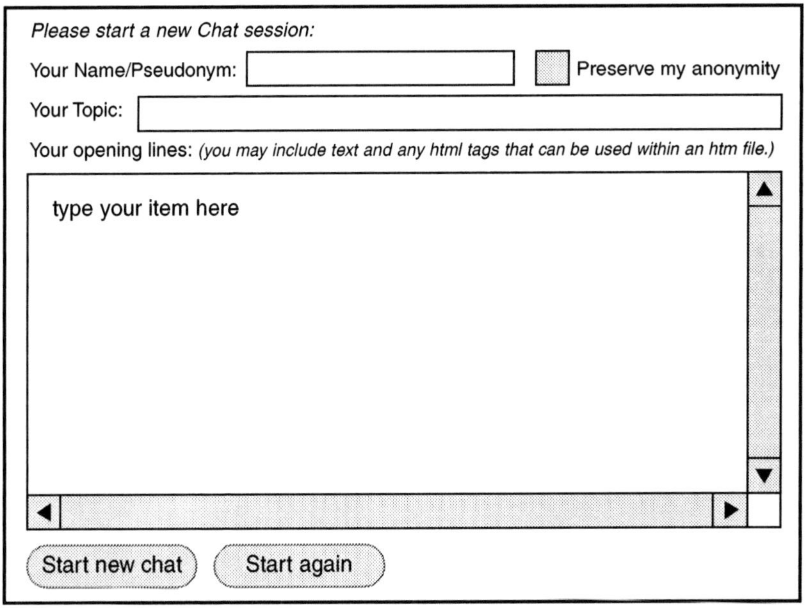

- …

Please start a new Chat session:

Your Name/Pseudonym: [_____] ☐ Preserve my anonymity

Your Topic: [_____]

Your opening lines: *(you may include text and any html tags that can be used within an htm file.)*

    type your item here

(Start new chat) (Start again)

Figure 2: Linked Page of BBS

Conseils pour répondre au dialogue de l'examen écrit

D'abord, il faut lire la question au moins deux fois. Notez vos idées, ensuite mettez-les logiquement en ordre …

Posted by Simone and George via Someone at IP: 149.171 …

Comments on this item:

- Richard and Susanne:

  Chers Simone et George,
  Nous avons bien lu vos conseils et nous vous en remercions. Il nous semble que malgré vos conseils…
  Submitted by Richard and Susanne via Someone at IP: 149.171…

- …

Please start a new Chat session:

Your Name/Pseudonym: [_____]   ▨ Preserve my anonymity

Your Topic: [_____]

Your opening lines: *(you may include text and any html tags that can be used within an htm file.)*

```
type your item here
```

(Start new chat)   (Start again)

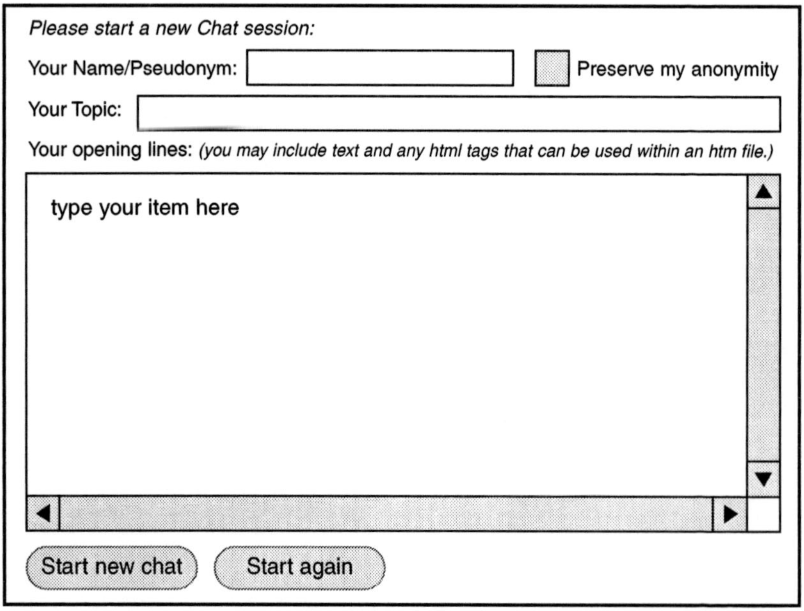

What makes a successful e-mail tandem partnership?

Lesley Walker
University of Sheffield

This paper is concerned with a group of language learners using the medium of email, and paired with a target language correspondent, to complete a task designed to develop their communicative, linguistic, and intercultural competence. At the same time these students are given the opportunity to develop their autonomy, by independently managing the completion of the task within a semester. By means of analysing the content of emails in these electronic bilingual learning partnerships, a picture is built up of the partnership skills necessary for a successful outcome.

1 Introduction

1.1 Tandem learning

Tandem learning involves a partnership of two native speakers, learners of each other's language who learn from each other and help each other to learn. As well as an exchange of language there may well be an interchange of intercultural knowledge. Tandem learning is underpinned by the principle of reciprocity, the reciprocity generated by individuals working together for the mutual benefit of both. Tandem learning also observes the principle of autonomy, which establishes that each partner is responsible for their own language learning and for establishing objectives and deciding on methods and materials. Each partner may have very different language goals.

The success of such partnerships as a form of autonomous learning is shown by students taking part in Face to Face tandem partnerships who remark on how much more motivated they are to learn when they can set their own agenda and learning rhythm, and use materials of specific interest to themselves. The support and encouragement between partners in such a learning relationship also plays a vital role in their mutual progress, with partners taking pride in the advances they see one another make through their input and help. In the hope of enabling such motivating factors and individual progress in written language learning and intercultural knowledge, e-mail tandem partnerships have been formally integrated into the students' language programme. From the relatively straightforward mode of speaking and listening to a real live partner, tandem learning has been introduced into the sphere of written communication with an on-line counterpart.

1.2 E-mail tandem learning

Drawing on his corpus-based study of e-mail discourse, to compare e-mail with speech and writing, Simeon Yates concludes that computer-mediated communication (CMC) is a complex mode of communication, being 'neither simply speech-like nor simply written-like' (1996: 46). E-mail then is not simply a very fast way of sending written missives but has its own properties, namely the advantage of a medium which combines the immediacy and fluency of spoken discourse and yet, as Yates points out, retains the written form. Elsewhere Yates presents both the pros and cons of e-mail interaction, setting out the arguments as to why the medium of CMC might be perceived by users as friendly or unfriendly. On the one hand, the lack of face-to-face cues might lead to a perception of the medium as distancing and cold. On the other hand, lack of an active visual feedback channel [might] lead to greater rather than less self-awareness. Indeed, lack of physical presence and the use of CMC allow individuals to construct alternative or virtual identities (1997: 284–286). Helmut Brammerts too is overwhelmingly positive in his account of this mode of communication, though for somewhat different reasons, arguing that 'many tandem partners – often due to the relative anonymity of the medium – lower their 'affective filters' and form very open and frank personal relationships without ever having seen each other' (1996: 15).

This innovative and empowering way of using IT for language learning also has practical advantages for learners. Speed and low costs are obvious factors but students also have the opportunity of working at their own rhythm, as in most universities the provision of IT facilities around the clock means that they can go on-line at a time which suits their needs.

Through the server of the International E-mail Tandem Network<URL: http://www.shef.ac.uk/uni/services/mltc/tandem/engfra.html> British students can be paired up with native speakers of the language they are studying. The network, whose members are drawn from universities throughout the European Union, has been set up with the aim of promoting e-mail tandem learning among HE students, because of the potential of such collaborative learning and peer support on-line to enable successful foreign language learning. It is then into this dynamic realm, one which is full of both problems and potential, that our language learners are cast.

1.3 Learning strategies and communication strategies

Of particular interest are the learning strategies that may be used in an effective e-mail tandem partnership. O'Malley and Chamot (1995: 8) describe as metacognitive strategies, 'thinking about the learning process, planning for learning, monitoring of comprehension or production while it is taking place, and self-evaluation after the learning activity has been completed'. The act of monitoring is particularly relevant to our analysis. Good learners distinguish themselves from poor learners precisely by their ability to 'analyse the demands of the task and to respond appropriately, to recognise and manage the learning situation' (*op. cit.* : 48–9).

We shall also consider some of the communication strategies used by our successful learners, exploring how individuals set about achieving their goals using their own linguistic resources, adapting them to the situation in which they find themselves and the means of communication available to them. In other words, we shall attempt to examine the pragmatic dimension of e-mail tandem interaction. We shall see how, in CMC, individuals are able to use, with various degrees of effectiveness, the strategies usually associated with face to face communication.

2   The learners and their task

The e-mail project, which is the focus of this paper, is set as an assessed writing assignment for Post A level students in Spring semester courses in French, German and Spanish. Many of them are reading Engineering, Maths, Physics, Chemistry or Geography, on courses, which include an Erasmus year or semester spent in the target language community studying their main subject. We will be examining the work of some of the students of French. Their partners are for the most part students in French institutions but some have partners who are working in commerce and industry.

Students have 12 weeks in which to complete their project. Though they will normally be allocated a partner by their course tutor, they are expected to complete the work for the project in their own time, with a minimum of formal supervision. The students are thus given the opportunity to organise their own learning and develop their independent study skills. The principles of tandem learning, and their application to the e-mail project are explained to the students. The importance of the negotiation of a topic, as well as negotiating how often to write, the distribution of both languages, and how much error correction to include are also underlined. The assessment of the assignment is also explained. The students are made aware of the joint aims of the project: broadening linguistic and intercultural knowledge as well as promoting autonomous learning, and its concomitant transferable skills, such as planning, reviewing and time-management.

As can be seen from the cover-sheet for the assignment in the appendix, students are asked to discover and write up in the foreign language, firstly, information on their partner, e.g. what they have in common and how they differ. Secondly, they are also required to research, with their partner's help, an aspect of France or French culture. This will subsequently form the basis of an oral presentation. Lastly, they are asked to reflect on the language they and their partner have used and to note which aspects of the language, for example vocabulary, idioms, constructions, they have consciously learned, acquired, or simply noticed for reuse. Students hand in the written report on the project in French, together with a portfolio of e-mails they have written to and received from their partners.

Reflecting the tandem principles, the criteria for the assessment of the assignment are based on the elements of 'partnership', 'intercultural knowledge' and 'language learning'. To be deemed to have had a successful e-mail tandem partnership, a student must complete the assignment in all respects. He or she will sustain an effective correspondence, successfully negotiating in order to accomplish the information-gathering and language-learning aspects of the task.

It is proposed in this paper to analyse several partnerships judged to be successful in varying degrees, in order to discover what elements lead to the happy conclusion of the e-mail project. Of the eight e-mail assignments under scrutiny in this chapter, one was awarded a first class grade, five an upper-second class grade and two a lower-second class grade. Thus we are identifying, across a range of attainment, factors identified by examiners as contributing to success. Tandem partnerships deemed unsuccessful because of overuse of native language and under-use of the target language, and a deficiency in the communication skills required to keep a partnership going, will not be examined here.

Our data comprises the text of the assignment plus the text of the e-mail messages exchanged. Quotations from all the texts are reproduced literally. The purist, reading what a French native speaker writes in an e-mail, may, at first, be disconcerted by the level of errors in spelling and morphology. Yet the documents are rich in accurate syntax and authentic idiom. This medium, which – though written – mimics the informality of verbal communication, entails a tolerance of grammatical incorrectness. In addition most of the e-mail partners, both French and English, chose not to use accents in their e-mails, since they are not transferred consistently between different e-mail software programs. For this and related reasons, as will become apparent, mistakes in the e-mails of the native speakers, as well as those of the English learners, preclude the identification of every typing error or linguistic mistake by means of the customary 'sic'.

3 Effective partnership skills

3.1 Negotiating a topic

The ability to accomplish the negotiation of a topic, which is of interest to both parties, is vital for a successful partnership. In our first example, an English student who is genuinely trying to engage with her partner writes such comments as 'Il faut que je dise à cette point que tu écris très bien l'anglais'. The learner seeks a rapport with her partner, writing, 'a propos puis-je te tutoyer, c'est plus amical n'est-ce pas?' She goes on to say, 'Comme tu sais il faut que je fasse un projet mais je n'ai pas encore décidée ce que je voudrais faire. Alors est-ce que tu as des idées? Peutêtre je peux faire quelque chose au sujet de tourisme en France ou où tu habites?' On receiving some information she thanks her partner and asks for 'plus information sur tourisme à Lyon et peutêtre les biens et mauvais effets du tourisme. Par exemple information sur pollution ou les nuisances sonores à cause des touristes.' Her partner replies this time by downloading and sending 'Tourisme, industrie du' Encyclopédie Microsoft Encarta 98, which consists of 8 pages of not very user-friendly material, the accents being shown as alphanumeric codes.

What happened here? The English student had prepared the ground carefully before asking for the favour of providing information for her topic. Because of the nature of her request and its potential for inconveniencing her partner, before the request for more detailed information, she had congratulated her partner on her English and had corrected several mistakes in the e-mail she had received. Responding to her partner but being asked for specialist information she cannot (or chooses not to) provide, or which she is not sufficiently interested in to pursue, the French partner has nonetheless replied with a positive politeness strategy and has either tried to help or at least gone through the motions. Perhaps if the English student had succeeded in formulating more concrete and specific questions about her partner's personal experience of tourism in Lyon, she might have gained information with which to complete her task. However her partner is not engaged by the topic. So although in subsequent e-mails the English partner finds out a good deal of detail on her partner's likes and dislikes, thus completing one element of the task for her assignment, the partnership is only partially successful in that the topic selected by the English partner, is not discussed at length by both partners. In fact the electronic information on tourism was not used subsequently by the English student. The request for information seems to have 'over-inconvenienced' the partner. After all the topic was not mutually agreed and it is not referred to again.

There is one more element to be taken into consideration. The English writer remained mistaken throughout the correspondence about the sex of her partner. When writing her report of the exchange, she constantly refers to 'il' when in fact the e-mails are signed with a girl's name. This could not have happened in a face to face conversation and one wonders if her strategies for communicating would have been different if she had been aware of this, and indeed if she construed her partner's responses as 'masculine' ones. Thus, although the project may be deemed successful with regard to language learning and practice, it was less than successful from the point of view of negotiation and indeed partnership.

In the next example, an English student writes to a French student of computer science and decides she would like him to explain his subject to her. The student has obviously given some thought as to what might, in theory, be a fruitful topic. However the topic was not mutually negotiated and her partner writes, 'you wrote me that you would like me to explain computer science to you but I don't know what you want to know. So if you are thinking of something precise just ask me and I will try to answer it. I find it hard to explain in French and of course even harder in English.' His subsequent e-mails echo those of other French partners who are trying their best, 'as I really want to help you in this project, can you please ask me more precise questions about a subject?' Several e-mails later he writes, 'Comment se fait-il que tu ne m'as pas reparlé de ton projet de français? la date est-elle passée? Si c'est le cas, je suis confus de n'avoir pas répondu à temps, sinon je veux bien t'aider.' It would seem that, in many cases, the project topic threatens to get in the way of what is otherwise a successful partnership and becomes an embarrassment to the English student who does not wish to encumber e-mails with any further reference to it. The English student in this partnership writes on her project coversheet, 'Selon moi les partenaires à l' émail sont trés bons pour améliorer son niveau de français spontané mais pour apprendre quelque chose sur un sujet, ils ne sont pas si utiles.'

How then do the partners decide on a topic of mutual interest that is fruitful from the point of view of intercultural knowledge and language learning for those students working on an e-mail project? The next learner has already exchanged a few e-mails with her partner and has offered reciprocal support. When she discovers that he lives 'dans les Hautes-Alpes près de Briançon à la station de Serre-Chevalier' and is very enthusiastic about the region he lives in, she writes, 'je veux faire un petit projet sur le tourisme dans la vallée, mais est-ce que tu penses que c'est une bonne idée?' The topic although obvious still needs to be mutually confirmed. When the French student agrees to the topic, the English student follows up with some questions, which will lead to an interesting discussion. 'Peut-tu m'envoyer quelques informations sur les deux saisons et les activités principales? Est-ce que le tourisme a les désavantages pour la vallée comme la congestion, la pollution, les prix élevés dans les supermarchés, etc ????' The use of the four question marks seems to indicate that the English partner recognises the size of the favour she is asking and, in this case, the partner appears not to have been inconvenienced and agrees to the topic suggested. Perhaps the four question marks were cues which the partner picked up on and can be classified, according to Oxford (1990), as a compensation strategy, the written equivalent of using mime or gesture to get help. Although the French partner is required to give information, the management of the topic has not become his responsibility. The English student assumes responsibility for the learning and decides on the direction to be taken in the topic discussion. As we stated at the beginning of the article, tandem learning seeks to promote autonomy through the individual taking decisions on his or her learning. Within the framework of the e-mail project the learner has the scope to complete the task in his or her own way once the approval and co-operation of the partner has been gained

Another example shows that a successful topic negotiation can also be a matter of good luck as, for example, when two partners find a mutual interest very early on in their e-mails. In one of the first e-mails received by the English student, her partner writes, 'You are interested by the French political system… .me too, so I'll try to explain it from my (objective!) point of view – but in French to be really clear.' She goes on to talk about the main political parties of the left and right in French. Her English tandem partner, who tentatively suggested the topic, has struck gold. She in turn replies 'Je suis très heureuse que le sujet t'intéresse aussi.' She explains: 'Je pense … décider pendant mes vacances les détails exactes que je veux savoir. Et puis je peux te demander des questions un peu plus specifique!' We can see that once the topic has been successfully negotiated then the effective autonomous learner takes responsibility for the direction and planning of the learning and does not expect her partner to execute the project for her.

In a subsequent e-mail the English partner sends a list of questions in French on the Assemblée Nationale, le Sénat, les élections législatives, l'élection présidentielle and le perchoir. It is a very long list and she adds 'si tu pouvais répondre à une ou deux questions ça maidera beaucoup..je suis désolée.' She is aware of making a heavy demand on her partner but is still negotiating, one or two questions answered would be helpful and she goes on to apologise. This e-mail was sent 27/4/98. The English partner writes again on 1/5/98. The pattern of the exchange has been one of e-mails exchanged every three or four days. She has not heard from her partner and sends a very chatty letter with no mention of her topic. Her next letter with the heading SALUT!!! goes out on 6/5/98. It is now ten days since she sent the list of questions and she has heard nothing from her partner. At the end of another chatty letter she writes, 'Je suis désolée si j'ai t'effrayée avec toutes les questions pour le projet!! J'espère que tu m'écriras bientôt!' In the continuing silence she writes to the Eng-Fra e-mail forum, a subnet of the International Tandem Network where native English and French speakers exchange e-mails on topics of mutual interest. Our student asks the forum at large the questions she put to her partner and is rewarded with replies from members interested in the subject. She is a determined and resourceful on-line learner. There is in fact a happy ending, for on 15/5/98 the English student does receive a letter from her partner, explaining 'I'm realy sorry for this late. Now we can use the computers again. In fact the technicians were 'en grève'. She goes on to answer all her partner's questions and to talk about the other subjects of conversation that have cropped up in the meantime.

Unlike our own students, most of the French partners do not have a formal assignment. Those French students who do have one, have been told specifically what topic to investigate. Immediately three different kinds of e-mail exchanges are apparent, each of which will have very different outcomes in terms of the skills to be developed. Learners can be left to communicate with no specific objective or topic. They can be given a specific topic on which to gather information. On the surface this may simplify matters but could give rise to difficulties in the partnership. Thirdly, as with the students above, they may be left to negotiate a topic, but given specific objectives in terms of the amount of information they were expected to collect. The purpose in doing this was to give them the opportunity to develop their skills in managing and monitoring their learning, transferable skills which, combined with IT literacy, should enhance their 'employability'.

3.2 Shifting from transaction to interaction

Michael McCarthy (1991: 70), writing on discourse analysis, notes that 'conversation is a joint activity that has to be worked out.' In this sense an exchange of e-mails is more akin to a spoken interaction than to a conventional exchange of letters between penpals because of the dynamism which stems from the possibility of an immediate response from one's partner. Obviously the context of the e-mail project will constrain the way learners express themselves, especially at the beginning of the exchange when, as well as coming to grips with expressing ideas in the target language, the learner is tentatively discovering how to perform effective speech acts in an exchange with a complete stranger. One student offers an almost parodic embodiment of Grice's co-operative principle (1975: 45–50) with its maxims of quality, quantity, relevance and manner, and truthfully states, giving as much information as is necessary in a relevant and unambiguous fashion, that, 'This semester I have to do an e-mail project and I hope you can help me with some information. I'd be glad to help you if I could of course.' Even though in his request he uses a mitigating device in the form of an offer of possible reciprocal input, he asks too much of his partner, who replies, 'Ben, non je n'ai pas d'idées pour ton projet.' His reply of 'Moi non plus, je n'ai pas encore des idées pour mon projet' leaves both a gap in the communication and possibly in the formation of a bond between the two. The French partner cannot respond to the request in a way which appears helpful, even though he has couched his answer in terms which soften his refusal with 'Ben' and the use of the familiar 'ton' which a pragmatist will recognise as, in fact, a face saving act (1996: 61) avoiding a threat to the burgeoning partnership, but which the average student may see only in terms of a refusal to help, bearing out the theory that the medium of CMC might be perceived as unfriendly. The partner has in fact previously mentioned an interest, 'Je lis pas mal de livres de science fiction, c'est sympa' and we also find out he is doing his military service. Neither of these potentially rich veins of information is explored or alluded to at all by his English partner. Another e-mail from the French partner begins, 'Je suis désolé mais je ne m'intéresse pas vraiment à la politique.' However, while not being interested in politics (and apologising for it), he does go on to give some basic information about the French system and recommends a web-site on the book written by President Mitterrand's doctor and banned in France at the time. 'thank you Mr Internet!' he writes. Again this encouraging lead is not followed up by his English partner who subsequently uses other resources to find out about French politics.

If we examine the competence shown by the English partner in communicating we can see that he is successful at only a basic level of competence. He understands his partner's French. However it would appear that he is less successful at the level of sociolinguistic competence. The English partner, at this point, is performing at the level of *transactions*. He asks questions without engaging with his partner. There is certainly a lack of *interaction* evident in his disregarding the wealth of information provided by his partner. The lack of follow-up to his partner's mention of his interests, his situation in life and also his provision of useful information, inhibits natural discourse (although his partner keeps trying) and so restricts the learning process to the disadvantage of both partners. This bears out David Little's observation that 'difficulties will arise if either partner attaches greater importance to personal learning objectives than to the maintenance of a collaborative learning partnership' (1996: 29).

In striking contrast to this failure to both negotiate a topic and sustain an effective partnership, let us look at the moves of the learner who successfully negotiated the topic of tourism in the Alps. Once the learner has established the 'formal' topic for her project she goes on to establish an informal topic of discussion, writing 'apprends-moi quelques phrases et quelques mots d'argot'. In his next letter her partner sends back a list of argot 'ne pas aller à un RDV = poser un lapin, un garçon = un mec' and sends some cruder words too. The ice is broken. 'Voilà de quoi apprendre !' he adds. The informal topic has moved the relationship on to an informal footing. Sending over slang becomes a regular feature of their exchanges. The partners are engaging with one another. The e-mails show us interaction taking place and not a transaction with one of the pair interviewing the other. At one point the French partner explains 'Je ne suis pas sur de l'orthographe car je le dis mais je ne l'écris jamais.' His partner replies 'merci pour les mots d'argot que tu m'as envoyé ; j'essayerai de les utiliser le prochaine fois que je parle en francais.' Here is a very good example of a successful e-mail tandem partnership where intercultural information is being exchanged while providing the basis for language learning. Interestingly, though this is a written exchange it involves sharing information about the spoken language and the learner writes that she will incorporate this into her spoken output.

An important next step is to help our learners to acquire or develop the sociolinguistic skills with which to communicate effectively. McCarthy (1991: 136) defines interactional talk as having as its primary function, 'the lubrication of the social wheels, establishing roles and relationships with another person…, confirming and consolidating relationships, expressing solidarity, and so on'. This is the 'talk', which our e-mail tandem learners need to be conversant in. We need to raise their awareness of the need to apply to the electronic medium those skills usually associated with spoken discourse. Successful learners know how to use such discourse. To many good language learners this comes naturally. They appear readily to transfer their usual effective strategies to the on-line context. If these sociolinguistic skills are not present, learners may need more support to develop them and also the language in which to express them. Just as McCarthy goes on to advocate the need to design speaking activities with the development of interactional skills in mind, perhaps there is a need to design activities, which promote effective interaction using e-mail. With a heightened awareness of the competencies required, the attention of our learners may then be directed to looking for whatever cues may be present in an e-mail communication. In turn, their own use of effective cues in the electronic medium can be developed.

3.3 Deployment of learning and communicative strategies

If we analyse what makes the previous partnership a successful one, we can identify communicative competence on three levels. The English partner understands and manipulates the target language effectively, showing grammatical competence. She uses effective strategies to engage with her partner, showing sociolinguistic competence, and – within the framework of the tandem partnership – reciprocity. She also displays discourse competence, compensating for her inability to use the kind of paralinguistic cues that would be normal in a face-to-face encounter by means of her non-verbal '????'. However, most importantly, in addition to all of this she is managing her learning efficiently. We have evidence of her planning opportunistically and taking advantage of the information present in the message in order to complete the task. Here is evidence of the metacognitive strategy of monitoring as previously discussed in section 1.3, where the learner is deploying all necessary procedures to complete the task set.

We have seen other examples where a successful outcome is achieved because of the communicative competence of the English student, expressing gratitude, apology and regret at key stages. However we can also recognise an underlying competence which is not merely communicative. It is a matter of knowing when and how to use such moves to advance the partnership and the learning.

Thus the successful establishment of partnership on the part of an effective language learner, is characterised by grammatical competence, and discourse competence in the successful deployment of interactive techniques and follow-up moves, such as thanks and personal remarks. Sheer persistence plays a role too. We have also seen that rather than being hampered by 'cuelessness' in this medium the learner can make use of basic non-verbal compensation strategies, for example exaggerated punctuation, such as ???? and !!. Finally we can see the metacognitive strategies, such as planning and monitoring, that the learner brings into play in order to ensure that learning goals are attained.

3.4 Support and collaboration

'Il serait bon d'avoir des nouveaux amis sur l'Internet.' Because of the nature of tandem learning and its potential for the mutual benefit of the pair, from the first e-mails exchanged there was an obvious predisposition to communicate and help out. If there was some breakdown in communication due to underdeveloped skills in interactive discourse, the fact that each of the learners was paired with a peer of a similar age and with a background of the same youth culture seemed to minimise the danger of cross-cultural differences impeding the development of the partnership. For example 'Je suis pret a discuter avec toi de n'importe quel sujet dont tu auras envie de parler.' and 'Tu dois me dire dans quelle optique ton projet s'oriente, de quoi as-tu besoin?' It has been obvious that partners gave concrete support to each other in providing the information sought and in language practice, for example, 'I will write in English now so hopefully you can get some good phrases to use from it' and in another case 'I will now write you a little in English so that you can practice reading too.'

In the case of error correction in successful partnerships, partners find ways in which to avoid giving or taking offence with the associated risk of inhibiting communication. Encouragement accompanies correction, as we can see in the following examples taken from 6 different e-mails.

One English student wrote:

'Your English is very good – however I did notice some small errors'

A second comments:

'Il faut que je dise à cette point que tu écris très bien l'anglais'

Another example reads,

'J'ai corrige tes fautes, il n'y a pas beaucoup, ton anglais est beaucoup mieux.'

Three French students wrote:

'Je vais maintenant corriger tes fautes et je suis très fière de toi car il y en a très peu.'

'Quoiqu'il en soit, je te rassure, ce ne sont que de petites fautes, peu importantes.'

'The first part of your letter is 'perfect French' only little mistakes. Congratulations.'

Such an encouraging and supportive attitude helps to build the rapport which holds the partnership together and which underlies successful collaborative learning. In the most successful partnerships there is an empathy between the partners which has its beginnings, on the one hand, in successful interaction, and, on the other, in language management techniques which combine with a genuine desire for mutual benefit and fruitful communication with a peer from the target language community. The successful partners are aware that there is a person at the other end of the line and that they are not merely taking part in an academic exercise or talking to a computer. Empathy too comes from what they have in common. 'We are european students, we use e-mail or the internet and we both need money.' 'La tension et le stress sont à son maximum! les finances sont au plus basses.' The personal element which enters and is recognised puts the partnership on a sound footing. Partners become people. 'dans une station de ski a Paques j'ai appris le surf- c'etait tres amusant et j'avais de mal partout'. They wish each other 'bonne chasse (sic) pour tes examens' et 'bon anniversaire.' The extra element that we can call empathy is present in successful partnerships. Students are aware of its importance too. 'J'ai bien aimé faire ce projet – mon correspondant était sympa. Je pense qu'on va continuer à se parler pour que nous puissions apprendre tous les deux plus sur un pays étranger.' Compare this to 'Peut-être que si lui et moi avaient plus en commun, nous aurions envoyé plus courriers électroniques.'

3.4.1 Error correction

When the partners are first paired up their attention is directed to the tandem network's web pages *<URL: http://www.shef.ac.uk/uni/services/mltc/ tandem/tips.html>* where they may find advice on how best to manage their partnership for their mutual benefit. One English student alludes to the advice in one of his first e-mails. 'Est-ce que tu as lu le documentation des organisateurs de tandem? Ils suggerent que nous ecrivons la moitie des messages en notre propre langue.' His partner replies 'Effectivement je n'avais pas lu les recommendations des organisateurs de tandem!' Whether they have read the recommendations or not, effective learners manage the correspondence so that it is of mutual benefit to both learners with respect to writing and reading the foreign language. Most partners automatically write in their native tongue and then try out the target language. 'I will try to write a few words in English because I have to perfect this language. I'm sure I'll make many mistakes in orthograph; please correct me;' and the equivalent from a learner of French 'Je sais que je fait beaucoup de fautes, donc, si tu veut corrigé quelleques'un, je serai très content!' The native speaker's first reaction may well be 'where do I start?' However in a tandem partnership, which is underpinned by reciprocity, receiving such messages in one's native language from one's partner triggers a successful negotiation and management of error correction. One French student writes 'Veux-tu que je corrige les quelques fautes qui sont dans tes lettres? Si tu a le temps, je veux bien que tu corrige mes fautes en anglais ou que tu m'indique de meilleures tournures.' Another suggests, 'Je pense que c'est une bonne idée que l'on se corrige mutuellement'; yet another, 'est-ce que je peux te demander de corriger mes e-mails, pour essayer de faire un peu de progrès! Je te renvois ta derniere reponse avec des corriges. J'espere que tu le trouveras utile.'

From a study of the e-mails we see that there are varying methods of correction. One very well organised French student writes,

'Je vais me transformer en professeur et corriger tes fautes: Les lignes commencant par > sont les tiennes et celles commencant par # contiennent des corrections.'

He illustrates his method:

>'J'espere que tu as passe des bonnes vacances, et que tu as mange bien
de bonnes vacances   tu as bien mange'

As the correspondence grows he develops his method further,

'J'utilise des phrases entre parentheses pour indiquer des formulations plus jolies mais que ta phrase est exacte.'
'tu n'as que me le dire,
(dis-le -moi).'

An English student brackets her partner's mistakes and gives the correct usage.

'I'm a student (in the) at Le Havre university but it's near to (from) Paris.'

Another English student decides on a different method. 'Je crois qu'il sera tres utile si tu corrige mes fautes. Peut-être je peux faire la meme chose? Alors voici ta dernière lettre et les équivalents anglais sont en capitales':

do you want that I reply to you including your message corrected?
(ME TO SEND YOU A CORRECTED VERSION OF YOUR LETTER

WHEN I REPLY TO YOU)

Yet another method is that of the student who writes COR: in front of the corrected version. Some students explain without using brackets or capital letters or signs. They explain 'on dit' or 'on écrit'. One student merely sent a completely corrected version, saying that he hoped his partner had kept the original for comparison.

Whichever method the pair decided on, it is a measure of a successful partnership that error correction takes place. 'Lorsque tu corriges mes fautes, je peux parfois apprendre quelques choses sur la langage, donc si tu peux continuer avec cela ce sera tres utile' is a typical comment. In successful partnerships mutual error correction occurs and is kept within bounds. In other words it does not become a chore which puts off partners from communicating with each other.

It must also be said, however, that one of the projects deemed most successful in that the English student had got to know her partner well, had gathered quality information on her topic and had acquired and reused new language, was the result of a correspondence conducted entirely in French. At no stage did the pair discuss what language to write in. The English student began the correspondence in French and her partner continued it. At no point was there any error correction by the French partner. The pair exchanged views and information very successfully, with the English partner noting and reusing new vocabulary and idioms. At first sight, benefits seem to be very one-sided, with an apparent lack of reciprocity. However the French partner's main objective seemed to be information seeking. On this score he was evidently content with the arrangement, as it still continues.

In most partnerships both partners write mostly without accents. 'J'ai essayer de mettre des accents mais je ne sait pas comment tu les reçois et il est difficile d'en faire car il faut utiliser un code spécial.' This is not therefore an aspect of the language on which they focus. Learners are tolerant of each other's mistakes – a point highlighted by Brammerts (1996: 15). There is however a broad pattern to the mistakes corrected by both sets of native speakers. They both most commonly corrected obvious spelling mistakes, for example 'le travaille' to 'le travail'; 'convennient' to 'convenient'. The next most common correction on both sides was of prepositions. Partners tend to correct mistakes by giving the correct version without any grammatical explanation. For example 'they still live at (with) their parents'. 'I'd like to go back in (to) the area of Lyon.' 'COR: I will help you for //with// your project' and a French student corrects, 'Les filles s'occupent avec leur macquillage # de leur maquillage.' Apart from spelling and prepositions the corrected mistakes do not appear to conform to any obvious pattern across the languages. Because of the differences between the languages, French partners corrected adjectival agreements, position of pronouns and adverbs whereas English students tended to correct idioms, 'I offer you to sleep at home (YOU CAN SLEEP AT MY HOUSE).' However there was one compelling common element in the correction of mistakes and this was the supportive attitude of the partners.

3.5 Mastering the technology

Up till now we have looked at the internal working of the e-mail partnerships to analyse successful factors and have taken it as read that the external framework of the technology enabling such partnerships is a resource with which our language learners are at ease. Axiomatically, partnerships failed when technology failed, with returned mails from addresses which were incorrect and so on. There were also a few examples of glitches getting in the way of communication. 'I am very sorry not to have replied to you earlier but I have had a big problem with my computer (I had to change my motherboard).' Also 'Les ordinateurs n'a pas marché depuis dimanche l'après-midi.' We have already seen the example of the technicians' strike, However on the whole our tandem students have a positive attitude to technology and its use is a skill they have acquired. One French partner is a case in point, 'Actually I thought twice before answering you since you are my fourth tandem partner. But I think I'll write to you because other students of my english class already have e-mail partners in Sheffield and they told me you had a videoconference together. So it might be fun to see each other on a video conference.' Technology is actually an incentive for her to become involved. All partners seemed competent, some having their own web pages which they invited their partners to visit. We have seen partners give Internet references for research purposes and the use of software for the same purpose. There is proof that partners use news-groups and forums. They are also familiar with Internet-Relay Chat (IRC), which is a synchronous form of CMC as opposed to the asynchronous e-mail. One student goes as far as to state: 'I don't like writing, I prefer direct conversation such as on IRC'. This perception of IRC , not as writing, but as 'direct conversation' is very revealing. This implies that for her IRC is more authentic and perhaps easier than e-mails, which she seems to view as a more formal exercise and a more difficult medium of communication, even though both involve writing.

Most students have proved competent in using the medium to communicate and to correct but they do have reservations about it. One English student writes, 'En utilisant les ordinateurs je n'avais pas préparé une lettre avant de l'envoyer par e-mail, donc, je n'ai pas utilisé un niveau de langue élevé. C'est pourquoi j'ai fait assez de fautes fondamentales. Quand j'écris des e-mails il faudrait quand même que je verifie tous les mots. En conclusion, la solution à tous ces problèmes serait d'utiliser un dictionnaire pour verifier l'orthographe, le genre et tout.' This student is aware of her own shortcomings when using a computer to communicate. She feels the impoverishment of register and the number of mistakes made because of lack of preparation beforehand. Taking along a dictionary would help, an on-line dictionary would be even better: and yet we remember the words of a previous example – 'les partenaires à l'émail sont très bons pour améliorer son niveau de français spontané.'

There are in fact two related problems to be confronted. Firstly, when we look at the level of the target language written in the e-mails, we see many mistakes but we also see real communication taking place and mistakes corrected by partners in subsequent e-mails. This exemplifies the very real advantage of attention being given to individual mistakes by an 'expert' in the target language. Secondly if we also look at mistakes made in their own language by the native speakers, we might think that the conditions for second language acquisition are not ideal. And yet, when a successful relationship is established, the motivation for communication and collaboration provides fertile ground for language learning. We remember that 'good language learners'(1975: 47) seek out native speakers for practice. E-mail can be regarded as a medium for spontaneous communication practice. Reflection on information received and language used or corrected can come later. There may always be an element of error in e-mail messages just as there is in verbal communication. However the possibility of communicating authentically with a native speaker, when such an opportunity may not be otherwise given, clearly outweighs the disadvantages. We have indeed seen that, on most occasions, learners may choose to prioritise content over form and that the very attraction of e-mail may be communication without preparation. However for those who choose to take it, there still remains the alternative opportunity to 'rehearse' their e-mails.

Whatever kind of e-mail is sent, the learner has the opportunity to 'converse' with a native speaker regularly, deciding his or her own rhythm. Benefiting from the provision of computers throughout the campus and their 24-hour availability, the learner chooses time, place and frequency to suit his or her individual needs. Thanks to the benefits of technology, writing and receiving e-mails appears to be a more attractive and gratifying alternative, in keeping with the pace and spirit of the age, than writing a letter.

We must also remember that in our assignment the language in the e-mails was not assessed. The basis for language assessment was a retrospective, written report on the e-mail partnership. Here the partners could reuse the idioms and the structures they had noted in their partners' e-mails. In fact, the assessment procedure has been revised in the light of experience to take into account conscious re-use of such language in subsequent e-mails. Thus we can work on helping students to improve their e-mail methodology, by using such standard IT features as spell-checkers, grammar programs, on-line dictionaries and the alphanumeric keypad, to produce foreign accents using ASCII code.

4   Conclusion

We have seen from the analysis of the e-mails exchanged the partnership skills necessary for a successful outcome, namely:

- Successful negotiation of topic
- Shifting from yransaction to interaction
- Effective learning strategies
- Support and collaboration
- Mutual error correction
- Mastery of the technology

If electronic mail is a distinctive medium combining aspects of writing and speaking, then teachers have a new skill area, with its own set of protocols and strategies to be acquired or developed, in which their students will need support and training. If we can provide our students with the supportive technology to improve the standard of their electronic communication, then, in advancing uninhibited language practice, we need also to instil the skills inherent in a successful partnership. What these are will depend to a large extent on the framework in which learning takes place. Because the topic to be investigated during the e-mail exchange is left to the students to decide, the context described above places a premium on negotiating skills. At the same time it favours the emergence of strategies we have chosen as appropriate for our learners to acquire or develop. Since it is our aim to encourage our learners to successfully direct and manage their own learning, the principle of autonomy is explained and nurtured. Together with their responsibility for their own learning, the principle of reciprocity, with its emphasis on the importance of negotiation and mutual help, is also central.

If our approach achieves its aims, then more of our students will become successful e-mail tandem partners and benefit fully from collaborative learning via the Internet. From all the evidence available, there are native speaker partners willing and able to help, not just with ideas and information, and the very valuable input of language correction, but with support and encouragement, thereby creating a virtual environment in which language learning may flourish.

References

Brammerts, H. (1996) 'Tandem language learning via the Internet and the International E-Mail Tandem Network', in D. Little and H. Brammerts (eds), *A guide to language learning in tandem via the Internet*, CLCS Occasional Paper No 46 Summer 1996 (ISSN 0332 3889).

Grice, H.P. (1975) 'Logic and conversation', in P. Cole and J.J. Morgan (eds), *Syntax and semantics: Speech Acts* (vol. 3), pp. 41–58, New York: Academic Press.

Little D. (1996) 'Learner autonomy and learner counselling', in D. Little and H. Brammerts (eds), *A guide to language learning in tandem via the Internet*, CLCS Occasional Paper No 46, Summer 1996 (ISSN 0332 3889).

McCarthy M. (1991) *Discourse Analysis for Language Teachers*, Cambridge University Press.

Nisbet J. and Shucksmith J. (1986) *Learning Strategies*, Routledge & Kegan Paul quoted in O'Malley & Chamot (1995) *Language Strategies in Second Language Acquisition*, pp 48–49, Cambridge University Press.

O'Malley J.M. and Chamot A.U. (1995) *Language Strategies in Second Language Acquisition*, Cambridge University Press.

Oxford R. L. (1990) *Language Learning Strategies. What every teacher should know*, Heinle & Heinle.

Rubin J. (1975), 'What the Good Language Learner Can Teach Us', *TESOL QUARTERLY* Vol. 9 No 1, pp. 41–51.

Yates S. J. (1996) 'Oral and Written Linguistic Aspects of Computer Conferencing: A Corpus Based Study', in S.C. Herring (ed.), *Computer-Mediated Communication*, pp.29–46, Amsterdam/Philadelphia: John Benjamins Publishing Company.

Yates S. J. (1997) 'Gender, Identity and CMC', *Journal of Computer Assisted Learning* 13, 281–290.

Yule G. (1996) *Pragmatics*, Oxford University Press: chapter 7: Politeness and Interaction.

Appendix

FEUILLE D'EVALUATION DU PROJET E-MAIL DU PRINTEMPS

Au cours de tes échanges e-mails avec ton/ta partenaire, tu devras relever les informations suivantes :

- 5 choses que tu as en commun avec ton/ta/tes partenaire(s)

- 5 choses que tu n'as pas en commun avec lui/elle/eux

- 8 choses que tu as découvertes au sujet du pays, de la région, de la culture de ton/ta partenaire

- 8 nouvelles particularités de la langue que ton/ta partenaire t'a apprises (par exemple des phrases d'argot, des points de grammaire, du vocabulaire spécifique).

Fais un bilan écrit en français (400 mots) sur cette feuille d'évaluation. Pour chacun de ces points, tu dois faire référence aux e-mails correspondants (grâce à un système de numérotation et/ou en soulignant les termes).

Utilise tes propres mots plutôt que de reprendre ceux de ton/ta partenaire afin de montrer que tu as compris et assimilé ce que tu as appris.

Remets cette feuille d'évaluation accompagnée de tes e-mails afin d'être noté(e). **Tu dois également apporter comme preuves les e-mails envoyés à et reçus de ton/ta partenaire.**

Continue au verso si nécessaire

'What do they get up to?' Activity in a Spanish–English discussion list

Jane Woodin and Liz White
Modern Languages Teaching Centre,
University of Sheffield

1   Introduction

There has been a significant amount of interest over the last few years in the use of e-mail for educational purposes, not least because of the explosion in use of computer-mediated communication.

Computer-mediated communication (CMC) is used for a variety of purposes in higher education; perhaps the most common are for teacher-student discussions, as an alternative to face-to-face feedback, and for linking students together either one-to-one or many-to-many, to complete an educational task. Although audio- and video-conferencing are also forms of CMC, this paper deals specifically with the use of the written word and in particular of e-mail, as a form of CMC.

CMC is often cited as having a levelling effect. Participants cannot judge others by their appearance, age or accent; all participants have the same opportunity for their thoughts and ideas to be taken into account (Ellington & Race, 1993: 232, Bartholomae, 1993: 261), Sproull & Kiesler, 1991, cited in Warschauer, 1997).

Some have found student-to-student communication to have a liberating effect on learners (Batson, 1993, McConnell, 1994). Others, however, (e.g. Miller, 1993) have found that different groups produce completely different results and that the CMC experience is not necessarily positive for everyone.

1.1 Computer-mediated communication and language learning

CMC for language learning differs in one fundamental way from other educational purposes; the medium used for communicating is also an object of learning. Messages themselves are authentic texts and communication often occurs between native speakers of different languages, in the form of one to one communication and also between groups of learners.

The language used in CMC differs from conventional spoken or written texts; it contains features of both written and spoken discourse (Murray, 1991). Examples of these include reduced use of punctuation (Woodin, 1997) and reduced register and discourse markers (González-Bueno, 1998).

Computer-mediated communication cannot presently accommodate the complexity or range of oral communication such as voice tone, pitch or speed of delivery. Despite the use of, for example, capital letters to indicate the raising of the voice, or the use of emoticons to convey the sender's attitude to his/her message, CMC lacks the wealth of paralinguistic aids present in face-to-face communication. With the possible exception of emoticons such as a smile [:)], the learner must rely upon the words alone.

Neither does computer-mediated communication allow the opportunity to check one's utterances with one's interlocutor until after the utterance has been made; utterances cannot be modified in mid-flow, depending on their effect. Both of these are central to oral communication. (Lewis *et al*, 1996, Little & Ushioda, 1998).

These factors can make CMC challenging for language learners, but at the same time as struggling with understanding and conveying messages, they are equipping themselves with a skill necessary for life in the twenty-first century.

1.2 Tandem learning

Tandem learning takes place between two people, who are learning each other's native language. It has two main principles:

Autonomy: You are responsible for your own learning

Reciprocity: You are responsible for ensuring mutual benefit.

(http://www.slf.ruhr-uni-bochum.de/learning/idxeng11.html) Traditionally, tandem partners have worked face-to-face, communicating orally. However since 1993, tandem learning has been extended to include working with partners at a distance, through the Internet. The International E-Mail Tandem Network[1] service offers support for learners of a variety of different languages. An EU-funded programme involving tandem learning between universities in over 10 European countries, it currently has 30 bilingual subnets.[2] Each subnet offers the following:

- access to the central Tandem Agency which will find you a partner, who is a native speaker of the language you are learning;

- the chance to participate in a bilingual discussion list, which provides many-to-many communication between members of the subnet;

- a database of teaching and learning materials, to which participants can also contribute.

  (adapted from IETN information for participants: http://www.slf.ruhr-uni-bochum.de/email/infen.html)

The tandem principles of autonomy and reciprocity apply whether face-to-face or at a distance and e-mail tandem participants are made aware of these through the welcome message sent to all subscribers (See Appendix 1).

Initially set up to cater for students from universities participating in the project, the International E-mail Tandem Network facilities have, since 1996, been openly available to interested participants via the World-Wide-Web and as a result the number of people seeking one-to-one partners has increased, together with the number of people taking part in the discussion lists. Some of the high traffic lists have in turn become less directed by tutor input into the list and 'discussion' is now partly decided upon and moderated by the participants themselves. This is the case with the English-Spanish subnet (ENG–ESP), and it is therefore particularly interesting to examine contributions made to it.

Whereas one-to-one partnerships have received some attention (Tella, 1992, Lewis *et al*, 1996, Woodin, 1997, Little & Ushioda 1998, Appel 1998 to cite some examples), discussion lists have received relatively little attention. This is another reason for further investigation of the list.

2   The ENG–ESP discussion list

Each e-mail discussion list which is part of the International E-mail Tandem Network is called a forum. The Spanish-English forum will from here on be referred to as the ENG–ESP forum.

The ENG–ESP forum was one of the first lists to be set up, and to date is jointly co-ordinated by the Universities of Oviedo and Sheffield. It is a relatively high-traffic list in comparison to the smaller subnets (over 800 messages were sent to it in 1996–7, over 1000 in 1997–8 and 1998–9).

The educational aims of the forum are:

> *to enable participants to improve their foreign language skills and to gain better understanding of the culture of the target language country by reading the contributions to the forum and by posting messages themselves.* (Hedderich, 1996)

and, as cited in information for participants:

> *ENG–ESP is a forum for discussion in Spanish and English in which people who have a command of one of the two languages are learning the other and wish to know more about members in other countries.*[3] (Appendix 1, Welcome message for participants 1998)

The learning aims of the forum are thus clear to all; indeed a survey of participants in the 1997–8 forum revealed that their principal reason for belonging to the forum was to learn English or Spanish. We shall therefore assume that participants would leave the forum if they felt that they were not learning from it.

Because of the world-wide nature of the forum, participants' backgrounds vary greatly. We have no control over other influences on their language learning (for example, exposure to native speakers or the formal language classes they might be following) and it is therefore not feasible to attempt to ascertain exactly what they were learning through the forum. We chose, therefore, to focus on evidence of the *opportunity* for learning, in the form of the following questions:

1 Who participates in ENG–ESP? To give us a profile of those in the forum, consideration was given to:

- the number of participants;
- their origin;
- their gender;
- the frequency of their contributions.

2 How do they participate? To investigate something of *how* these participants chose to learn through the forum, we considered:

- the nature of the contributions made
- the language used in the contributions
- the different topics discussed and their duration.

To this end, the following steps were taken:

- All messages sent to ENG–ESP forum over the academic year 1996-7 were stored in a specifically designated e-mail folder.
- At the end of the year, messages were categorised according to their content, and those which we considered to have most opportunity for participation were analysed further.

3   Results

Over the year, 859 messages were sent. This does not include repeat or erroneous messages such as blank ones, or messages requesting to join or leave the forum, but it does include messages which were sent to the forum but were clearly intended for a single recipient (see 'personal' category in Table 1).

None of the participants were required to participate in the forum as part of a formal course. However, students from the University of Oviedo (43 in all) were among the privileged few allowed Internet access free through their university. Before gaining this access they had to demonstrate that they were interested in improving their English, but their participation was not formally assessed as part of their English studies. These students were therefore clearly motivated and keen to make the most of the ENG–ESP experience.

The majority of the English students participating from the University of Sheffield (32 in all) were given the task of working one-to-one with an e-mail partner as one of their assessed projects; participation in the forum was an optional activity. These students were at lower-intermediate level, having studied Spanish for an average of 2 years (100–150 contact hours in total.) Approximately half of them reported having difficulty with understanding the messages sent to the forum as well as the practical challenge needed to read and discard the messages every day or two days, to avoid their e-mail account being frozen for exceeding their filestore limit. These students reported that the one-to-one work with partners was more rewarding, where, in the privacy of e-mail partnerships, the terms of the learning partnership can be discussed and agreed (such as the frequency of messages or language used or the kind of corrections wanted).

3.1 Participation

In all, 256 participants sent at least one message. Figure 1 shows the distribution of messages by participants and reveals that half of them sent only one message. In many cases this was a presentation to the forum, something which the introductory message asks them to do on joining (see Appendix).

Interestingly, only 6% of participants sent more than 10 messages. Data on which of the participants had a one-to-one tandem partner are not available, but between August 1996 and July 1997 there were 246 tandem pairs. It is therefore likely that many forum participants were already in these partnerships.

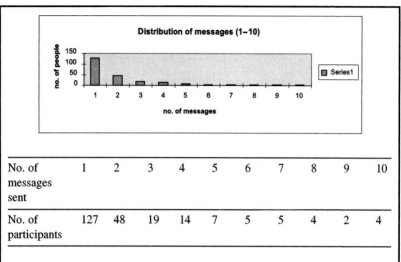

No. of messages sent	1	2	3	4	5	6	7	8	9	10
No. of participants	127	48	19	14	7	5	5	4	2	4

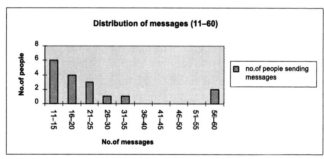

no. of messages sent	11–15	16–20	21–25	26–30	31–35	36–40	41–45	46–50	51–55	56–60
no. of participants	6	4	3	1	1	0	0	0	0	2

Figure 1: Number of messages sent by participants (includes messages requesting to join or leave the forum)

The location of participants (Figure 2) varied widely, from the mountains of Peru to the coast of New Zealand. This was probably because information about the E-Mail Tandem Network was openly available on the World-Wide-Web, as the previous year's membership had been mainly limited to Europe, with some interest from the United States.

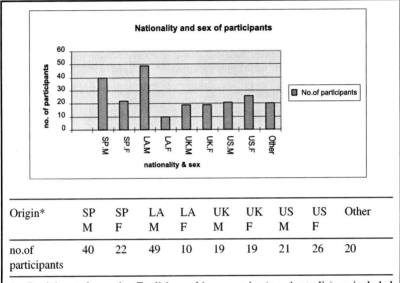

Origin*	SP M	SP F	LA M	LA F	UK M	UK F	US M	US F	Other
no.of participants	40	22	49	10	19	19	21	26	20

* Participants from other English-speaking countries (e.g. Australia) are included in US, those whose mother tongue was neither English nor Spanish are included in Other.

Figure 2: Origin of participants

There was a gender imbalance among the participants. Spanish-speaking female participants totalled just over a quarter (26%), but there were more female English-speaking participants (57%) than male. While this figure alone is not particularly significant (more men go to University in Spanish-speaking countries than women), it is interesting to note that in Latin America, Spain and the United States, messages from male participants outnumber those sent by female participants (see Figure 3). The fact that there was a high proportion of English-speaking participants may be explained by the fact that the Sheffield students who made up most of the UK group were mainly women.

With 121 Spanish speakers and 95 English speakers, one would assume that the languages used would also be more or less equal. However this is not the case. Figure 3 shows the distribution of messages according to sex and nationality.

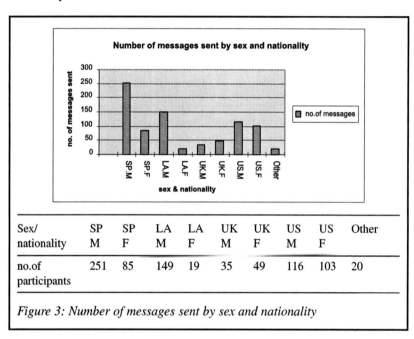

Sex/ nationality	SP M	SP F	LA M	LA F	UK M	UK F	US M	US F	Other
no.of participants	251	85	149	19	35	49	116	103	20

Figure 3: Number of messages sent by sex and nationality

While there were 27% more Spanish speakers than English speakers, Spanish speakers actually sent 66% more messages than their English-speaking counterparts, without taking into account the category Others (Figure 3). This was commented upon by the native Spanish speakers who at times felt there was little participation from the English speakers.

It would appear that Spanish-speakers tend to participate more. Is this a cultural difference? Spaniards reputedly talk more than Britons (Launay,

1993), but factors such as motivation and language level also require consideration.

Maintaining a balance between the number of Spanish and English-speaking participants may be difficult; ensuring equal participation is even harder on an open access forum, particularly when there are so many native Spanish speakers wishing to learn English.

This is further aggravated by the fact that, although the vast majority of people were sending messages in both languages (Figure 4), there were in fact twice as many messages sent in Spanish only (108) than in English only (54). Mexicans notably used Spanish the majority of the time, some of the most prolific participants were Spaniards who used mainly Spanish, particularly when they became emotionally involved about the topic under discussion (see section 3.3.1).

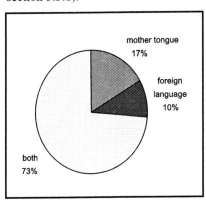

Figure 4: Percentages of people sending messages in mother tongue, foreign language or both languages

3.2 Co-ordinator input

In all, 22 messages were sent to the forum by the subnet co-ordinators and the Spanish Language Assistant. The role of the Language Assistant was principally to support the Oviedo students, through offering advice on taking part in tandem learning, answering language queries, correcting set pieces of written work undertaken voluntarily, and introducing possible topics for discussion. There was no equivalent language assistant based in Sheffield, although native English students also benefited from the services of the Spanish Language Assistant, through her contributions to the ENG-ESP forum. In some cases topics suggested were taken up by forum members, but many times this did not happen. Two topics which were brought up by the Language Assistant in Oviedo ('Pronunciation learning' and 'Simple questions') led to a number of responses, with students taking the floor.

3.3 Messages

The 859 messages were categorised according to their content. As it is not possible for us to analyse the actual learning from the forum (external variables were outside our control) we found a categorisation of topic to be more practical. This was not an easy task, as some messages, overlap with more than one category, or evolve from others. We chose the following 7 categories of messages:

Presentations – the first message to the forum, in which the participant gives a brief introduction to him/herself

Personal – messages which should have been sent to one individual

Process – asking about finding partners, how to unsubscribe, complaints

Information – information-seeking or information-giving, such as asking for help with a project

Miscellaneous – greetings such as Happy Christmas/Valentine's Day/ holidays, 'hello everyone', chain letters, problems with e-mail address, welcome messages

Language – discussions on vocabulary, idioms, pronunciation

Topic – exchange of ideas on a particular theme such as bullfighting, regionalism

Category	Total number of messages
Presentation	159
Personal	147
Process	60
Information	21
Miscellaneous	84

Language	99
Topic	289

Table 1: Messages by category

The subject heading on an e-mail message is frequently misleading about the actual content of the messages. Of 20 messages which were headed on 'Pronunciation Learning', for example, 13 were on a previous topic of animals and violence. (All messages have been kept in their original category.) In addition, a subject may start out as a language exchange, but develop into a discussion of ideas, or vice versa. Because of the difficulty with overlap, we chose to keep all messages in the category of their subject header.

The last 2 categories in Table 1 – language and topic – were chosen for further scrutiny on the basis that they are more 'open' than the other categories and responses are not so predictable. The first five categories are either not meant for all to read (as in the case of 'Personal') or prompt only one response (as in the case of 'Information'). Those messages in the 'Miscellaneous' category were also considered to be of a more 'closed' nature, being largely messages requiring no response

3.3.1 The category 'language'

The language exchanges include 7 messages on pronunciation learning. The subject was introduced on 15 April, by the Spanish Language Assistant, in both languages. This discussion lasted from 15 April until the 29 April and involved 6 different people, 3 of whom were native speakers of Spanish (one Argentinean and 2 Spanish nationals) and 3 of English (all American). Most of the messages were written in Spanish, or a mixture of both languages. An extract from these exchanges, between four people, is below. (Note: The Languages Assistant's comments are marked LA, participant U's comments are marked U, participant S's comments are marked S and participant P's comments are marked P.) Author' translations are in italics and no linguistic or orthographic corrections to participants' messages have been made.

From:	'P...............'
To:	ENG–ESP@tandem.uni-trier.de,
Date:	Tue, 29 Apr 1997 15:45:28 +0100

Subject: Re: PRONUNCIATION LEARNING
\> Date: Tue, 29 Apr 1997 11:12:31 +0200 (METDST)
\> From: B. .... (Language Assistant)
\> Subject: Re: PRONUNCIATION LEARNING
\> To: ENG–ESP@tandem.uni-trier.de

LA Hello everybody;
Let me introduce a new topic for discussion.

U Good idea

LA Which word do you find more difficult to pronounce in English/Spanish? For me
it used to be 'yoghurt'. When I started learning English I could hardly pronounce the phoneme /j/ as in 'yoghurt', of course!, 'yellow', 'yolk', etc. So, when I first visited England at the age of 12 I did a lot of practice for the simple reason that I love them, yoghurts I mean!

U A mi me gusta este asunto. (*I like this topic*)

LA En una ocasion unos amigos ingleses me dijeron que a los espanoles se nos 'cazaba' facilmente con solo pronunciar las palabras 'yes' y 'very', which we tend to pronounce as 'lles' and 'beri' (sorry phoneticians! I'm afraid phonetic transcription is not possible). (*Once some English friends told me that you could tell Spaniards just by saying the words 'Yes' and 'very'...*)

S Esta me sorpresa un poco. Yo creia que el 'y' de 'yes' y el 'y' de 'yo' eran lo mismo. Es posible que todos los hispanohablantes no pronuncien 'y' (o 'll') de la misma manera? Es verdad que a veces 'y' es como 'j' (en ingles), at least in Mexico. Where are you from?

(*This surprises me. I thought that the 'y' from 'Yes and the 'y' from 'yo' were the same. Could it be that not all Spanish speakers pronounce 'y' (or 'll') in the same way? It's true that sometimes it is like 'j' (in English) at least in Mexico...*)

U I'm from Spain, from Leon (in the NorthWest)

S The difficulty with 'v' and 'b' I can understand easily. In Spanish I have the most difficulty with 'rr'. I can 'roll' my r's, but in the context of a word or a phrase I often stumble. I guess I need a lot more practice.

What kinds of pronunciation errors do you hear most when native English speakers speak Spanish?

U Well 't' and 'd' are quite different, but I agree with you that your 'r'
> doesn't sound very nice in Spanish. You also tend to lengthen your 'o' which
> is just /o/ in Spanish and sometimes you make them as /ou/.>

S Hasta luego,

S.......

P It's really embarrasing sometimes, isn't it?, not to be able to pronounce English words properly. But it is, however, quite encouraging to find out that even English people can not sometimes understand each other. If you don't believe me ask any Londoner to speak to a Welsh or viceversa. Then sit back, and relax.

End of message...

It is interesting to see how language issues which are usually reserved for speaking, such as pronunciation, can be discussed through e-mail; this is probably helped by the interactive nature of the e-mail medium and the fact that others' comments can be included in one's message.

Another language discussion within the forum was on the meaning of 'short of'. This took place between the 3 and 11 July, involved 4 people and continued until the person who asked the original question Al, a native Spanish speaker, understood. His first message, in English, was asking for an explanation of the phrase 'short of' as in 'a few ants short of a picnic'. The 8 exchanges which followed involved the originator on four occasions, writing some messages in English and some in Spanish, and 3 Americans, writing mostly in Spanish. It took three attempts at explanations before he understood; below is his question and the first attempt at the explanation: (Al's comments have one >, S's comments have none. Authors' translations are in italics.)

Date: Thu, 3 Jul 1997 16:27:45 -0500 (EST)
From: 'S...........................
To: ENG-ESP@tandem.uni-trier.de

Cc:foro <ENG-ESP@tandem.uni-trier.de>
Subject: Re: Duda dudes

On Thu, 3 Jul 1997, Al.... wrote:

> I don't understand the expression 'short of' in the following sentences.
> Could you help me?
> a few ants short of a picnic.
> 'A few fries short of a Happy Meal'.
> Al....
Or a few cards short of a full deck.

If you are supposed to have 3 dozen apples (36) and only have 34, we could say that you are short 2 apples (sic) (that is, you have two too few). So if you are a few cards short of a full deck, you are missing some cards. Similarly, if you are a few fries short of a Happy Meal, you don't have a complete Happy Meal (from MacDonald's). Except in these expressions, you are actually saying that someone is a little stupid or maybe not completely sane. (They're missing common sense, or normal intelligence, or something.)
S...........

End of message..

A new participant then entered the discussion, pointing out, in English, that it is not necessary to understand such idioms; what is needed is to know when to use them. The final message, from the originator in Spanish, was to say that he did not agree with this idea, and that in order to learn, it is necessary to understand. He concluded this set of exchanges with reference to a WWW site giving more examples of 'short of'. Even though only 4 people were involved in this discussion, it was of general interest and all members could have learnt from it. A similar set of exchanges was on the meaning of 'bunking off'. Thirteen messages were also sent on the meaning of 'bitch'. This evolved from a joke which was sent to the forum.

These examples of specifically language-oriented discussions illustrate the particular benefits of tandem learning to higher level learners:

1   Learners are exposed to language as it is used by native participants, such as colloquial terms, or idioms. This can be different from the language used in the classroom setting. Neither is it graded for ease of comprehension as is often the case in textbooks for language learners or classroom language.

2   They experience first-hand discussions on points of language. Questions put to the forum reach a wide audience and are therefore more likely to elicit a varied response than if they were handled in a one-to-one paired exchange. This can contribute to their understanding of the multiplicity of interpretations that can occur when more than one native speaker is involved.

3.2.1   The category of 'topics'

Table 1 shows that the most popular category for discussion was 'Topic'. Within this, the greatest number of responses on a single theme related to 'Silly questions' and 'Jokes'. Between 27 May, when the Spanish co-ordinator suggested a set of 'Simple questions and difficult answers', and 27 June, 94 messages were sent. The initial suggestion was that people should send in answers to seven specific questions such as: 'Why do we drive so fast?', and 'Why do we admire beauty?' (These questions were in English.) One Brazilian, three Spaniards and one American sent in their answers, all in English. A Spanish native speaker then suggested that more silly questions and answers should be sent; the subject title of these emails then changed from 'simple questions, difficult answers' to 'silly questions, silly answers'. Various questions were submitted, such as: 'Why do little balls form on sweaters?'; 'What makes a noise in a storm?' and 'Why do dogs bite mailmen?' The ways in which people participated in these exchanges can be seen below. Interspersed among these messages were a few of more limited interest which have not been included.

Here is an extract from one conversation, started by the Language Assistant, B.....: (Authors' translations are in italics)

Date: Tue, 27 May 1997 11:00:03 +0200 (METDST)
From: B........
Subject: NEW TASK
To: eng-esp@tandem.uni-trier.de

Technology and the advanced language learner

Hola a todos; (*Hello everyone*)

Creiais que me habia olvidado de vosotros? (*Did you think I had forgotten you?*) Pues no, here I am ready for a new task. This is called: SIMPLE QUESTIONS – DIFFICULT ANSWERS. I'll give you a list of questions you have to discuss with your partners. It won't
be easy I'm sure! Then, write back to me and let me know the most original, surprising, sincere, witty, or shocking replies from both of you.

1.– Why do we drive fast?

2.– Why do we admire beauty so much?

3.– Why do we feel frustrated if we fail an exam?

4.– Why can't we manage without being loved?

5.– Why do we want to have curly hair if ours is deadly straight or vice versa?

6.– Why do we smoke more when we are nervous or depressed?

7.– Why do we learn a second language?

Buena suerte con los examenes y no os olvideis de las ventajas de

practicar idiomas mediante el correo electronico. (*Good luck with your exams & don't forget it is good to practise languages using e-mail*)

Lots of love,

B........

Question (see key below)	No. of messages in Spanish	No. of messages in English	No. of messages in both languages	No. of participants	Duration of discussion
A	0	5	0	5	2 days
B	2	1	2	5	2 days
C	6	4	0	5	5 days
D	4	16	1	11	6 days
E	4	3	1	5	3 days
F	0	5	2	5	2 days

G	2	1	1	2	2 days
H	3	1	0	4	2 days
I	5	0	0	4	4 days
J	3	2	1	5	2 days

Table 2: Messages on 'Silly questions'

Key to questions:

A. 7 questions e.g. why do we drive so fast?

B. Why do little balls form on sweaters? *¿Por qué se forman bolitas en los jerseys de lana?* (introduced in both languages)

C. What makes a noise in a storm?

D. Why do dogs bite mailmen?

E. Can you have your cake and eat it?

F. Why call it the EURO not PEAN?/ Why do good students wear glasses?

G. *¿Hay más tiempo que vida?* (Is there more time than life?)

H. *¿Por qué cuando un coche adelanta a otro, sus ocupantes miran al coche adelantado?*(why do people look at the car they are overtaking)

I. *¿La popularidad no es una preocupación de los colegiales latinos e ingleses?* (does popularity matter to English and Latin American students?)

J. Why do bad films make more money?

It could be argued that the first set of seven questions (A in Table 2) was only of value to Spanish speakers since all the responses were in English. However, it led on to a variety of related issues which produced messages in both languages and increased the number of participants. The forum was extremely active in this period, with a high intensity of exchanges over a limited period.

In addition to the 'Silly questions' discussions, jokes provided a fruitful source of exchanges within the forum. Participants took the opportunity to write at greater length. Many jokes rely on a play on words, and can require a level of language commensurate with advanced learners. The subject of jokes was introduced on seven different occasions, and involved 12 people sending in their favourite jokes, and in some cases, commenting on previous ones. There was less interaction in this topic, possibly due to the fact that a joke does not necessarily require a response. 15 topics were popular enough to stimulate more than 4 responses. Among these were bullfighting, drugs, horror films and cloning. None of these was introduced by a co-ordinator. If we take the case study of '*si eres motero*' (if you drive a motorbike) we see that this topic involved 10 messages, from 9 participants between 12 May and 16 June. The participants came from the following places: Sheffield (2), Peru (1), Oviedo (4), USA (3). 6 of the messages were in Spanish, and 4 in English, but only 3 people wrote in their mother tongue. The first message was sent in Spanish by an English student, asking for statistics on motor cycle accidents in Spain, to help her prepare for a presentation. The following two messages were asking for clarification of, and then giving an explanation of, the word 'motero'. Another English student, in Spanish, commented on the number of accidents in England because of rain. The subsequent messages all concerned the weather in Spain. It is possible that the information the original student wanted was sent to her individual e-mail address. The topic of Terror (films, books, crime) elicited 31 messages, between 11 March and 23 April. Fourteen people, of whom the majority were Spanish, joined in the discussion. It was started, in Spanish, by someone wondering why horror films are so popular. The next few messages, in Spanish, recommended specific films and authors; then the emphasis turned to true crime, with messages in English, Spanish or both languages. Exchanges were quite heated at times, with opposite opinions being expressed on capital punishment. In this set of exchanges, people tended to use their mother tongue, and write longer messages, particularly as they became more emotionally involved. This increased use of participants' mother tongue enabled all members of the forum, including those who were not participating actively, to have the opportunity of reading authentic material. Here is an extract from their messages, in particular illustrating how students revert to using their mother tongue when becoming emotional: (M's comments have one > R's original comments have two>> and his current comments have none, Authors' translations are in italics,)

Date: Wed, 16 Apr 1997 08:47:51 -0500
From: R.....
To   ENG–ESP@tandem.uni-trier.de
Subject: Re: terror & real crime answers

M...wrote:

>

> > I'm certainly not trying to be morbid, as an American we are tought (*sic*)
> > to keep an open mind about things. Peaple (*sic*) read terror to get a rush
>
> I don't really understand what u're trying to say with that
> sentence, could you be more explicit about what you mean with
> that? I'm not saying I don't understand it, I mean textually, I
> do, I just (maybe I'm I bit fool) (*sic*) cannot understand what you
> mean.
> I'm refering to that 'as an American we are tought (*sic*) to keep an open mind
> about things'.
>
> Thanks in advance, J.... Sorry it takes me so long to respond what I mean by that is if you live
in a sociaty (*sic*) where things like true crime do not happen I believe
its much easier to say I don't want to hear about it, deal with it
or know anything about it. Like starvation in Africa, we all know it
happens, but what can I do? So don't tell me about it.
I can understand this I lived in Spain for 5 years and felt very safe
nobody carries guns there these types of things don't happen so much in Europe.
But here in the States where just about everyone carries a gun (not me)
you need to think some of this.
I give an example that happened just today.

A friend at work I have been working with for the last 8 months
was seperated (*sic*) from her husband because he was abusive. Last week
she filed for devorce, (*sic*) last night he went to her house shot and killed
her and shot and wounded her father,she was one of the nicest peaple (sic)
I personaly (*sic*) have ever known.
But the answer to your question may be that Americans may be interested
in this because it has become a part of our everyday lives.

   Sincerly (*sic*) Richard

The topic ended when an Australian suggested euthanasia as a different area
of discussion since some participants were becoming rather irate:

Date: Tue, 15 Apr 1997 00:20:15 +1000

To: ENG–ESP@tandem.uni-trier.de
From: A..............
Subject: an end to the terror – hurray!!!

L........ I do not think R.......meant to be offensive – I, too, am an
English speaker but have not replied because I did not find the topic
interesting. But it's true, we humans do at times have a sick fascination
for what R....calls 'true crime'. It is interesting because it is so
difficult to understand what drives a person to do such terrible things.
It's like reading stories about how sharks rip people apart! Anyway, YES,
let's get onto a new subject. Did you know a doctor in the Northern
Territory (Australia) is trying to make euthanasia (hope I spelled it
correctly!) legal? What do you think about this?

This member of the forum is monitoring messages, trying to clear up
understandings and ensuring that the forum discussions do not get out of
hand; this provides an opportunity for language learners to manage real
interaction within the relative safety of an educational list.

4   Conclusion

Clearly the ENG–ESP forum is a high-traffic forum with exchanges occurring
between large numbers of people. However, large numbers of people also do
not participate on a regular basis. Messages predominate in Spanish, but there
are enough in each language to enable all to benefit.

Assuming that all ENG–ESP members belong to the list mainly to learn
English or Spanish (see Section 2), it follows that even those who participate
little believe that they are benefiting from the participation of others through
reading the messages and thinking about the issues raised. As mentioned
previously, one can assume that they would leave the forum if they were not
learning from it. While others are 'talking' they may feel no need to do so
themselves.

As shown in section 3, discussion was stimulated to a high degree with short
messages such as the questions and answers. Perhaps these are the kinds of
messages easily exchanged by large numbers of people as they require little

on-line reading and are possibly the kinds of questions which can be thought about while doing something else. They are also the kinds of questions which can be exchanged between large numbers of people from different backgrounds who do not know each other. One might draw a parallel between social chat in a large group face-to face which, in order to include everyone, exchanges jokes and sayings across the table.

It would appear that native speakers of both languages have the opportunity of being exposed to their target language; some are taking the opportunity to practise it actively, others are reading it. The English-speaking participants have more opportunity to read authentic texts in the language they are learning than do the Spanish. While participants are asked to ensure that both Spanish and English native speakers benefit, in practice it is not easy for them to regulate this. It would be interesting to research this question in the forum over other years to find out if the uneven split in language use is also evident in these.

Whatever the calibre of exchange and topic discussed, it is clear that participants can learn at first hand the triply difficult skill of communicating at a distance with large numbers of people from a variety of cultures in a foreign language. This provides a unique and valuable experience, particularly for advanced language learners.

References

González-Bueno, M. (1998) 'The effects of electronic mail on Spanish L2 discourse', *Language learning and technology*, 1,2 (URL: <http://polyglot.cal.msu.edu/llt/vol1num2/article3/default.html>).

Hedderich, N. (1996) 'Language and intercultural learning in the forum', in D. Little and H. Brammerts, *A guide to language learning in tandem via the Internet*, CLCS occasional paper no.46, Trinity College, Dublin.

Launay, D. (1993) *The Xenophobe's Guide to The Spanish*, Ravette.

Levy, M. (1998) 'Two conceptions of learning and their implications for CALL at the tertiary level', *ReCall*, 10, 1: 86–95.

Lewis, T. Woodin, J. and St John, E. (1996) 'Tandem Learning: Independence through Partnership', in E. Broady and M-M. Kenning, *Promoting Autonomy in University Language Teaching*, London: Association for French Language Studies in association with CILT, pp. 105–20.

Little, D. and Ushioda, E. (1998) 'Designing, implementing and evaluating a project in tandem language learning via e-mail', *ReCALL*, 10, 1: 95–101.

Murray, D. (1991) *Conversation for action: The computer terminal as a medium of communication*, Amsterdam: John Benjamins.

McConnell, D. (1994) Managing Open Learning in Computer Supported Collaborative Learning Environments', *Studies in Higher Education*, 19, 3: 341–358.

Schwienhorst, K. (1998) 'Third place – virtual reality applications for second language learning', *ReCALL* 10, 1: 118–126.

Sproull, L. & Kiesler, S. (1991) *Connections: New ways of working in the networked organisation*, Cambridge, Massachusetts: MIT Press.

Warschauer, M. (1997) Computer-Mediated Collaborative Learning: Theory and Practice,, *The Modern Language Journal*, 81, 4: 470–481.

Woodin, J. (1997), E-mail tandem learning & the communicative curriculum', *ReCALL* 9, 1: 22–33.

Notes

1 Further information on the International E-Mail Tandem Network, set up by Helmut Brammerts of Ruhr-Universitaet, Bochum, can be found at: page http://www.slf.ruhr-uni-bochum.de/email/infen.html

2 The project title is 'Telematics for Autonomous and Intercultural Tandem Learning', Socrates/ODL ID N.: 25192/CP/1/96/1/DE/ODL.

3 Participants are also informed that they can look for a one-to-one tandem patrtner via the discussion list, if the pairing agency is not currently able to find one for you.

Appendix

Welcome message from the ENG–ESP subnet. This message is sent in both languages; here only the English is shown.

International E-Mail Tandem Network

Welcome to ENG–ESP

ENG–ESP is a forum for discussion in Spanish and English in which people who have a command of one of the two languages are learning the other and wish to know more about members in other countries.

1 The forum

In order to take part in the discussion of this forum, the only thing you have to do is to send your messages to the forum address and the computers will automatically send them on to all the other members.

The address of the forum is: eng-esp@tandem.uni-trier.de

To begin with, we suggest that, as a beginner, you introduce yourself to the other members writing just a few lines in your mother tongue, or better still, in both languages. It is possible that in this way other members might get in touch with you and, by having things in common, will find out more about you.

In this forum you will be able to write what you want: you can ask for and give information, give your own opinions, relate your personal experiences, etc. Each person can write in his/her own language, in the foreign language or in both. The important thing is that the number of contributions in both languages is more or less equal so that everyone has the same opportunity to read and write in the foreign language.

2 Tandem partners

You will benefit even more if you have a link with a tandem partner. (The term 'tandem' is used when two people of different languages collaborate in the learning of their partner's language.) In pairs you can not only discuss topics that you may not want to share with everyone but also, which is more important, you will have the opportunity to give each other help through corrections, advice, questions, etc.

So that we can find a tandem partner for you, you can write a brief message to the 'dating agency': 'Forum ENG–ESP. First language: English. I am learning Spanish. Looking for a tandem partner.'

The address of the 'dating agency' is: tandem@slf.ruhr-uni-bochum.de

Teachers who want to include e-mail tandem in their Spanish or English classes, should contact both of the ENG–ESP co-ordinators (addresses at the end of this text).

3   Other network services

In this network we have a program which to take care of the administration to which you can send commands of different types. But these commands must be well formulated (one command per line) so as not to confuse the program. At the present time the program only understands and 'speaks' English.

The address of this service program is: majordomo@tandem.uni-trier.de

If, for example, you don't want to receive any more ENG–ESP mail, you can send it this command: unsubscribe eng-esp to leave the network for ever

Other important commands are: help to know more about the commands of the service program.

For further information you can contact ENG–ESP or us, the co-ordinators of this subnet.

Have fun!

Juan Antonio Alvarez González: jaag@PINON.CCU.UNIOVI.ES
Facultad de Informática Universidad de Oviedo E-33007 Oviedo España

Jane Woodin: .Woodin@sheffield.ac.uk, Modern Languages Teaching Centre, The University of Sheffield, Sheffield S10 2JA, United Kingdom

Ana Ojanguren Sánchez: ana@etsiig.uniovi.es, Dpto. de Filología Anglo-germánica y Francesa, Universidad de Oviedo (E), España

News travels fast: Multimedia and current affairs in the advanced language class

Ursula Stickler and Elke St John
Modern Languages Teaching Centre
University of Sheffield

1 Introduction

One of the issues which confronts anyone seeking to employ technology to promote learning is the level of complexity of the proposed learning instrument. While a high-tech option may provide a greater range of potential learning opportunities, the complexity of its manipulation may mean that these are rarely fully realised. A low-tech option may be more limited or more labour intensive, for both learner and tutor, but its accessibility and ease of use may mean that both of them are more ready to invest effort in using it.

Since – by its nature – much of the authentic material used for second language learning is inherently obsolescent, the developer has to make judgements about the level of sophistication to which it is worthwhile developing it, given its intrinsic lack of durability. The quest is on therefore, not so much for definitive learning resources (they are a chimera), but for structures which offer the possibility of regularly renewing such material at relatively little cost, in terms of labour, to tutors and producers.

Nowhere is this dilemma more acute than in the exploitation of news broadcasts – one of the staples in the use of satellite television and video for language learning. Nothing is as stale as yesterday's news. Yet how many teachers have the energy or the opportunity to daily renew the listening comprehension (or other) exercises they want their learners to undertake, merely in order to keep them topical? One possible solution to this dilemma is offered by the growing number of instances in which news producers combine and support their transmissions with a WWW-based textual information service, offering actual transcripts of newly broadcast material.

This is an account of one such combination by the German language broadcaster ARD and of the way that combination has been exploited both for classroom use and independent study.

1.1 Advantages of news

According to Evard (1996), awakening an interest in current affairs among young people can be a challenging task even when these are part of their own culture (cf. Evard 1996); all the more so when the news is taken from a foreign one. News bulletins are delivered rapidly, the news is very context-dependent and demands a high level of background knowledge which can make it difficult for the language learner to understand the content properly.

On the other hand, news programmes[1] are a useful vehicle for developing the cultural awareness of learners. Raising cultural awareness in a second language learning context is not simply achieved by presenting information on the target language country as in traditional area studies or 'Landeskunde'. A more learner-centred approach starts by alerting the students to possible differences and similarities between their own culture(s) and the target language culture(s).

Even if the news is presented – as is often unavoidable in second language teaching – as disembodied snippets of culture rather than one facet of a whole in context, news programmes are particularly well suited for familiarising students with the target language culture(s), for various reasons:

• Expectation

Most learners will be familiar with the concept of news and the format and content of news programmes in the L1 culture. This allows them to approach foreign language news with some expectations in mind and makes it easier to spot and analyse differences for themselves.

• Comparability

Assumptions about the status of news in their own country will give learners some ideas about where to place the news of a foreign language country in the overall cultural context, i.e. they will be disposed to treat the content as factual or 'truthful'[2] rather than fictional and they will be familiar with the role of the news programme as a day-to-day source of factual information.[3] The topics selected for programmes can give some indication as to the significance an event has for the intended audience of the news bulletin. These three features (factuality, source of information and relative significance) mean that news will most likely be perceived by second language learners as indicating how the world is perceived at a certain point in time by the recipients of news in the target language culture.

With some background information on the relative status of specific news organs in the target language culture, learners will be able to compare and contrast the view of reality purveyed to target language consumers with that provided by specific organs of their own culture.[4]

• Variety

The variety of different areas covered by news features in any one programme or publication (e.g. politics, culture, sport, weather) means that news can offer something of interest to a wide range of individual learners. This characteristic of news is important if cultural awareness is to form an integral part of students' language education and a varied programme can offer a better chance of holding an individual student's attention.

1.2 Conditions for independent study

This last point also leads to one of the reasons why we considered it desirable that students should be able to use news programmes in independent study mode. The limited amount of class contact time in foreign language learning makes it impossible – in choosing topics and material – to cater for every individual interest. In independent study time, on the other hand, learners can focus on topics which are of genuine interest to them.

In this respect the role of the tutor in language classes is a changing one: in addition to presenting chosen aspects of the target language culture, tutors also need to prepare students for the task of finding, selecting and using appropriate material for independent study.

Learners need to acquire certain skills – apart from the computer skills necessary for the tasks we will describe – to be able to exploit the masses of authentic material on offer in a fruitful way for their independent language learning and the development of cultural awareness. These are as follows:

- finding and selecting material:

News can make this task easier in that a specific news programme shows an overview of topics and information relevant for the target language culture at a certain time. In other words, news is a good starting point to check one's assumptions of 'what is going on' in the target language countries and decide – according to one's own interests – on features or topics for further study.

In this respect, the more up-to-date the news, the more 'authentic' it is as a representation of the target language culture.

- language skills:

As language teachers, we expect and encourage students – especially at higher levels – to use a variety of resources to develop their receptive skills outside the classroom and independently of the course requirements. These include printed texts, the broadcast media, films and latterly the WWW.

For this purpose, news has two advantages over other material as stated above (see 1.1): predictability of format and – to the extent to which learners are aware of international news in their own language – of content, which facilitates listening and reading comprehension. If learners are already aware of the news in their own language, it will be easier to guess at the meaning of a news item, since the content is already broadly familiar.

- language learning strategies:

However rich such materials are in linguistic, factual and cultural terms, learners will need some form of strategic competence to make appropriate use of them. Some of the abilities students need for independent language learning are manifested in the kind of metacognitive language learning strategies described, e.g., by Oxford (1990), such as organising, preparing for a listening or reading task, and self-evaluation.

Worksheets and timetables can help students to organise their tasks in relation to news programmes. For this some input from the tutor can be helpful (e.g., offering worksheets, information on resources). Students can prepare for a listening or reading task by paying attention to the news in their own country and making predictions about the target language news.

Self-evaluation, finally, is indispensable for independent study. If a language learning task is intended to lead to enhanced cultural awareness or linguistic proficiency, students will need access to feedback on how successful their attempt at understanding was, firstly, to prove that their assumptions about the target language culture are correct and, secondly, to monitor their own strengths and weaknesses in comprehension. This individual feedback is difficult for a third party to provide, especially for input which is changing so rapidly as up-to-date news, hence the need for students to develop their capacity for self-evaluation.

In our project we endeavoured to use technology to improve teaching and learning in two main areas: materials preparation and independent study. On the one hand we tried to exploit the benefits of the new media to counteract some of the problems inherent in using news for language learning or teaching: i.e. their rapid delivery in spoken form, high context dependency, rapid obsolescence and the high level of effort demanded from the tutor to prepare suitable material. On the other hand we tried to stimulate students' interest in the current affairs of the target language country to open up a new area of independent study for them to pursue.

2   Background

News is now readily available in the foreign language classroom thanks to broadcasts and off-air recordings as well as newspapers. Moreover, technology has made the news in written form instantly and globally accessible. Nowadays, most language tutors, in Higher Education at least, also have access to Internet-based news resources such as foreign language newspapers on the WWW, news bulletins or foreign language news digests which may be sent by email to the recipient (e.g. 'Germnews').[5]

Despite its advantages, the rapid out-dating of the material and the pressure on tutors' time makes news a less than ideal basis for worksheets and independent study. Therefore, commercially available self-study material often takes the form of CD-Rom based multimedia programmes. The advantages of these for language learning have been widely recognised (e.g. Brett 1996): they integrate listening and reading skills and offer interactive opportunities and feedback for users. A multimedia package can enhance learners' receptive skills as well as giving opportunities for speaking and, in some cases, writing practice. *TV und Texte* (1994) is an example of a German CD-ROM for advanced language learners based on a news programme (*Reportage*, on SAT 1). In this package, users can watch a news reader announce the headlines, see the news feature, read the transcript of the texts in German and in an English translation, and use a notepad for summaries or to prepare their own bulletin which can be recorded and played back (cf. St. John 1996).

The major disadvantages of these multimedia packages are: CD-Roms are time-consuming to produce and quite expensive to purchase, the amount of choice for users is limited, and – of particular relevance in the case of news programmes – they very soon become dated. Old news is no news. Instead of topical and authentic cultural information, *TV und Texte* offers an aspect of German public life, frozen in time in the year of production. For the sake of high-tech interactive options for users, contemporary relevance is foregone.

We started to look for a way to overcome these disadvantages without losing too much of the ease and range of practice opportunities of a multimedia package.

3   The material

3.1 Tagesschau [6]

Tagesschau is a news programme, broadcast two or three times a day, which lasts approximately 15 minutes, offering brief factual information on current affairs. It is the flagship and trademark of *ARD*, one of the main German television channels. *ARD* stands for *Allgemeiner Rundfunk Deutschland*. It is the 'National Radio and Television Network of the Federal Republic of Germany'. *Tagesschau* is the most widely broadcast news on German language television. The related programme *Tagesthemen*, which lasts 30 minutes, is broadcast later in the evening and *Nachtmagazin* is broadcast just before midnight.

3.2 The Tagesschau *website*

Tagesschau and *Tagesthemen* were the first news broadcasts to go on the Internet in their entirety in August 1996. Transcripts of the news bulletins, video clips on VDO[7] and an archive of the broadcasts and transcripts of the past few months are available, in addition to similar services for the more detailed programmes, *Tagesthemen* and *Wochenthemen*. Details of the news appear on the *Tagesschau* website[8] straight after the transmission of the ARD programme. Since 1996, a new broadcasting system offers better-defined videoed reports on computer screens and the *Nachtmagazin* has been added to the website. An average of 125,000 users access the *Tagesschau* page every day. 70% of the interest comes from Germany with the foreign interest coming from over 100 countries. All the programmes remain stored on the Internet as a publicly accessible archive. The newscasters' scripts and presenters' interventions are also stored here in textual form. In addition to these items, background information about ARD is offered. The work of editorial staff is presented, there are also short profiles of news readers and presenters.

The *Tagesschau* website provides a multimedia alternative to other sources of news for students of German, it is easily accessible and regularly and speedily updated. It offers less scope for interaction than a CD-Rom like *TV und Texte*,[9] but is a vast source of authentic up-to-date material that can be just as stimulating for users and certainly gives a better insight into German culture today.

A fulltext search option of the archives is now available,[10] which extends the possible uses for language learners. Entering a term, the search engine will look through the archives to find any news bulletins connected with the topic. This means that users can research a particular topic strand over an extended period, reconstruct the development of a current story, or focus (in the sense of Krashen's 'narrow reading' or 'narrow listening'[11]) on one particular subject for reading and/or listening practice. It gives learners the opportunity to explore a topic for themselves, in instances where it is necessary to have some information on past events to understand the most current news.

3.3 Proposals for use of Tagesschau

Quite apart from its potential for self-access use by independent learners the *Tagesschau* website can reduce the effort required from tutors for the preparation of worksheets for in-class use. The headlines on the homepage[12] offer a quick overview of the different news items and facilitate selection of a news broadcast suitable for a certain stage, class or topic. The availability of transcripts means that the tutors needing these can download the text and adapt it for gap-filling, multiple choice, direct question or true-false question exercises very easily.

Transcripts can also be used in class to prepare exercises such as mock presentations or matching exercises. The availability of the same material via two different channels can be used to alert the students to the advantages of multi-channel input for independent use of the material, e.g. by asking them to compare their reading and listening comprehension. The transcripts can be scrambled or adapted for reading comprehension or grammar exercises, e.g. by substituting all capital letters or deleting verb endings; or they can be pasted into available text jumbling software for reconstruction exercises or even simple spelling practice.

The opportunities for self-study use are manifold: not only is access to the webpage simultaneously available to large numbers of students (in our self-access centre every networked computer can access the WWW), but the multi-channel input offers students the flexibility to choose their tasks, according to their level of language comprehension and their learning purpose. Information gleaned from the news programme or the WWW-based news resource can supply topics for discussion in class as well as stimulating interest in the whole area of German current affairs and increasing students' familiarity with German culture.

4   The *Tagesschau* project

4.1 Aims/goals

Our goal in introducing the use of the *Tagesschau* website into our language classes was twofold: to further cultural awareness and to offer students access to attractive resources for independent learning. To make it possible for students to use *Tagesschau* for their independent study tasks, we found it necessary to prepare them in class for the technical side of using the *Tagesschau* website and archives, and to make sure that they had the necessary computing skills and became familiar with the format. According to Warschauer, Turbee and Roberts: 'One very important aspect of empowering students is that they should learn to use the computers, rather than feel used by them' (Warschauer, Turbee and Roberts, 1996:9). Once the students had mastered the basic computing skills necessary to access the resources, we suggested different activities according to their relative level of language proficiency.

4.2 Users

Tagesschau was used with five groups of students. Two groups were intermediate (Stage 2: post GCSE), two advanced (Stage 3: post A level) and one very advanced (Stage 4: A level + 1 year at university). Most of the students were specialists in other disciplines, such as Engineering, Pure Science, Social Science and Arts. Their language classes comprised 3 hours of class contact time and 3 hours of independent study per week for which a well appointed self-access centre was provided. In the self-access centre students could use networked computers, television (with satellite channels) and audio playback and recording equipment. All networked computers on campus had access to the Internet, and 13 of the 27 computers available in the self-access centre were equipped to play video using the VDO software.

4.3 Procedure

After an initial training session for tutors on how to access the website, it was decided to employ different activities with each class to explore the potential of this experimental introduction of WWW-based news resources. Classes were introduced to *Tagesschau* in the following ways:

The two Stage 2 classes were asked a week in advance to watch at least three different issues of *Tagesschau* on video to familiarise themselves with the format and structure of the programme and to avoid a 'shock' in class when they first came across rapidly delivered, topical news in the foreign language. Considering that some of the students had previously undertaken only one year of German it was quite likely that they had never seen an authentic German news programme before. They were also asked to make notes on one item that was of interest to them. Specifically they were asked to watch the same edition of *Tagesschau* once only, to encourage them to concentrate on and elicit information at first hearing, as in an authentic situation.

The Stage 4 group was prepared for this task by asking them to pay particular attention to the (English) news over the week following these instructions in class.[13] Paying more attention to the equivalent medium in their own culture, allowed them to form hypotheses about the likely content of news in the foreign language. This group and the two Stage 3 groups were asked in class to fill in a grid to establish their awareness of news topics and current affairs, nationally, internationally and with specific reference to Germany (see Appendix 1).

The preparation for Stage 2 students familiarised them with the format and structure of the German news, the language used, the speed of delivery and some of the topics which were reported on the video shown in class.

In their next language classes all groups were given the video of *Tagesschau* and an accompanying worksheet containing listening comprehension exercises (see Appendix 2). Immediately afterwards, they were shown how to access the *Tagesschau* website, use the VDO player and the *Tagesschau* archives on the Internet. They then were asked to fill in worksheets identical to those used for the listening task.[14] We left the preparation of computing skills for classtime, considering that, although some of our students are highly computer literate, these skills might be best introduced with help at hand.

In the following week, students of all groups were first presented with short transcripts from *Tagesschau* and were then shown a video recording of the *Tagesschau* news programme from one of the previous days.

Watching *Tagesschau* on satellite television, video or the Internet and completing the accompanying worksheets was an optional self-study task over the next weeks.

4.4 Evaluation procedure

Students' evaluation of the different *Tagesschau* tasks was collected in class discussions in Stage 2, Stage 3 and Stage 4 groups. In addition, Stage 3 groups were invited in week 8 of the semester to give a written account of their independent study tasks and to assess their usefulness. This could be done in the form of an essay, detailing their listening practice and the use they make of the self-access centre for independent study or by handing in the language learning diaries which they kept over the semester.

5   Results of in-class use of *Tagesschau*

5.1 News awareness

The first pre-viewing exercise asked students of the Stage 3 and Stage 4 groups to give an account of the most recent news they had heard, seen or read and to guess which of these news items would be important from a German point of view, in other words, to predict the headlines of German news reports. The results of the exercise and following discussions showed that the students' perception of news was rather localised or even personalised.[15] Some students reported that they had not heard any news or read any newspapers for days. The small number of items of information they produced were either of a very local nature (i.e. concerning Sheffield or the university community) or of very specialised interest (e.g. the results of their favourite football club). The only notable exception to this was the debate about the British budget, which was at that time taking place in Parliament. This was mentioned by three students, but in the following class discussion most of the students thought it might not feature prominently in German news.

Generally, students felt that the information they had produced would not be relevant for German news recipients:[16] of the 31 news items mentioned by the 21 students who took part in this exercise, only 6 were felt to be of potential interest to Germany; only one student chose 2 of his items of information for their relevance to the German news market. There was remarkably little difference in the number of items produced by the Stage 4 group which was asked to prepare for the task a week in advance (average of 1.66 items) and the Stage 3 groups which were unprepared (average of 1.83 items).[17]

5.2 Use of video recordings

Conventionally, listening tasks based on the video recording of a news programme consist of true-false questions, gap-filling exercises and a grid to fill in details of the news items. Three worksheets with listening exercises in this format were produced for video recordings of *Tagesschau* which was shown in class to three groups of students on different days. By using the transcriptions of *Tagesschau* news bulletins available on the WWW, the production of the worksheets was made considerably easier for the tutor. Instead of having to transcribe recordings, text could be downloaded from the website and adapted for gap-filling and true-false questions. The facilities of the *Tagesschau* website made it possible to use an up-to-date news bulletin for each class instead of preparing one recording and using it throughout the week.

Showing a video of the news programme in class has disadvantages compared to working with news recordings in self-access mode: students cannot stop and rewind the video as and when they need; the limited class time makes it impossible to show the recording as often as students would like to hear it; and the sound quality of television or video in class is poorer than when students can use the headphones in the self-access centre.

This combined with the lack of awareness of current news topics shown by students (see 5.1, above) resulted in a relatively low success rate for the listening comprehension exercise for stages 3 and 4. The average success rate of students was 20.6% of all possible correct answers. The best achieved approximately 39% and the weakest 17%.

Most students reported that they found the exercise difficult[18] and gave various reasons for this: the speed of the delivery, the unfamiliarity of the content, lack of knowledge about German politics, and the nature of the task (having to concentrate on listening and writing at the same time).[19] 8 of 11 students mention these problems again in their diaries; three refer to their lack of knowledge about German politics (see below, 6.3, Table 3). Only one student found the class exercise easy. He reported having watched the news programme in the self-access centre two days before.

5.3 Use of Tagesschau website

The website of *Tagesschau* was new to all the students and was enthusiastically received by them as an alternative source of information after the difficult listening task. Although access to the video replay of the news items is technically not easy (four students reported technical difficulties when using *Tagesschau* independently), the main advantage of the webpage was seen to be the transcripts it provided of the headlines and news reader's reports which allowed students to assess their performance in the listening tasks and to compare their listening and reading comprehension. Some quotes from students' diaries:

> *Später sind wir in Computerraum gegangen und das Tagesschau 'Website' gefunden. Es war sehr gut, weil wir konnen das Video auf Computer sehen und auch die Abschrift haben. Auf dem Computer habe ich mehr verstanden als vorher.*[20]

> *(Later, we went to the computer-room and found the website of the Tagesschau. It was good because we could watch the video on the computer and read the transcript. I understood more on the computer.)*

> *Es war ziemlich interessant um der Unterschied zwischen meines Verständnis der schriftlichen und gesprochenen Information zu sehen. Es war einfacher die Tagesschau zu lesen als hören. Ich habe gelernt, daß es besser ist, etwas zu hören, und lesen, weil wenn ich etwas nur hören, gibt es viel, was ich nicht verstehen kann.*

> *(It was rather interesting to notice the difference between my comprehension of written and spoken information. It was easier to read the Tagesschau than to listen to it. I learned that it is better to hear and read something because when I only hear it, there is much that I cannot understand.)*

The second quote in particular shows that the exercise alerted students to the benefit of having two channels for input: it obviously facilitates comprehension of the content. Once the learners have become familiar with the structure of the programme and find that they can understand a good deal of the information by using a combination of different media, we would hope that they may get used to accessing German news broadcasts not only as a beneficial listening exercise but also as a genuine source of information on events in German speaking countries, e.g. in preparation for a period of residence abroad.

5.4 Prepared listening in class

An alternative way of presenting video recordings of the news programme in class was chosen for the following week, to alert students to the advantages of preparing for a listening task to be undertaken in independent study. Transcripts of the headlines and short summaries of the news items were downloaded from the first page of the *Tagesschau* website and handed out in class as hardcopies.[21] Students were asked to first read the transcripts, categorise the news items into different types of news features[22] and summarise them. They could then discuss the outcome with fellow students and check their understanding of the content in class. After this preparation, students were shown the recording of the news programme and asked to summarise their understanding in a grid and answer some detailed questions.

In the feedback to this exercise, students showed an increased awareness of the advantages of two channels of information input – i.e. reading the transcripts and listening to the tape – and commented on the relative merits of the different modes of input. Whereas some students found it easier to summarise the written information even before listening to the full reports, others saw the video with its visual clues as their main source of information. Generally, the combination of written information and video recording was seen as an aid to understanding.

> *Es ist leichter zu verstehen, wenn man die Abschrift habe.*
>
> *(It is easier to understand when you have the transcript.)*

The worksheets for this exercise, slightly edited for independent use, are now available in the self-access centre[23] and students follow a similar procedure when using the news independently.

> *Persönlich genieße ich am meisten die Tagesschau auf dem WWW.*

Manchmal ist das Video ein bißchen langsam aber ich finde es nützlich ein bißchen von jedem Beitrag zu lesen, bevor ich mir das Video ansehe. Ich glaube, daß ich sehr viel von diesen Sendungen gelernt habe.

(Personally, I appreciate most the Tagesschau on the worldwideweb. Sometimes the video is a bit slow, but I find it very useful to read a little about every report before watching the video. I believe that I have learned a lot from this programme.)

Others choose to watch the news programme on video or live satellite television first and utilise the website for self-assessment. They can fill in the worksheets when watching the video or live satellite television, and afterwards check their answers against the transcripts on the web.

Im „Self-Access Centre' sehe ich „die Tagesschau' in Fernseher und ich versuche die Hauptthemen der Nachrichten zu verstehen. Nach den Nachrichten in Fernseher benutze ich normalerweise einen Computer in dem „Self-Access Centre' und ich besuche die Tagesschau „World Wide Web' Seite.

Auf der Tagesschau-Web Seite lese ich die Geschichten die ich vorher gesehen habe.'

(In the self-access centre, I first watch the Tagesschau on television and try to understand the main topics of the news. After the news on television, I normally use a computer in the self-access centre and visit the website of the Tagesschau.

On the Tagesschau webpage, I read the stories I have been watching before.)

5.5 In-class preparation for independent study

Using *Tagesschau* does require some preparation to familiarise students with the technology and the material. Part of this can be done in class by alerting the learners to the topic, asking them to pay attention to the news in their own language and making them guess beforehand which topics will be dealt with in the foreign language news. This is not only a valuable preparation but can also stimulate interesting discussions about the relative impact of events in different cultures.

Showing a video recording of a news programme without any preparation or supporting material in class can be frustrating for students and is unlikely to predispose them to using this particular kind of listening comprehension for self-study. In contrast, by good practice in class, students can be shown that there are ways in which they can facilitate their understanding of the content. It is worthwhile to draw students' attention to the advantages of more channels of input which allow them to compare their own performance in the respective skills and gives them more control over the material they can use for independent study.

The major benefit of *Tagesschau* is the easy accessibility of reading and listening material on the same topic which allows for a combination of different media. We are aware of the danger that students might be tempted to avoid the input they perceive as the more difficult (either reading or listening) and attempt to glean the information in the easier way but our evaluation has not shown any such tendency in our students.

6 Evaluation of students' reaction and up-take for independent study

A relatively comprehensive evaluation of the *Tagesschau* project by a group of 25 Stage 3 (post A level) students offers useful insights into students' attitudes towards recorded news bulletins as well as the use they made of *Tagesschau* for independent study. In the following, views gleaned from the written accounts (essays and diaries) of these students will inform our conclusions.

The difference in the data collection tools means that we deal with two slightly different sets of data: in their essays, students have carefully chosen what type of listening exercise they want to present and, in most cases, give an evaluation of the task. This means that not everything that was presented in class will be mentioned but only those exercises deemed useful for independent study. In interpreting these accounts, we would assume that a detailed description of a *Tagesschau* exercise offers evidence that students find value in the task.

The language learning diary used for the German classes is much more structured than a blank diary. It contains rubrics which encourage students to set themselves goals for improving their language and to evaluate the success of their self-study tasks. However, diaries are usually more conducive to recording affective responses to learning situations than objective assessments of what has been learnt (cf. Numrich 1996). Learners may use them to comment on tasks done in class and to report on the follow-up tasks they have elected to undertake independently. Accounts from the diaries, therefore, can show learners' immediate reactions to the perceived benefits or disadvantages of an exercise, whether undertaken in class or as a self-study task. Such immediacy makes the judgements recorded of crucial importance.

6.1 Awareness of news

Of these 25 students, 11 handed in their diaries and 14 wrote an essay describing and evaluating the listening tasks they used in the self-access centre. Of the 14 essays, 13 mention having listened to news programmes. Only 5 students referred specifically to the webpage of *Tagesschau* and the multimedia application. Three students mentioned *TV und Texte*.

News broadcasts are mentioned in all of the 11 diaries, the Internet application is mentioned in 7. No diary entry refers to the CD-Rom *TV und Texte*.

No. of students in Stage 3	overall	essay	diary
	25	14	11
Nachrichten/ news in general	24	13	11 8 in class, 7 for self-study
WWW *Tagesschau* 12	5	7	
TV und Texte	3	3	0

Table 1: Media used by Stage 3 students

The high number of students who refer to news programmes in their essays is in part influenced by timing: just two weeks after they were introduced to the *Tagesschau* news programme and the WWW-based news resources, they were asked to write about listening tasks. The diary also reflects events in the classroom, although it is interesting to note that 7 of 11 students mention listening to the news as self-study tasks.

In his research on students' evaluation of multimedia programmes, Paul Brett (Brett, 1996: 209) is in some doubt about whether the initial favourable opinions of users will persist over time. He feels that the initial enthusiasm sparked by any novelty can easily fade. In our experience this seems to have happened to the CD-Rom *TV und Texte*, which was shown to the students approximately 6 months before the start of the *Tagesschau* project, and is only mentioned in 3 of 25 written accounts.

If, on the other hand, the information content is more important than the practice aspect,[24] *Tagesschau* has an undeniable advantage over the pre-fabricated multimedia package. Legenhausen and Wolff (1990) warn against multimedia packages where the computer seems more of a distraction from the language learning task than a help. In the case of *Tagesschau* and its WWW-page the computer is merely a necessary instrument for accessing authentic information on the Internet. It is the topicality of the news broadcasts themselves which is used to generate an interest in events in the German speaking countries,[25] which then motivates learners to access the WWW-page of *Tagesschau*, using the computer.

In the words of one student:

> *Am Internet gibt es wieder die Möglichkeit das Video mit Ton zu sehen und für Zuschauer, die noch immer Schwerigkeiten haben die Sendung zu verstehen, gibt es auch ein Transkript der Sendung bei diesem Website.*

> *(On the Internet you have again the opportunity to watch the video [i.e. the Tagesschau] and for listeners who still have problems to understand the broadcast, a transcript of the broadcast is given on this website.)*

6.2 Students' motivation for using news programmes

Of the 25 post A level students 12 mentioned the information content as reason for watching news, regardless of whether their motivation for using it was instrumental or integrative:

Erstens, um meine Hörfähigkeit zu üben und zweitens, weil ich in zwei Jahren in Deutschland studiere und hoffentlich ich viel über Deutschland durch die Nachrichten lernen kann.

(Firstly, to practise listening skills and secondly because I will study in Germany in two years time and, hopefully, will learn a lot about Germany through the news.)

Bei der Nachrichten kann man beide, die Horchgeschick und die Kenntnisse der deutschen Geschehen verbessern. Ich höre oft die Nachrichten zu, weil es mich für die Tagespolitik interessiert.

(With news you can do both: improve your listening skills and your knowledge of German affairs. I often listen to the news because I am interested in current affairs.)

The news was valued for the authenticity and immediacy of its content by 11 out of 25 students. And 12 out of 25 mentioned news broadcasts as particularly well suited for listening tasks.

Reasons for watching news	overall	essay	diary
No. of students in Stage 3	25	14	11
Authenticity/current affairs	11	8	3
Relevance of information	12	6	6
News for improving listening skills	12	7	5

Table 2: Reasons given by Stage 3 students for watching news

Of the main reasons given for watching news programmes, the last – suitability for listening exercises – seems the most prone to changing 'fashions' in self-study habits and tasks: there is a vast range of listening material available in our self-access centre. The other two reasons, authenticity and relevance, are inherent to authentic, up-to-date news programmes. This motivation is connected with a genuine interest in the content of the programme and could therefore help to sustain students' interest in *Tagesschau* over a longer period of time.

Die tägliche Nachtrichen Sendungen sind besonders nützlich, weil sie über Tagespolitik berichten.

(The daily news programmes are especially useful because they report on current political events.)

Once developed, students' appetite for topical news can be met by *Tagesschau* whether live, on video, or on the WWW, as it cannot by any package, however sophisticated, which employs 'old news'.

6.3 Perceived problems

The most encouraging finding of the evaluation is the comparatively low rate of reported technical problems which tends to bear out some of our initial assumptions about the immediate benefits of 'low-tech' options. Only 4 students reported technical problems with the webpage at one time or another. A more widespread problem was a perceived lack of background information about German politics or the political system.

	Overall	Essay	Diary
No. of students in Stage 3	25	14	11
Problems understanding content of news[26]	9	1	8
– lack of political background	4	1	3
Information			
– speed	2	0	2
– concentration	1	0	1
– unspecified	4	0	4
– does not work	2	0	2

Table 3: Problems reported by Stage 3 students

This is encouraging because the students themselves identify the remedy for this problem: watch more news programmes, find out about the situation in Germany.

(Ziel) Mehr über aktuelle politische Themen herauszufinden.

(Schritt) 'S.A.C. Internet, Tagesschau'

(goal: Find out more about political topics.

step: S.A.C. Internet, Tagesschau.)

Watching *Tagesschau* obviously stimulates their interest in other aspects of German culture and in broadening their horizon. This curiosity could be further exploited for language learning by offering links on the WorldWideWeb to sources of information on German history, the political system and background information to news events. The Internet is the ideal tool for this kind of research because it gives every individual student the opportunity to choose areas of interest and to follow up his or her own lines of inquiry.

7 Evaluation of the material

The particular combination which *Tagesschau* offers, of satellite TV broadcasts using the aural/oral channel and WWW-based textual information, has a number of advantages for both learners and teachers.

7.1 Materials preparation

The advantages of the *Tagesschau* website for the tutor should not be underestimated: headlines can be rapidly skimmed in preparation for showing the news programme in class; the transcripts can be used to produce up-to-date worksheets with relatively little effort; archives can be searched for background information on specific topics and to check for news items of relevance to current topics of study.

Even the preparation of worksheets for self-study is made considerably easier for the materials developer: detailed answer sheets for every exercise become unnecessary since the website offers students the possibility of checking their answers to listening tasks or of using the webpages to practise 'prepared listening' after skimming the written information on the main news.[27]

The use of new media puts considerable pressure on teachers to constantly update and expand their skills. To encourage teachers to actually employ these skills in their everyday work, the benefits have to outweigh the effort. Apart from the fact that students need some training to use the new medium, the teacher's attitude can also work as a model for students. No level of expert introduction can substitute for the teacher's own enthusiasm for the use of new media.

7.2 Suitability for independent study

Judging from students' reflections and evaluations, we can conclude that our project has been at least partially successful:

Of the 25 students taking part in the detailed evaluation, 12 mentioned news programmes as a valuable source of information on German-speaking society and culture; 8 students were made aware of gaps in their understanding, which 4 suggested could be remedied by more background information on specific topics, e.g. German politics. The benefits of input presented through more than one channel (written text, spoken information and the accompanying pictures) were recognised (predominantly in their diaries) by 9 students. And 9 students described various learning strategies for use in connection with news programmes, e.g. planning, organising, summarising, preparing and extending vocabulary. The importance of interest or motivation for comprehension was mentioned by 4 students.

Not all students will choose to use the *Tagesschau* website for independent study, but most of those who do, find it very rewarding. It lowers their anxiety at not being able to understand the rapidly delivered news bulletins, whether live or recorded. It raises their chances of gleaning details from reports by offering a 'back-up' when needed. They can work at their own speed and with a flexible set of worksheets. The transcripts can also be used to monitor their own listening comprehension, and – reciprocally – video images can support the understanding of the written information. The enhanced opportunity for self-evaluation is an important consideration in the planning of self-study material: if we want our students to become more independent language learners, we must provide for all aspects of autonomous learning, including self-assessment and evaluation.[28]

An interest in cultural information, stimulated by news reports, can be fed, using the WWW search engines or the *Tagesschau* archives to locate more detailed information on specific topics.

7.3 Limitations of the material

Some of the obvious technical difficulties (access to the Internet, slowness of the software), can be counteracted by an informed and imaginative use of the available resources: the slowness of video on the Internet can be offset by using a video recording of the same news programme.

Other limitations to the use of the *Tagesschau* multimedia programme for independent study are more difficult to overcome: for independent study *Tagesschau* is best suited to more advanced (post A level) learners. For lower or intermediate stages the material may be used for classroom tasks, with preparation and support from a tutor.

Whether in the classroom or in independent study, *Tagesschau* and its website primarily offer practice in the receptive skills. Transcription, summary and note-taking tasks also offer a ready source of writing practice, for relatively little tutor input. Even greater dividends may be derived from simple tutor-devised worksheets. Of itself, however, the *Tagesschau* material provides no opportunity for speaking practice. Yet the stimulus provided to genuinely communicative exchanges by such rich authentic material is almost certainly greater than even the most interactive CD-Rom can offer.

As indicated above, preparing learners for independent study is not only achieved by setting specific tasks but relies heavily on flexible exploitation of the available material and on students' own motivation to make use of it. In this sense, the *Tagesschau* website is one of a growing number of possibilities for learners. The main responsibilities of tutors are: (a) to produce suitable material to enhance/exploit the qualities of a combination of media and (b) to make sure that the learners are able to employ the available material to their best advantage. Both these tasks are made considerably easier to achieve by the features of the *Tagesschau* WWW-site.

8 Conclusions

Our experience shows that a low-tech option is not always second best. On the contrary, with inventive use of readily available technology, language learning and teaching can be made more exciting, can make use of more authentic material and lead to more independence. While the easy accessibility and handling allows learners to develop independent study skills which are useful both in the immediate context of second language learning and in the wider area of university study and subsequent employment, the tutor gains independence of a different kind: instead of being dependent on pre-fabricated multi-media packages, a plethora of authentic material can be accessed and used in class or for independent study material.

The number of news organs in different languages which are represented on the WWW is constantly increasing and it can be assumed that the combination of news broadcast on satellite television and transcripts on the WWW – which we used for our *Tagesschau* project – will soon be offered from other European television channels, as well. The task for language teachers is to 'pick and choose' material from different media depending on quality and suitability.

We hope that our project has shown – apart from one vignette of teaching with multi-media which may or may not be useful for other tutors – that the way forward in using technology for language teaching is not to advocate one or the other 'new' medium as the be-all and end-all for language learning but to stay up-to-date and exploit the variety of media and the vast range of material with imagination rather than high-tech specialism.

References

Bender, W., Chesnais, P., Elo, S., Shaw, A. and Shaw, M. (1996) 'Enriching communities: Harbingers of news in the future', *IBM Systems Journal*, 35, 3–4; http://www.almaden.ibm.com/journal/sj/mit/sectionb/chesnais.html

Brett, P. (1996) 'Using Multimedia: An Investigation of Learner's Attitudes', *System*, 9, 2–3; pp.191–212.

Cho, K.-S. and Krashen, S. D. (1994) 'Acquisition of vocabulary from the Sweet Valley Kids series: Adult ESL acquisition', *Journal of Reading* 37, 8 pp.662–7.

Evard, M. (1996) 'Children's interests in news: On-line opportunities', *IBM Systems Journal*, 35, 3–4.
Available at: <URL ttp://www.almaden.ibm.com/journal/sj/mit/sectionb/evard.html>

Holec, H. (1981) *Autonomy and Foreign Language Learning*, (Council of Europe) Oxford: etc. (Pergamon Press), p3.

Hummelmeier, A. (1997) *Nachrichten im Ersten*, Hamburg (ARD-aktuell, Chefredaktion).

Krashen, S. D. (1996) 'The Case for Narrow Listening', *System* 24, 1 pp.97–100.

Legenhausen, L. and Wolff, D. (1990) 'CALL in Use – Use of CALL: Evaluating CALL Software', *System* 18, 1; pp.1–13.

Numrich, C. (1996) 'On Becoming a Language Teacher: Insights From Diary Studies', *TESOL Quarterly* 30, 1; pp.131–51.

Oxford, R.L. (1990) *Language Learning Strategies: What Every Teacher Should Know*. Boston, Mass.: Heinle & Heinle Publ.

St.John, E. (1994) 'TV + Texte CD ROM', *ReCall Journal* 6, 2; pp.72–3.

Warschauer, M., Turbee, L. and Roberts, B. (1990) 'Computer Learning Networks and Student Empowerment', *System* 24, 1; pp.1–14.

Website:
Die Tagesschau (ARD: Allgemeiner Deutscher Rundfunk). Available at: <URL http://www.tagesschau.de>

CD-Rom:
TV und Texte. Interactive Video-based Language Learning. Authors: Loftus, G, Dyson, P., Mckeown, A. and McAleavy, M. (1994). Oxford University Press. Satellite news clips: Sat.1 1993.

Notes

1   We use the words 'news programme' when we are referring to specific television (or radio) broadcasts or their recordings on video. WWW-based news resources are all forms of news that can be accessed via the Internet, e.g. WorldWideWeb-sites, e-mail circulars. The word 'news' is used in the broadest sense for the specific content, i.e. factual, up-to-date reports on current events.

2   In an everyday sense of the word 'truth'.

3   To a variable degree viewers will also be aware of the cultural norms, e.g. attitudes, prejudices, also contained in or transmitted by news.

4   e.g. *Bildzeitung* (a German tabloid comparable to the *Sun*) or *Frankfurter Allgemeine* (a German national newspaper similar to the *Times*).

5   This service is accessible by subscription to LISTSERV@LISTSERV.GMD.DE

6   Cf. Hummelmeier (1997).

7   VDO is a software package that allows the viewing of video material on the Internet. It can be downloaded from various Internet sites, e.g. the *Tagesschau* homepage, without charge. In the near future the *Tagesschau* will also be available on live video.

8   http://www.tagesschau.de

9   The webpage offers the possibility to read the headlines on the homepage, access the full text of the news reader's announcement on selected news items and play back and stop the video clips. It does not allow any other manipulation of the video clip or simultaneous perusal of text and video.

10 This service is also available for the ARD server which can be used to lead to news reports and links to background information to *Tagesschau*.

11 Krashen (1996) argues that 'narrow listening' has the advantage of letting the learner gain familiarity and feel more comfortable with a topic or area which interests him/her and thereby makes comprehension easier. The learner (or 'acquirer' in Krashen's words) can choose and prepare for the topic. 'Narrow input' also provides the amount and level of input the learner needs at that particular stage in his/her language development. (cf. Cho and Krashen 1994).

12 For an example, see Appendix 5.

13 This activity might also benefit the Stage 2 group and help them focus on the content of news, rather than preparing them for the format of foreign language news. This might, in the next step, alert them to cultural differences in format and presentation of news.

14 Using the same worksheet made it easier (for students and for the tutor) to compare the success in understanding the different input and alerted the students to the advantages of the multi-channel input.

15 There is a tendency in a high-tech culture with high information input to narrow the scope of news that is actually taken in. This can reach a degree where the actual information content is relevant or interesting for no more than one person, creating a newsorgan that might be called the 'Daily Me'. Cf. Bender *et al*, 1996.

16 This perception of difference between the L1 culture and L2 culture news might be an interesting topic for future research and could certainly be exploited for the development of more in-depth cultural comparison material to be used in class.

17 This could either be due to a lack of serious preparation work on part of the Stage 4 students or simply indicate that a certain awareness of news is common to all students and does not need a preparation task specifically geared towards eliciting it.

18 For an alternative exercise using transcripts and video recording of the news in class, see below 5.5

19 Although this can be a good exercise for taking notes in a second language, it is a task that is easier in self-study, when students can choose mode of delivery and speed or pauses in recordings.

20 All students' quotes in German are given in their original form. Consequently, the German is not always accurate. In the translations obvious mistakes have been disregarded.

21 For an example of worksheets, see Appendix 2.

22 For categories, see the worksheet in Appendix 3.

23 For examples of worksheets for independent study, see Appendices 3 and 6.

24 Which is, according to our analysis of students' motivation (see 6.2, below), the case for approximately half of our users.

25 'Auch habe ich die Videobänder der deutschen Nachrichten benutzt. Sie sind sehr interessant, weil sie über augenblickliche Sache sind. Ich finde, daß meine Konzentration immer besser ist, weil die Nachrichten so interessant sind.'

(I have also used the video tapes of the German news. They are very interesting because they are about current things. I find that my concentration is always better because the news is so interesting.)

26 Some students mention more than one problem, e.g. speed and lack of background knowledge.

27 For an example of worksheets for 'prepared listening', see Appendix 3 and 4.

28 cf. Holec 1981, p.3.

Appendix 1

Die Schlagzeilen des Tages

Vorinformation

Was ist gestern geschehen? Denkt an die englischen Nachrichten, an Zeitungsmeldungen und an alle anderen Informationen, die ihr über aktuelle Ereignisse in Europa habt.

Was geschah?	Wann?	Wo?	Schlagzeile

Über welche dieser Ereignisse wird auch in Deutschland berichtet? Unterstreicht sie!

Was glaubt ihr, wie lauten die Schlagzeilen der Tagesschau in Deutschland? Die Tagesschau ist das 15 minütige Nachrichtenprogramm der ARD und wird täglich um 20 Uhr (mitteleuropäischer Zeit) gesendet.

Was geschah?	Wann?	Wo?	Schlagzeile

Dr Ursula Stickler   Tagesschau Vorbereitung   TAGAPPA   09/05/00

Appendix 2

Die Tagesschau vom _____

Ihr seht die Videoaufzeichnung der Tagesschau einmal. Schreibt so viel wie möglich mit, macht Notizen zu den einzelnen Schlagzeilen und beantwortet einige Fragen!

Überschriften	Details	Wer?	Was?	Wo?	Wann?	Wie?/Warum?
1. Schlagzeile: ___ ___						
2. Schlagzeile: ___ ___						
3. Schlagzeile: ___ ___						
4. Schlagzeile: ___ ___						
1. Auslandsmeldung: ___ ___						

Technology and the advanced language learner

2. Auslandsmeldung: ___ ___	3. Auslandsmeldung: ___ ___	1. Inlandsmeldung: ___ ___	2. Inlandsmeldung: ___ ___	1. Sportbericht ___	2. Sportbericht ___	Die Wettervorhersage:

Appendix 3

Vorbereitetes Hören

TAGESSCHAU

A   Lest die Transkripte der Meldungen aus der Tagesschau!

A1   Schreibt zuerst in die erste Spalte links, um welche Art von Beitrag es sich handelt.

Neben den **Schlagzeilen** (den wichtigste Meldung(en) des Tages) gibt es:

Berichte (ausführlichere Meldungen) und Meldungen (kurze Beiträge) zu den Themen **Inland/Ausland/Europa/Sport/Kultur/Wetter.**

A2   Schreibt die Überschriften der Beiträge darunter!

A3   Faßt jetzt die Beiträge in der zweiten Spalte von links kurz zusammen und diskutiert euer Verständnis des Texts mit einem Kommilitonen/ einer Kommilitonin! Habt ihr die gleiche Zusammenfassung? Versteht ihr den Text oder braucht ihr Hilfe/Vokabeln/ein Wörterbuch?

B   Seht euch jetzt das Video der Tagesschau an!

B1   Überprüft, ob ihr die Transkripte richtig verstanden habt.

B2   Berichtigt eventuelle Fehler in den zwei Spalten auf der rechten Seite des Arbeitsblattes.

B3   Schreibt neue und zusätzliche Informationen von den längeren Berichten in die Spalte „Details" auf der rechten Seite des Arbeitsblattes.

C   Nachbearbeitung

Beantwortet die folgenden Fragen!

C1   Wie unterscheiden sich Berichte und Meldungen?

_____

_____

C2   Welche sind leichter zu verstehen und warum?

_____

_____

Appendix 4

Arbeitsblatt zu den deutschen Nachrichten

Die Tagesschau vom _____

Lest zuerst das Anweisungsblatt: Vorbereitetes Hören!

A: Vom Transkript

	Art des Beitrags/ Überschrift	Details
1		
2		
3		
4		
5		
6		

B: Vom Video

	Art des Beitrags/ Überschrift	Details
1		
2		
3		
4		
5		
6		

Art des Beitrags/ Überschrift	Details
7	
8	
9	
10	
11	
12	
Wetterbericht:	

Art des Beitrags/ Überschrift	Details
7	
8	
9	
10	
11	
12	
Wetterbericht:	

Die Tagesschau ist das Nachrichtenprogramm des ARD. Die Beiträge der **Tagesschau** werden im Fernsehen und auf dem Internet veröffentlicht. Die Webadresse für die **Tagesschau** ist: **http://www.tagesschau.de/** Im MLTC wird **die Tagesschau** täglich auf Video aufgenommen.

Appendix 5

Die TAGESSCHAU vom 24. März, 20.00 Uhr

Stasi-Vorwurf gegen Gysi

Gregor Gysi ist nach Einschätzung eines Bundestagsausschusses inoffizieller Mitarbeiter der DDR-Staatssicherheit gewesen. Mit deutlicher Mehrheit stimmte der Ausschuß heute einem entsprechenden vorläufigen Bericht zu. Danach soll der PDS-Gruppenvorsitzende seine Position als Anwalt für Stasi-Zuträgerdienste mißbraucht haben. Eine schriftliche Verpflichtungserklärung liege allerdings nicht vor. Gysi selbst bestreitet die Anschuldigungen nach wie vor. Er will sich gerichtlich zur Wehr setzen.

Richtungsstreit

Bündnis 90/Die Grünen wollen sich offensiv darum bemühen, die Diskussion über Benzinpreise und Flugbenzin einzudämmen. Die Bundestagsfraktion beschloß, der Konflikt um eine Kerosin-Besteuerung könne nicht im deutschen Alleingang, sondern nur EU-weit gelöst werden. SPD-Kanzlerkandidat Schröder reagierte auf den Streit verärgert. Die Grünen hätten sich aus einer ernsthaften politischen Diskussion in Deutschland verabschiedet. Unterdessen zeichnet sich neuer Zündstoff bei den Bündnis-Grünen ab. Es geht um die Entscheidung im Bundestag über eine Ost-Erweiterung der Nato.

Mugabe in Bonn

Der Präsident von Simbabwe, Mugabe, hat einen dreitägigen Besuch in Deutschland begonnen. Bei einem Abendessen in Bonn rief Bundespräsident Herzog die Führung des afrikanischen Landes auf, für mehr Rechtssicherheit und eine stabile Demokratie zu sorgen. Dies sei auch im Interesse ausländischer Investitionen. Mugabe dankte Bonn für die bisherige Unterstützung des seit 1980 unabhängigen früheren Rhodesiens.

Clinton-Rede

US-Präsident Clinton hat seine Afrika-Reise heute zu einer überraschenden Geste genutzt. In Uganda drückte er sein Bedauern über die Rolle der USA bei der Sklaverei aus. 'Weiße Amerikaner haben vom Sklavenhandel profitiert und das war falsch', so Clinton wörtlich. Gleichzeitig stellte er ein Hilfsprogramm in Höhe von 120 Millionen Dollar in Aussicht. Gestern hatte Clinton dem schwarzen Kontinent eine neue Partnerschaft mit den USA angeboten.

Regierungsbildung

In Rußland hat der geschäftsführende Ministerpräsident Kirijenko mit Gesprächen über die Bildung einer neuen Regierung begonnen. Präsident Jelzin hat ihm dafür eine Woche Zeit gegeben. Jelzin deutete an, daß einige der gestern entlassenen Kabinettsmitglieder wieder ihr Amt übernehmen werden. Er lobte ausdrücklich die Arbeit von Außenminister Primakow und Verteidigungsminister Sergejew.

Appendix 6

Arbeitsblatt für die Taggesschau

Please record on this sheet when and in which style you watch the Tagesschau in the Self-Access-Centre! Tick in the first line, which media and support material you used. In the second line record how successful/unsuccessful they were and why!

Arbeitsblatt

Datum der Übung	Tagesschau vom:	Video	Internet Transkript	Internet mit Ton (Video)	Vorbereitung („Schlagzeilen‘) mit Ton (Video)	„Tagesschau"	„Vergleich" Transkript/ Video	Andere:

Un corpus électronique au service de l'apprentissage de la langue

Marie-Noëlle Guillot
University of East Anglia

1   Introduction

L'exploitation pédagogique des corpora en classe de langue présente pour l'apprentissage des langues vivantes des avantages pratiques et didactiques qui ne prêtent pas à controverse en soi. C'est le cas notamment de celle de quotidiens produits sur CD-ROM, comme *Le Monde* pour le français, qui servira d'exemple dans cet article (voir autres possibilités en annexe).[1] Ceux-ci représentent en effet un fonds tout prêt, diversifié et stable d'information factuelle et linguistique, que les paramètres de recherche de leur interface permettent en général d'aborder de points de vue divers (sujet, mais aussi registre ou fonctions langagières, par exemple, dans le cas du *Monde* – voir Guillot, 1996 et plus loin); ils ouvrent par là même la voie à une approche en direct de la culture et de la langue, dont ils reflètent l'évolution d'année en année. Qu'ils soient utilisés seuls ou en conjonction avec un concordancier électronique (*Microconcord* ou *Wordsmith Tools* par exemple)[2], ils constituent ainsi un outil précieux de support direct aux activités de production (rédaction, traduction, auto-correction, par exemple). Ils se prêtent parallèlement à une analyse inductive, individualisée de la langue et du discours, propre à en stimuler l'apprentissage critique et autonome, qui dépasse, elle, le cadre de l'utilitaire et s'inscrit dans une optique d'apprentissage à long terme, plus intégrée et plus globale.

Mais il n'est pas si simple en pratique de tirer parti de ces avantages, et de concilier ces différentes options. La poursuite des objectifs plus abstraits qui correspondent à une optique intégrative de longue haleine se heurte sur le terrain, comme on le verra, à un certain nombre de difficultés, d'ordre pratique et méthodologique (investissement de temps, formation à l'exploitation et à l'analyse des données, perception des buts recherchés). L'exploitation essentiellement utilitaire des corpora, plus susceptible de satisfaire la motivation instrumentale des étudiants – axée sur le concret et le rentable à court terme – risque, elle, de se limiter à un travail ponctuel, disjoint, peu propice, en particulier, à l'ouverture sur le discours. Compte tenu des contraintes auxquelles est soumis l'enseignement, ce deuxième type d'approche offre cependant des possibilités sur lesquelles construire pour en transcender les limites, et ménager le passage à une analyse d'ensemble du discours au niveau avancé qui est celui qu'on attend d'étudiants de troisième cycle. La question qui se pose alors est celle de la méthodologie.

C'est à ces divers aspects de l'intégration du travail sur corpora dans la pratique pédagogique que s'attache cet article. Chacune de ses trois parties – aspects généraux et limites en pratique, perspective instrumentale, stratégies d'approche du discours – y sera traitée par le biais d'exemples basés sur l'utilisation du *Monde* sur CD-ROM, illustrant différentes formules d'exploitation et pistes de travail à explorer.

2 Intégration pédagogique du travail sur corpora: aspects et limites

2.1 Attributs généraux

Parmi les propriétés des activités didactiques promues par l'exploitation des corpora en classe de langue, McEnery et Wilson, dans un article de synthèse sur la question, citent les suivantes en introduction: elles placent les apprenants en position de recherche; elles permettent une approche individualisée et différenciée de l'apprentissage; elles donnent lieu à un apprentissage inductif basé sur l'interaction directe avec les données; elles se prêtent à un apprentissage dirigé mais non pour cela directif (McEnery et Wilson, 1997: 6–7; voir aussi Leech, 1997). A ces attributs sont associées des formes complémentaires d'apprentissage (*'discovery learning'*, *'divergent learning'*, *'mediated learning'*, *'directed learning'*) qui définissent de façon générale la portée éducative du travail sur corpora en classe de langue et

209

caractérisent de ce point de vue le potentiel du *Monde* sur CD-ROM. L'exemple du *Monde* permet par ailleurs d'en mettre en relief une propriété supplémentaire, d'ordre cognitif et métacognitif.

Comme c'est en général le cas pour toute banque de données, il est impossible d'accéder au contenu du *Monde* sur CD-ROM sans se soumettre au processus graduel de sélection qu'impose son interface. Tout travail de recherche, documentaire ou linguistique, suppose en ce sens une démarche raisonnée, que la tâche à accomplir définit dans une certaine mesure, mais pas entièrement, et qui doit se (re)négocier à chaque étape en fonction des résultats obtenus à la précédente. Chercher des informations sur l'attitude des Français envers l'environnement, par exemple, ou encore se créer un répertoire de verbes ou d'expressions pour étayer un argument, sont des questions qui ne s'abordent pas de la même façon, même si certains choix s'imposent ou s'excluent dès le départ: le choix du paramètre 'sujet' va ainsi pratiquement de soi dans le premier cas (recherche sur l'environnement), mais paraît par contre peu indiqué dans le second (recherche centrée sur la langue); quel paramètre choisir alors, et pourquoi – 'genre de texte'? l'un des termes de l'index hiérarchisé donné sous 'sujet', comme 'politique' ou 'société'? 'taille' [d'article]? une combinaison de termes…? Comment, donc, lancer la recherche, et comment ensuite la faire progresser: quel termes de l'index sélectionner parmi ceux qui s'affichent sur l'écran après sélection, par exemple, dans ce deuxième cas, de 'genre de texte': 'entretien'? 'libre opinion'? 'revue de presse'…? Et là encore, pourquoi? Quels textes choisir de parcourir parmi ceux dont les titres sont proposés sur l'écran après les différentes étapes de sélection? Et suivant quels critères?

Que le travail soit ou non guidé par l'enseignant, la part d'inconnu qui le caractérise du point de vue de la démarche et de la collecte des données lui confère nécessairement un caractère individualisé, différencié et inductif qui se reporte sur l'apprentissage. Du fait des décisions qu'exige la procédure d'accès aux textes et de ce que celles-ci demandent (réflexion sur le rapport entre tâche à accomplir et caractéristiques des ressources disponibles, révision de la démarche à chaque étape), il a, outre ces qualités – déjà citées – celle de promouvoir une prise de recul cognitif dont la recherche dans ce domaine souligne l'importance pour la qualité de l'apprentissage (voir par exemple McLaughlin, 1987; O'Malley & Chamot, 1990). Le développement de facultés cognitives et métacognitives, stimulé pour les mêmes raisons par les activités qui font intervenir le concordancier (voir plus loin), est à cet égard particulièrement important dans les contextes où la formation antérieure des étudiants ne les habitue pas beaucoup, ou pas souvent, à l'analyse ou à l'auto-évaluation.

Cela dit, d'un point de vue plus terre-à-terre, le corpus est aussi, tout simplement, un outil de support concret aux exercices de langue, comme la rédaction ou la traduction, qui se prête à un travail en rapport direct avec des préoccupations immédiates, et tangibles (recherche d'idées, de vocabulaire, d'expressions à investir sur le champ dans un travail donné, par exemple; voir section suivante). Or si l'on peut mettre en cause les attributs généraux du travail sur corpora récapitulés plus haut, ce n'est pas tant du point de vue de leur pertinence éducative en soi ou de la perspective pédagogique dans laquelle ils s'inscrivent, que de celui de leur mise en oeuvre en pratique.

La conception de l'apprentissage sous-jacente à la synthèse de McEnery et Wilson, qui se révèle dans leur conception de référence de l'enseignement – 'teaching as mediated learning, rather than teaching as imparting knowledge' (McEnery & Wilson, 1997: 6; Laurillard, 1993: 13–15) – correspond, disent-ils (voir aussi Leech, 1997), à la philosophie dominante de l'enseignement tertiaire au Royaume Uni des vingt dernières années, et se retrouve dans la plupart des comptes rendus relatifs à l'exploitation des outils informatiques en classe de langue. Elle trouve ainsi un écho direct dans l'article suivant de la même revue, consacré, lui, à la question de l'auto-évaluation assistée par ordinateur:

> *the learning experience has increasingly been seen to be as important as its outcomes, which has resulted in a move away from measuring recall of knowledge, which encourages students to adopt a 'surface' approach to their learning, towards an appraisal of the acquisition of skills and subject understanding which is more likely to lead to deeper learning.*
> (Kane-Iturrioz, 1997: 15)

Le bien fondé de la synthèse que font McEnery et Wilson des qualités didactiques du travail sur corpus en classe de langue dans une telle perspective se trouve pour une grande part confirmée par l'expérience de travail sur laquelle s'appuie cet article, qui en révèle cependant aussi les limites.

211

2.2 Exemple d'expérience d'intégration

En bref, il s'agit d'un cours général de français de 2ème année dont les deux objectifs principaux, pour ce qui est du travail sur corpus, sont les suivants:

i) initier inductivement les étudiants à l'exploitation rationnelle du *Monde* sur CD-ROM, i.e. les aider à découvrir par eux-mêmes les moyens de maîtriser son interface et de tirer le meilleur avantage de son contenu de différents point de vue (sur ce point, voir Guillot, 1996);

ii) procéder à une recherche factuelle et lexicale sur des sujets donnés (travail et environnement pour les principaux), y compris avec l'aide d'un concordancier électronique (*Microconcord*), à partir d'un sous-corpus thématique copié du *Monde* sur disquette (voir plus loin).

En rapport avec la conception de l'apprentissage définie plus haut, le cours fait porter l'accent autant sur la méthodologie et l'analyse à des fins de transfert à d'autres ressources et à d'autres tâches que sur l'assimilation de connaissances. Les types d'activités qu'il fait intervenir dans ce cadre sont assez courants, comme le montrent les trois exemples suivants:

• préparation à la recherche à partir de textes de sources, thèmes et registres différents, utilisés pour poser des questions de départ et définir des directions de travail, factuelles et linguistiques (voir par exemple celles que peuvent engendrer, directement ou indirectement, les textes reproduits dans la section suivante en Appendice 3a [extrait du livre de John Ardagh *France in the 80s*] et 3b [extrait d'un article de Geoffrey Gibbs paru dans le *Guardian*], qui traitent chacun d'aspects différents de la question du travail: comment les modalités du travail ont-elles évolué en France depuis 1980? (cf. 3a); combien gagne-t-on quand on travaille en France? y a-t-il un salaire minimum? à combien s'élève-t-il? quelles sont les conditions de travail pour les femmes (cf. 3b)? etc; quel vocabulaire, quelles expressions rechercher pour pouvoir s'exprimer en français sur les thèmes de ces textes, ou pour les traduire?);

• recherche individuelle et en sous-groupes soit en fonction des directions de travail définies au cours de la préparation, soit en fonction de thèmes identifiés par exploration des possibilités de l'interface du CD-ROM (comme ceux donnés sous 'travail' dans l'index alphabétique de 'sujet en

France' ['travail à domicile' ou 'travail clandestin' par exemple], ou ceux obtenus par combinaison de termes ['travail' ET 'aménagement', 'travail' ET 'femme' par exemple]) (travail hors-cours; rapport et discussion en classe);

- travail par inférence contextuelle sur les collocations, les nuances de sens et d'utilisation du vocabulaire, les variations lexicales liées au registres (voir par exemple les collocations verbales, adjectivales, substantivales à gauche et à droite de 'temps' dans la concordance de la table 1 [voir sous 'Recherche lexicale' dans la partie suivante; para. 1, 3, 2 et 4 respectivement] et, en Appendice 2 (même partie), les variations lexicales illustrées par les différents termes associés à 'temps de travail' (réduction, diminution, baisse, aménagement, annualisation), dont les différences de sens ou d'utilisation peuvent être étudiées par retour au contexte d'occurrence; des exemples et commentaires additionnels sont fournis dans la troisième partie).[3]

2.3 Portée et limites de l'expérience

Dans l'ensemble, les qualités attribuées aux activités d'exploitation de corpora se vérifient dans ce cas particulier. Le volume et la diversité du contenu du CD-ROM, la part d'imprédictibilité que ces caractéristiques confèrent au travail, l'individualisation et la complémentarisation des tâches d'exploitation stimulent un effort individuel ou coopératif du point de vue de la démarche et de l'analyse qui est stimulant pour l'apprentissage, et pour le travail en soi.

L'impact à plus long terme est difficile à évaluer sans procédure de vérification formelle, mais les commentaires des étudiants sur leur expérience linguistique et culturelle au cours de leur séjour à l'étranger l'année suivante suggèrent qu'ils possèdent, dans une plus ou moins grande mesure, les capacités correspondant à celles que leur travail de deuxième année vise à développer: capacité d'aborder et d'exploiter les ressources disponibles de façon critique; d'être sensibles à leurs registres et autres caractéristiques linguistiques et culturelles; d'évaluer les progrès; de faire le diagnostic de leurs difficultés et de se donner des pistes de travail pour y remédier (voir exemples de commentaires en annexe).[4]

Ces remarques demandent toutefois à être qualifiées, à plusieurs égards:

i) celui, terre-à-terre mais déterminant, du temps et de l'investissement en travail; même sans parler de l'initiation à la manipulation des outils, moins problématique maintenant qu'elle se généralise, définir des lignes de travail, faire des recherches et parcourir des textes à ces fins, en faire la synthèse et le compte rendu, constituer, analyser et exploiter des concordances, suppose: a) disposer d'un capital de temps qui dépasse de loin celui qui peut en général être consacré aux cours de langue dans le tertiaire aujourd'hui (deux heures de contact par semaine sur douze semaines dans ce cas, qui ne suffisent jamais à aller au bout du travail, encore moins à le systématiser et à s'assurer, pour ce qui est de l'assimilation de connaissances, qu'il se transforme en acquis); et b) pouvoir compter sur un travail personnel des étudiants hors cours plus important que celui qu'ils veulent ou peuvent fournir.

ii) celui, lié au précédent, de la perception des objectifs et des progrès accomplis, et de son impact sur les réactions des étudiants au cours et sur leur motivation: les capacités que le cours s'attache à développer ne s'actualisent à proprement parler que dans le plus long terme, et ne correspondent pas, même dans ce plus long terme, à une réalité aussi tangible que l'assimilation de connaissances. Cette part de 'non-tangible' se traduit par un certain scepticisme quant à l'efficacité du cours, voire une certaine résistance au travail, du moins pour ceux pour qui l'impact des activités langagières se mesure plutôt par l'assimilation instantanée et concrète de faits de langue, ou leur inculcation.

Autrement dit, pour que le travail prenne tout son sens, qu'il tienne les promesses intégratives qui correspondent aux qualités exposées plus haut, il doit s'accommoder dans les faits de contraintes pratiques et psychologiques que le bien-fondé pédagogique de ses objectifs à plus longue échéance ne suffit pas en soi à minimiser: si souhaitable qu'il soit pour la qualité de l'apprentissage d'encourager les étudiants à transcender les limites d'une 'surface approach' fondée sur l'obtention de résultats identifiables (voir Kane-Iturrioz, 1997: 15 et plus haut), motiver un investissement en travail plus important de leur part qu'ils puissent, surtout, voir se concrétiser plus nettement dans le court terme, reste un facteur déterminant pour étayer la poursuite d'objectifs génériques à plus long terme, du moins dans le type de contexte présenté ici.

3 Perspective instrumentale

Or le travail des étudiants, à plus forte raison en dehors des cours, tend à être plus productif s'ils y trouvent leur compte et voient leur effort se matérialiser, y compris par exemple par l'obtention de meilleures notes – autrement dit s'il fait vibrer la corde de leur motivation instrumentale. Quelles que puissent en être les limites (cf. Gardner & Lambert, 1972, mais aussi Savignon, 1972, ou O'Malley et Chamot, 1990, qui en soulignent aussi l'utilité), il s'agit là d'une forme de motivation incontournable, qu'il vaut donc mieux exploiter qu'ignorer.

D'où l'intérêt d'une approche initialement plus instrumentale, tirant avantage du corpus et du concordancier d'un point de vue principalement utilitaire. De ce point de vue, il ne s'agit pas pour les étudiants d'utiliser un corpus énorme à des fins de recherches ouvertes, ou encore un corpus étiqueté susceptible d'en faciliter les modalités, mais de pouvoir se constituer des corpora restreints adaptés aux besoins immédiats: s'il leur faut par exemple rédiger une dissertation sur un sujet donné (relatif au travail ou à l'environnement, par exemple), de se créer un corpus qui puisse leur donner accès à une information factuelle et linguistique en rapport, de procéder à des vérifications ou des expansions, de se libérer du carcan de la grammaire ou du dictionnaire – bilingue en particulier – ou d'y trouver un supplément lorsque ces outils ne suffisent pas à leur fournir les réponses aux questions qu'ils se posent – ce qui suppose cependant qu'ils sachent se les poser.

D'où l'intérêt également d'un corpus comme *Le Monde* sur CD-ROM: en dépit de ses limites (relative uniformité de style, par exemple), celui-ci est cependant amplement diversifié du point de vue des sujets, des registres et des fonctions langagières qui y sont représentés; grâce aux possibilités de son interface, il permet en outre, suivant ces critères et d'autres (taille des articles, par exemple), de créer et de charger sur disquette des sous-corpora appropriés aux besoins concrets définis par la tâche de départ (comme celui dont sont tirés les concordances et exemples inclus ici).[3]

Ce que l'expérience d'exploitation du *Monde* sur CD-ROM décrite plus haut a ainsi mis en relief, outre ses limites, ce sont des fonctions du travail dont l'utilité immédiate a retenu l'attention des étudiants, sur lesquelles ils étaient prêts à construire seuls, et qui pourraient permettre d'ancrer dans le concret des objectifs intégratifs à plus long terme; autrement dit, il s'agit là de fonctions qui pourraient faciliter la poursuite de ces objectifs intégratifs d'un point de vue pratique (incitation au travail) et psychologique (perception de résultats tangibles).

Ce travail plus utilitaire, centré sur des besoins précis définis au gré des tâches à accomplir, a lui aussi ses limites: il risque de donner lieu à des remarques sur la langue trop localisées, ou fragmentées – ce que la décontextualisation caractéristique des données obtenues par concordance peut d'ailleurs avoir tendance à encourager. Mais il peut quand même, comme on va le voir, ouvrir de fil en aiguille la voie à des études plus conséquentes. Reste alors à concilier ces perspectives, à ménager le passage d'une exploration 'opportuniste', au coup par coup, à une exploration plus intégrée, et promouvoir une stratégie d'approche du discours plus globale, plus cohérente, qui s'inscrive dans le cadre d'une démarche académique à visée intégrative.

Des options ou fonctions qui ont mobilisé les étudiants se sont ainsi dégagées des applications, ou des possibilités d'applications, qui, de par leur à-propos à court et moyen terme, pourraient servir de base à négocier cette transition. Ces fonctions et applications, qui n'ont rien de particulièrement inédit pour la plupart, et ont l'avantage d'être relativement simples à mettre en oeuvre, relèvent de différents types d'activités: recherche lexicale, expression écrite, traduction, révision des textes produits; chacune sera illustrée ci-dessous par des exemples relatifs au sujet 'travail', tirés soit directement du Monde sur CD-ROM par le jeu des paramètres de recherche, soit de concordances réalisées à partir d'un corpus restreint d'une quarantaine de textes sur le sujet.[3]

3.1 Recherche lexicale

A un niveau élémentaire de recherche lexicale, c'est la fonction supplément au dictionnaire, dictionnaire vivant de la langue dont l'impact s'est révélé le plus sensible. Grâce aux possibilités qu'il donne d'isoler des textes sur des thèmes précis (le télétravail, par exemple), Le Monde sur CD-ROM s'offre en alternative ou complément au dictionnaire, en particulier pour ce qui concerne des domaines en évolution, comme l'informatique. Il permet aux étudiants, par parcours rapide des textes isolés, de se donner accès à des champs lexicaux que le dictionnaire ne couvre pas encore, d'identifier ou de reconnaître des termes, expressions (ou sigles) qui n'y figurent pas nécessairement (e.g. 'websurfer', 'to surf the internet', 'autoroutes de l'information', 'numérisation', 'CNPF'), ou d'en retrouver le sens par inférence contextuelle: il leur a par exemple suffi de faire une concordance de termes comme 'annualiser'/ 'annualisation', 'loi-cadre' (relatifs cette fois au thème de l'aménagement du temps de travail), de retourner au contexte d'occurrence grâce à l'option du concordancier qui permet de le faire par simple pression de la touche '*Enter*', pour découvrir par eux-mêmes le sens de ces termes, absents de leur dictionnaire.

Les applications immédiates de ce type de recherches pour leurs activités, la traduction en particulier, ne leur ont pas échappé. Mais ce qui s'est également trouvé renforcé, mieux perçu que par le biais des activités génériques du cours, c'est le sens que, par la même démarche, ils pouvaient, plus efficacement que par le truchement du dictionnaire, se constituer tout un lexis sur *n'importe quel* sujet, couvert par le dictionnaire ou non.

3.2 Expression écrite

La deuxième fonction qui s'est dégagée est une fonction de support à la rédaction, qui s'applique tout particulièrement, mais pas exclusivement, aux tâches de rédaction sur des sujets dont les termes se prêtent à concordance dans le contexte d'un thème particulier, comme celui du travail, qui l'a dans ce cas mise en évidence.

Pour un sujet comme le suivant: 'Faites une comparaison critique de deux formules d'aménagement du temps de travail' (donné dans le cadre du cours), il suffit de faire une concordance sur les termes principaux de l'énoncé pour accéder à une information substantielle d'un point de vue linguistique, et également d'un point de vue factuel (par retour au contexte global d'occurrence).

Mener la tâche à bien suppose procéder avec un minimum de méthode, mais la méthode de base se découvre et se maîtrise relativement aisément. Il est clair, ou il le devient vite, pour prendre un exemple très simple, que l'utilité d'une concordance du terme 'temps' seul, trop vague en soi, est limitée: elle fournit une liste d'exemples qui, lorsqu'elle est nettoyée et organisée (cf. Appendice 1), se prête à des remarques à exploiter plus avant, sur, par exemple, les collocations (verbales, adjectivales, substantivales à droite et à gauche comme déjà indiqué plus haut); mais sa pertinence pour le sujet à traiter est ténue puisqu'il y s'agit non pas de 'temps' mais de 'temps de travail'. Une concordance à double entrée sur 'temps' et 'travail' permet par contre de cerner les choses de plus près, et de trouver des informations en rapport direct, cette fois, avec le sujet. L'exemple donné en Appendice 2 d'une concordance là encore nettoyée et organisée pour en faciliter ici la lecture et, d'un point de vue didactique, le passage à une réflexion plus générique (voir plus loin), donne une idée de la manière dont les étudiants peuvent ainsi:

i) du point de vue de la langue:

- se donner accès à différentes formules, ainsi qu'à leur modalité d'utilisation dans un contexte ici limité, mais qu'ils peuvent élargir en déplaçant la concordance sur la droite et sur la gauche pour révéler l'ensemble de la phrase d'occurrence (par le biais des touches -> et <-), voire un contexte plus large si nécessaire (cf. par exemple 'moduler la réduction du temps de travail' [ligne 8]; 'adopter une formule de temps partiel de travail' [28]; 'fixer le temps de travail à' [35], etc);

- commencer, par la même occasion, à se poser des questions sur, par exemple, la fréquence respective d'utilisation de certains termes et les raisons susceptibles de la justifier (cf. 'réduction' [1 à 11] vs 'diminution' [15, 16] ou 'baisse du temps de travail' [19, 20]), sur les nuances de sens (cf. 'aménagement' [22, 24] vs 'réduction' [1 à 11]), les différences de registre ou encore sur les raisons justifiant l'utilisation d'une classe de mots plutôt qu'une autre (nominalisation vs verbe par exemple [1–11 vs 12–14; 15–16 vs 17–18; etc]);

ii) du point de vue factuel:

- se donner accès à des faits et idées en rapport avec le sujet par retour au contexte textuel global des termes de la concordance qui, comme le laisse entrevoir les exemples de l'appendice en fournit un large éventail (cf. par exemple les lignes 5, 12, 17, 18, etc qui font référence à des expériences sur le terrain d'aménagement du temps de travail).

Par des procédés assez simples, qui ne font appel qu'aux fonctions les plus élémentaires du concordancier, se créent donc des options de recherche qui entrent dans le cadre des besoins immédiats des étudiants, mais les invitent en même temps à la réflexion, peuvent déboucher sur l'analyse, et sur un travail sur le discours.

3.3 Traduction

Ces remarques s'appliquent à la troisième fonction, une fonction de support à la traduction qui s'inscrit dans la tradition thème d'imitation, mais avec une différence significative: la magnitude et la diversité de l'ensemble des données linguistiques disponibles sur le champ par simple appel mécanique.

C'est au cours de la traduction orale des textes en anglais initialement utilisés pour définir des pistes de travail (voir section précédente et Appendices 3a [texte John Ardagh] et 3b [texte Geoffrey Gibbs]) que se sont dégagées les possibilités, en réponse à des problèmes qui illustrent les limites définies précédemment. Lorsque, tout à la fin du travail, il s'est agi pour les étudiants de traduire ces passages, ils ont buté sur des formules qu'ils avaient pourtant souvent rencontrées au cours de leurs recherches, utilisées dans leurs comptes rendus et discussions, et qu'ils n'avaient de toute évidence assimilées que partiellement, ou de façon trop isolée.

La concordance (éditée) du mot 'heure/s', présent en anglais dans trois des phrases du texte de John Ardagh qui ont ainsi présenté des difficultés (voir les phrases soulignées dans le texte), illustre comment celles-ci ont été surmontées, et comment un corpus thématique exploité par le biais d'un concordancier peut servir de support direct aux activités de traduction (cf. Appendice 4): elle permet ici de retrouver à moindre effort des formules à utiliser ou à adapter dans la traduction des passages à problèmes centrés sur le mot 'hour' (cf. lignes 35 et 77 entre autres); elle en fournit également d'autres qui entrent en jeu à d'autres points du texte, soit directement (cf. par exemple 'd'ici à 1996' [ligne 26]/'*by 1985*' [13] dans le texte de Ardagh), ou 'sans baisse *des* salaires' [131], 'sans diminution *de* salaires' [132], 'sans perte de *salaires*' [134], 'sans diminution de *revenus*' [51] – qui amènent d'ailleurs

219

des questions: différence 'de'/'des' [salaires]? 'salaires'/'revenus'?), soit en déplaçant les lignes de concordances (cf. par exemple la ligne [3] qui permet de retrouver la construction de '[ob]jectif]' pour l'appliquer à la traduction de 'target of a 35-hour week' [13] [objectif des 35 heures]).

Parcourir la concordance suscite d'autres observations: 'prôner' dans 'ceux qui prônent les 35 heures' [152] contraste ainsi, même si le sens est différent, avec le 'want' de 'they want a reduction' [10] dans sa force et précision illocutoires. Et si l'on retourne au contexte global d'autres lignes de concordances pour y chercher des idées ou des formules, on y trouve d'autres exemples de cette tendance à la plus grande précision sémantique/illocutoire du français: cf. la ligne 20, par exemple, qui donne ainsi '...en préconisant une réduction...', ou la ligne 35, qui donne '[Quant à Mme Martine Aubry]... elle souhaite un autre partage...'. Là s'amorce un travail sur le discours, une analyse contrastive qui dépasse le cadre du strictement utilitaire.

D'autres points soumis à des vérifications dans le cadre du cours s'ouvrent de même à la réflexion: les possibilités de traduction de 'today' et de 'fight' [against unemployment], par exemple, dans la première phrase du texte de Ardagh ('aujourd' hui'? 'maintenant'?...; 'lutte' [contre le chômage]? 'bataille'? 'combat'?... [il n'y a pas d'exemples de 'combat' dans le corpus – pourquoi? – et 'lutte' y est beaucoup plus fréquent dans ce contexte que 'bataille'); celles, dans la deuxième phrase, de 'jobs crisis' ('crise de l'emploi'? 'crise du chômage'?) ou de 'full' [vs 'very'] dans 'full well' (pour lequel une concordance de 'bien' donne accès à 'fort bien', mais également à de nombreux emplois différents de 'bien' – à explorer). Dans tous ces exemples, la question n'est pas de décider ce qu'est la 'bonne' réponse, encore moins d'encourager à supposer qu'il y a une bonne réponse, mais d'inviter à s'aider des outils pour réfléchir de façon informée aux choix possibles, et aux paramètres susceptibles de les justifier (nuances de sens, mais aussi collocations, fréquence relative d'occurrence, etc).

3.4 Révision/correction de textes

Cette quatrième fonction découle directement des précédentes et couvre les même types d'activités, cette fois mises au service de la révision et correction des textes produits – dissertations, traductions, comptes rendus de film ou de livres, lettres, etc. Elle peut s'appliquer en cours ou en dehors des cours, en groupe ou individuellement, avant la remise de copies à l'enseignant ou, comme dans ce cas précis, après, sur la base des commentaires et conseils. Cette dernière option assure une prise en compte plus effective des remarques faites pas l'enseignant, et permet par ailleurs d'apporter aux étudiants un soutien individuel, linguistique et méthodologique.

Comme les précédentes, cette fonction s'applique à la diversification de l'expression (recherche lexicale pour éviter/supprimer les répétitions ou les imprécisions, par exemple); mais elle met plus nettement en relief les possibilités qui s'offrent de procéder à des vérifications d'ordre grammatical ou syntaxique, y compris sur des points difficiles à cerner ou à faire assimiler par le biais des ouvrages de référence:

- celui, par exemple, de l'emploi immodéré, sous l'influence de l'anglais *'only'*, de 'seulement' pour 'ne … que' – dont la concordance met en lumière la fréquence respective d'utilisation dans les contextes où les deux sont possibles;

- celui de la position de 'donc', que les étudiants s'obstinent à placer en début de phrase quoi qu'on leur en dise, alors que, comme la concordance leur en apporte la preuve immédiate, il y figure rarement (cf. Appendice 5);

- celui encore des constructions faisant intervenir des pourcentages, qui occasionnent des fautes (sur l'emploi des prépositions, l'expression de la comparaison, etc) qu'une concordance de '%' permet rapidement de corriger, tout en donnant l'occasion de se constituer inductivement une fiche de grammaire adaptée aux besoins sur la base des exemples divers qui y figurent (cf. Appendice 6); etc.

Compte tenu de ce que ces fonctions et applications, mises en relief par des activités à caractère utilitaire, ont de motivant pour les étudiants d'un point de vue instrumental mais aussi de potentiellement stimulant d'un point de vue intégratif, et compte tenu des contraintes et limites soulignées plus haut, l'option qui se dessine est claire. Il suffit de substituer à une approche définie par des objectifs génériques qui débouchent sur des applications concrètes, mais dont la mise en oeuvre prend du temps, et dont la portée pédagogique est plus tangible pour l'enseignant que pour les étudiants, une approche centrée, elle, sur les tâches à accomplir (i.e. task-based), donc plus mobilisante puisque motivée par des besoins immédiats, à laquelle assujettir le développement de capacités méthodologiques et critiques. Ce qui revient à dire faire d'exercices comme la rédaction sur un sujet défini, ou la traduction de textes donnés, plus faciles à circonscrire en cours, le médium premier d'exploitation des outils corpus/concordancier, à supposer que cela soit possible.

La traduction de sections des textes anglais mentionnés plus haut, que, pour le vérifier, j'ai essayé d'effectuer, à partir d'hypothèses très élémentaires, sans autre support que le sous-corpus relatif au sujet 'travail' créé en cours et le concordancier, s'est révélée assez concluante à cet égard. L'extrait de *France in the 80s*, plus général et uniforme dans son registre et traitement du thème du travail, et moins idiomatique que l'article du *Guardian*, se prête plus aisément à l'exercice (voir exemples plus haut), mais les deux passages en soulignent le potentiel. Pour la phrase suivante tirée de l'article du *Guardian*, par exemple,

> *...the average male wage in the industry is £169.90 per week, including overtime, based on an hourly rate of £3.80...*

les observations suscitées par les concordances amènent à substituer à une traduction littérale calquée sur la syntaxe de la phrase anglaise, du type 'le salaire... est...' (ou 'est de'? – point à vérifier...), une formule dont les échantillons mettent en relief la fréquence d'utilisation, i.e. 'les hommes gagnent/touchent... en moyenne...'; elles amènent de même à substituer au prévisible 'basé sur' des étudiants la formule 'sur la base de' (obtenue par concordance de 'basé', qui ne donne rien, puis de 'base'), qui, si elle se trouve dans le dictionnaire monolingue (également sous 'base'), est absente du dictionnaire bilingue dont les étudiants restent souvent dépendants. Les termes '*hourly*' et '*rate*' sont donnés dans le dictionnaire bilingue (y compris en combinaison dans un exemple qui contextualise '*hourly*', i.e. 'taux horaire') mais la concordance de 'taux', qu'on peut en principe supposer connu à ce niveau et qui donne 'un taux horaire de x francs', permet de s'assurer de la construction de la formule dans un contexte attesté d'utilisation (comme de retrouver 'horaire' sans dépendre du dictionnaire). Ceci s'applique à de nombreuses autres formules du texte (cf. par exemple la formule '*ranks as number three*' [5], absente du dictionnaire bilingue, pour laquelle une concordance de 'rang' (qui se suggère rapidement pour lancer la recherche) offre un choix de possibilités – 'se place/vient/figure au troisième rang' – qui authentifient les formules qu'on peut trouver dans le dictionnaire monolingue, à supposer qu'on y ait cherché '*rang*').

La démarche à adopter dans la recherche ne s'impose pas toujours d'elle-même et est appellée à être guidée en classe. Pour la phrase ci-dessus par exemple, pourtant choisie parce qu'elle y est relativement moins oblique et embrouillée à illustrer que pour d'autres, ce ne sont ni 'salaire' (qu'on peut supposer connu), ni 'mâle' (qui ne donne rien, ce qui suggère que ce terme n'est pas une collocation appropriée dans ce contexte), c'est-à-dire des termes qui semblent s'indiquer pour lancer la recherche, ni d'ailleurs 'homme/s' (possibilité dérivée), dont les concordances fournissent des informations à investir dans la traduction; c'est en fait 'femme' (qui donne 'salaire des femmes', '90% des femmes gagnent moins de 2000 francs par mois') ou 'francs' (pour '£'), qui donne accès à cette même deuxième formule comme à d'autres ('ne touche que… 6500 francs par mois', par exemple). Mais ce genre de gymnastique méthodologique et mentale, qui va de pair avec une prise de recul par rapport aux données et une mise en rapport des informations disponibles/recueillies propices, en soi, à un travail plus actif sur la langue, prend au jeu et fait vite boule de neige.

Reste quand même, pour éviter de s'y perdre ou de confiner le travail à la recherche de solutions *ad hoc* rapides, à l'inscrire dans une approche raisonnée, intégrée de la langue au niveau de la phrase, du paragraphe, du texte.

4 Stratégies d'approche du discours

Comment donc donner une direction au travail, et sans pour autant perdre de vue la perspective utilitaire, en élargir le cadre pour, par exemple, faire assujettir les observations à des problèmes d'ordre plus général manifestes dans l'écrit des étudiants, comme l'imprécision lexicale et le délayage syntaxique (cf. 'il y a des gens qui disent que…' par exemple) – qui, autant que les fautes de grammaire, nuisent à l'efficacité et à la qualité de leur expression, soutenue en particulier? Comment promouvoir l'ouverture sur le discours, mettre leur effort au service d'une réflexion plus globale et critique sur la langue (et les faits) qui les rendent sensibles au jeu des paramètres à prendre en compte, et qui puisse les préparer à tirer meilleur parti des ressources disponibles autour d'eux, en particulier dans la perspective de leur séjour à l'étranger?

Différentes options complémentaires peuvent être envisagées, y compris celle, traditionnelle et qui s'impose dans un premier temps, d'inviter les étudiants à la synthèse: de leur faire prendre note de questions qui peuvent se poser dans le feu de l'action des travaux pratiques, de points susceptibles d'être généralisés ou dignes d'intérêt pour d'autres raisons, de ceux qui retiennent particulièrement leur attention, et d'y revenir ultérieurement pour en faire le point et en dégager les applications et implications (méthodologiques, socioculturelles, linguistiques) – y compris dans des cours de type plus magistraux (cf. contraintes de temps). Pourquoi, par exemple, pour reprendre des points relatifs à la phrase traitée en exemple plus haut, le terme 'femme' est-il productif pour la recherche alors qu''homme' ne l'est pas? Est-il significatif que les rémunérations soient exprimées par semaine pour le contexte britannique et par mois pour le contexte français? Rapport avec *'wages'* vs 'salaires', avec l'évolution des modalités du travail au Royaume Uni et en France? Quelles remarques sur les collocations appelle celle faite sur 'mâles'? Quelles remarques appellent la substitution d'une formule attestée dans le corpus à une formule possible mais qui n'apparaît pas dans les exemples, et les différences syntaxiques entre elles? – tous points qui trouvent des échos ailleurs dans le texte.

Mais la question est aussi d'aller plus loin dans l'exploration du discours, et de ménager le passage d'une optique instrumentale à une optique intégrative, tout en préservant le caractère inductif et méta-cognitif du travail sur corpus qui en fait un agent d'autonomisation de l'apprentissage, et reste l'un de ses plus grands atouts. Une fois les fonctions et modalités de ce type de travail mieux ancrées dans le vécu des étudiants, des options axées sur le long terme de l'apprentissage et qui, sans le capital de confiance généré par des activités utilitaires, ont tendance à rester trop impalpables dans leurs objectifs, sont alors susceptibles de présenter une plus grande part de légitimité didactique.

Il y a ainsi l'option de construire sur les possibilités qu'offre *Le Monde* sur CD-ROM lui-même d'aborder le discours de différents points de vue. Celui-ci permet par exemple de regrouper des textes de même nature, ou d'opposer des textes de nature différente, pour effectuer des comparaisons ou identifier des contrastes, suivant différents registres (en passant par des termes de l'index hiérarchisé de 'sujet': 'arts et spectacles', 'économie', 'faits divers', etc), différentes fonctions (cf. index de 'genre de textes': 'chronique', 'courrier', 'dossier', etc) ou encore différentes tailles d'articles (cf. 'bref', 'court', 'moyen', 'long'), pour en étudier les paramètres – de contenu, de structure, de langue. Les textes en bref, qui doivent faire un impact immédiat sans grand effort de lecture, tendent par exemple à être aussi simples et concrets dans la langue que dans le contenu (prépondérance de phrases simples, paratactiques, préférant les syntagmes verbaux aux syntagmes nominaux plus abstraits, lexis référentiel, etc); les articles de fond comme ceux qui figurent sous 'dossier' et/ou 'longue', plus conceptuels et diversifiés quant au contenu, le sont aussi quant à la langue (phrases (hyper)hypotactiques auxquelles la syntaxe de l'anglais n'habitue pas beaucoup les apprenants, lexis conceptuel, fréquence des nominalisations, expression modale, etc). A ces possibilités s'ajoute celle de donner aux remarques une dimension comparative par mise en rapport, suivant une démarche parallèle, avec des sous-corpora équivalents de textes tirés de journaux anglais disponibles sur CD-ROM (*The Guardian*, par exemple).[1]

Il y a celle, dans une même optique comparative, d'utiliser le concordancier pour vérifier et développer des observations faites par ailleurs à partir de textes étudiés sur papier, comme celles que peuvent ainsi susciter l'analyse contrastive – quantitative et qualitative – d'un texte français et d'un texte anglais analogue:

- sur, par exemple, la longueur des phrases (qui ne sont pas systématiquement plus longues en français qu'en anglais, mais ont le *potentiel* d'être très longues) et son impact sur leur syntaxe (comment se construit une phrase de 10 lignes?);

- sur le début des phrases (proportion, en français et en anglais, de phrases commençant par une séquence sujet/verbe principal et de phrases commençant par autre chose (quoi?) dans différents types de textes? dans l'écrit des étudiants?);

- sur la précision lexicale (illocutoire, par exemple: cf. la fréquence respective d'occurrence de verbes comme 'to say' et 'dire', et les observations qui en découlent; cf. également la fréquence d'occurrence de formules ou termes dont les étudiants sont friands – 'il y a' vs 'there is/are', 'chose/s' vs 'thing/s' – ou dont ils le sont moins – 'il faut que' vs les modaux de l'anglais, verbes utilisés réflexivement); etc.

(Certains de ces exercices supposent pouvoir faire des concordances des signes de ponctuation, ce qui n'est pas possible pour tous avec *Microconcord*, mais l'est avec d'autres concordanciers (*Wordsmith* par exemple)).

Il y a encore l'option, centrée sur l'utilisation complémentaire du corpus et du concordancier, de reprendre les concordances produites dans le cadre du travail ciblé de traduction ou de rédaction, comme par exemple ici la concordance de 'temps'+'travail'. Le 'nettoyage' et l'organisation de cette concordance suivant des critères définis (cf. Appendice 2) peuvent ainsi déboucher sur des recherches plus ambitieuses, comme par exemple l'étude de la distribution verbe/nominalisation (cf. 'réduire'/'réduction', 'diminuer'/ 'diminution', 'aménager'/'aménagement' en Appendice 2) en fonction de caractéristiques des textes d'occurrence, là encore triés par le biais des paramètres de recherche du CD-ROM. Dans cet exemple précis, et avec le corpus très restreint de départ (voir plus haut), l'étude n'est guère concluante que pour le paramètre 'taille': les textes très courts font intervenir formes verbales et formes nominales, les textes longs privilégient la nominalisation, ce qui est logique compte tenu de leur nature plus conceptuelle. La recherche gagnerait de toute évidence à être étendue à un corpus plus substantiel (et motive d'ailleurs à le faire). Mais elle a au moins l'avantage de susciter des questions sur les critères de choix de ces formes et leur impact sur le discours: même si elles peuvent paraître abstruses aux étudiants, elles n'en ont pas moins des applications réelles pour eux, pour ce qui est de la maîtrise de la lecture des textes comme pour ce qui est de la maîtrise de la rédaction (hiérarchisation de l'information, jeu des reformulations – passage de l'abstrait au concret, du général au spécifique, de l'idée à l'exemple...).

Comme le met en relief ce dernier exemple, la démarche, lorsqu'on passe à un travail axé sur le discours, n'est pas toujours si simple. L'analyse ne l'est pas non plus. Il est vrai que, d'un point de vue tout à fait pratique, les avantages de l'exploitation d'un corpus comme *Le Monde* sur CD-ROM en conjonction avec un concordancier électronique en classe de langue passent d'abord par le volume des données disponibles, par l'efficacité d'accès à une information ciblée et susceptible de trouver des applications immédiates, tangibles, et par là même motivantes. Mais il serait dommage de négliger les possibilités qu'offrent aussi ces outils de transcender les limites du strictement utilitaire, de passer à un autre niveau d'analyse, de rationaliser l'exploration du discours. C'est là un domaine où tout, ou presque tout, reste à faire, du point de vue de la pédagogie comme du point de vue de la langue, et qui confronte enseignants et apprenants à un défi d'autant plus difficile à relever que les conditions de l'enseignement et de l'apprentissage ne se prêtent guère aujourd'hui à la flexibilité intégrative requise pour y faire face. Ce qui ne veut pas dire qu'on ne puisse, ou ne doive pas s'y essayer.

Références

Ardagh, J. (1982) *France in the 80s*, Harmondsworth: Penguin Books.

Garner, R.C. and Lambert, W.E. (1972) *Attitude and Motivation in Second Language Learning*, Rowley, Mass.: Newbury House.

Gibbs, G. (1995) 'Poor victims of a cutthroat industry', *The Guardian*, 9 September.

Guillot, M.-N. (1996) 'Resource-Based Language Learning: Pedagogic Strategies for Le Monde sur CD-ROM', in E. Broady and M.-M. Kenning (eds) *Promoting Learner Autonomy in University Language Teaching*, London: AFLS/CILT, 139–57.

Kane-Iturrioz, R. (1997) 'Computer-Based Language Assessment', *ReCALL*, 9, 1: 15–21.

Laurillard, D. (1993) *Rethinking University Teaching: A framework for the effective use of educational technology*. London: Routledge.

Leech, G. (1997) 'Teaching and language corpora: a convergence', in A. Wichman *et al.* (1997) *Teaching and Language Corpora*, London: Longman.

McEnery, T. and Wilson, A. (1997) 'Teaching and Language Corpora (TALC)', *ReCALL*, 9, 1: 5–14.

O'Malley, J.M. and Uhl-Chamot A. (1990) *Learning Strategies in Second Language Acquisition*, Cambridge: Cambridge University Press.

Savignon, S. (1972) *Communicative Competence: An Experiment in Foreign Language Teaching*, Philadelphia, Pa.: Center for Curriculum Development.

Wichman, A., Fligelstone, S., McEnery, T. and Knowles, G. (1997) *Teaching and Language Corpora*, London: Longman.

Voir également les ouvrages suivants (introductions à l'utilisation des corpora et logiciels d'exploitation, avec listes/discussion de corpora et logiciels disponibles):

Biber, D., Conrad, S. and Reppen, R. (1998) *Corpus Linguistics*, Cambridge: Cambridge University Press

McEnery, T. and Wilson, A. (1996) *Corpus Linguistics,* Edinburgh: Edinburgh University Press.

Sinclair J. (1991) *Corpus, Concordance, Collocation*, Oxford: Oxford University Press.

Svartvik, J. (ed.) (1991) *Directions in Corpus Linguistics*, Berlin, New York: Mouton de Gruyter.

Thomas, J. and Short, M. (1996) *Using Corpora for Language Research*, London: Longman.

Stubbs, M. (1996) *Text and Corpus analysis*, Oxford: Blackwell.

Notes

1 Autant que je sache, *Le Monde* est le seul grand quotidien français produit sur CD-ROM. Chaque CD, mis à jour tous les trois mois, couvre une année, et permet l'exportation rapide sur disquette de grands nombres de textes, et donc la constitution de corpora de taille plus ou moins importante et de caractéristiques plus ou moins spécifiques en fonction des besoins, à exploiter avec un concordancier électronique. Il est également disponible sur Internet (www.le monde.fr; éventail de paramètres de recherches et possibilités d'exportation de textes similaires), avec des archives qui remontent à 1987 (accès payant; licence multiple ou 'site' pour le CD-ROM). De nombreux journaux ou magazines français sont par ailleurs diffusés sur Internet (*Libération*, *Le Nouvel Observateur*, *Sciences et Avenir*, par exemple), la plupart avec des archives; les possibilités de recherche sont plus ou moins intéressantes suivant les cas, mais l'exportation (copie texte par texte plutôt qu'exportation en bloc) n'est pas aussi simple ou rapide qu'elle l'est avec *Le Monde*.

Parmi les journaux anglais disponibles sur CD-ROM (*The Independent, The Guardian/Observer*, par exemple), The Guardian/Observer est celui dont les paramètres de recherche sont les plus diversifiés (*keyword, publication, headline keyword, by-line keyword, section, date*): il permet comme *Le Monde* de constituer des sous-corpora suivants divers critères (sujet, mais aussi auteurs, fonctions ou registres, par exemple), comparables en ce sens à des équivalents tirés du *Monde* (*The Independent* ne permet lui que des recherches par mots-clés et dates, ce qui limite les possibilités de comparaison).

D'autres types de CD-ROM de type thématique sont également intéressants d'un point de vue didactique; cf. par exemple:

Conquête de l'histoire de 1945 à nos jours. Cube système multimédia, Collection Conquêtes, 1995.

2000 ans d'histoire de France (P. Bonafoux). Paris: Havas Editions électroniques, 1996.

Le cinéma français et francophone de 1929 à nos jours. Canal + Multimédia, Havas Editions électroniques, 1995.

Le Louvre (Brisson, D. et N. Coural). Paris: Montparnasse multimédia/Réunion des musées nationaux, 1994.

Musée d'Orsay (D. Brisson) Paris: Montparnasse multimédia/Réunion des musées nationaux, 1996.

2   *Microconcord* (Mike Scott et Tim Johns, 1993. Oxford University Press, Electronic Publishing, Walton Street, Oxford OX2 6DP) (très simple d'utilisation – le maniement s'en maîtrise en quelques minutes; fourni avec un manuel d'introduction au travail avec un concordancier et à ses applications en classe de langue très clair et utile (triage/organisation des lignes de concordance; analyses lexicales, syntaxiques, morphologiques, par exemple).

Wordsmith Tools (Mike Scott, 1996. Oxford University Press, Electronic Publishing, Walton Street, Oxford OX2 6DP) (plus technique et difficile à maîtriser/utiliser que *Microconcord*; mais plus diversifié dans ses possibilités: données statistiques plus détaillées, calcul de la fréquence d'occurence de tous les termes d'un corpus (liste alphabétique ou par fréquence), maniement des contextes, par exemple); se prête à des recherches plus avancées, en particulier d'un point de vue comparatif).

3   Ces concordances, comme toutes celles reproduites (partiellement) dans cet article, ont été réalisées à partir d'un corpus restreint d'une quarantaine de textes du *Monde* sur CD-ROM sur le sujet 'travail', chargés sur disquette par paramètre de taille ('bref', 'moyen', 'long').

4   Exemples de commentaires d'étudiants sur leur expérience culturelle et linguistique à l'étranger pendant leur 3ème année (tirés du premier des deux rapports d'auto-évaluation à remplir au cours de leur séjour; étudiants de niveau 2/1 en deuxième année):

J'essaie de lire dans divers domaines pour enrichir mon vocabulaire (par exemple Cosmopolitan, Le Monde, Le Nouvel Observateur et le Premier Homme de Camus) et bien sûr des messages, des pubs, des affiches qu'on lit sans s'en rendre compte. Tout me permet de me familiariser avec des styles différents français ... Je suis capable maintenant de parcourir rapidement les passages difficiles et de les comprendre ... J'ai remarqué que certains magazines et journaux utilisent des 'jeux de mots' et j'éprouve une certaine difficulté à les comprendre; à l'avenir, je demanderai à un Français si je ne comprends pas les 'jeux de mots' pour qu'il puisse me l'expliquer' (sic).

Maintenant, il me suffit de parcourir rapidement un livre pour en tirer les détails pertinents, et je suis plus capable de garder en mémoire les informations que j'ai lu parce que je ne dois pas consacrer autant d'attention à la lecture elle-même ... Quant il s'agit d'un niveau de français très soutenu (ex Le Monde et les livres académiques) j'éprouve de la difficulté à comprendre. J'ai donc souvent recours aux ouvrages de référence (dictionnaires, grammaires) ... Il me faut lire plus de français recherché pour m'habituer à ce style (sic).

Apppendice I

1	1	t à organiser, qui pourrait être du	temps consacré à sa formation ou, plus
2	1	eux que les Allemands ont mis du	temps à évaluer le coût véritable de leu
3	1	ises renoncent à comptabiliser les	temps effectués par leurs salariés. C'es
4	1	adultes y consacrent davantage de	temps une meilleure éducation des en
5	1	e multitude de questions. Celle du	temps qui déborde ses frontières usuell
6	1	e leur emploi. Ils n'ont pas pris le	temps de garder une zone d'autonomie d
7	1	sacrera désormais la moitié de son	temps à peaufiner ses spectacles de pr
8	1	A, va ainsi pouvoir consacrer du	temps à la petite entreprise qu'il a c
9	1	avail de reclassement demande du	temps, un temps donné et connu. Il ne p
10	3	autre conception de la gestion du	temps tout au long du cycle de vie, ils
11	3	demain ignorera la séparation des	temps sur laquelle nous vivons depuis l'
12	3	? On n'a même plus l'avantage du	temps :les adaptations sont souvent ra
13	3	odifier tous les ans les emplois du	temps, l'organisation de la production e
14	3	ganisation, son agencement dans le	temps. A la précarité de l'entreprise s
15	3	uvelle organisation du travail et du	temps. Elle passe par une réduction si
16	4	ployé qui accepte de travailler à	mi-temps perçoit une valorisation de s
17	4	les des horaires, horaires variables,	temps partiel généralisé voire annualis
18	4	partiel par rapport aux salariés à	temps plein. L'opinion de la plupart d
19	4	t morale qui en résulte ainsi que le	temps perdu, la dégradation de l'éducat
20	4	s partisans du partage, à la fois du	temps global de travail et de la masse
21	4	abillement ou l'automobile. Mais le	temps libéré créera une demande de serv
22	4	eux situations : le travail selon le	temps légal et le chômage à ' temps com
23	4	ortant. On sait aussi qu'il existe un	temps incompressible de transport, qui
24	4	indice du progrès : la conquête du	temps libre. Alors, on s'interroge sur l
25	4	'ou non ou les 'petits boulots' à	temps réduit ou partagé ; 3) procéder
26	4	rrons-nous conserver la rigidité du	temps industriel où chacun va à l'usine
27	4	ion croissante de la vie arrachée au	temps contraint pour être consacrée au
28	4	n de temps de mise à disposition de	temps subordonné ou de temps contraint
29	6	c de lourds horaires de travail, des	temps de transport longs, fatigants et
30	6	l'on voit bien que la diminution du	temps de travail proposée par certains p
31	6	tive qui lui permette d'alterner des	temps de plein emploi, des moments de
32	6	avantage d'accueil pour les enfants,	temps de loisir plus important, temps p
33	6	ble. Pour nombre d'entreprises, le	temps d'occupation des bureaux et des
34	6	contraint pour être consacrée au	temps de l'épanouissement individuel, de
35	6	s'agir que d'un compromis, car le	temps de l'entreprise et celui des pers
36	6	onomie des services, voici venu le	temps de l'économie de l'immatériel. Au
37	6	n du temps de travail, la notion de	temps de mise à disposition de temps sub
38	6	ent individuel, de la formation, au	temps de l'activité civique, culturelle

Appendice 1: MicroConcord search SW: temps

Appendice 2

1 1	dans les services, la réduction du	temps de travail sur une durée quotidien
2 1	n nombre à dire que la réduction du	temps de travail est une condition du re
3 1	s politiques actives de réduction du	temps de travail mises en oeuvre depuis
4 1	ent à se demander si la réduction du	temps de travail ne devrait pas être l'
5 1	emplois Accord sur la réduction du	temps de travail à la SFIM Plus de
6 1	rise par entreprise, la réduction du	temps de travail étant compensée par de
7 1	posée, l'option de la réduction du	temps de travail laisse pendantes de nom
8 1	'on y a appris que la réduction du	temps de travail devait être modulée en f
9 1	breuses d'emplois, la réduction du	temps de travail doit être massive, s'acc
10 1	nge d'une réduction sensible de leur	temps de travail, ceux qui font le même
11 1	les d'une réduction significative du	temps de travail, négociable par branch
12 1	t-quinze licenciements secs. Le	temps de travail sera réduit d'une heure
13 1	nt de politiques visant à réduire le	temps de travail, la question est délica
14 1	s possibles pour réduire la durée du	temps de travail: faut-il, comme on le
15 2	l'on voit bien que la diminution du	temps de travail proposée par certains po
16 2	du chômage ? La diminution du	temps du travail porte aussi en elle un p
17 2	diminuer de cinq journées par an le	temps de travail et de réduire très sen
18 2	ciera encore l'entreprise. Enfin, le	temps de travail ayant diminué de 30 % e
19 3	un discours malthusien, baisse du	temps de travail et amélioration du nive
20 3	revient à dire que toute baisse du	temps de travail serait, dans l'état ac
21 4	partenaires sociaux à aménager le	temps de travail. Il en prévoit le calcul
22 4	ro-mobilité 'et l'aménagement du	temps de travail. Les participants pour
23 4	vernement propose d'aménager le	temps de travail AVANT PROJET DE
24 4	mars un projet d'aménagement du	temps de travail qui doit permettre d'évi
25 5	u travail. Ainsi, l'annualisation du	temps de travail peut s'apparenter à un
26 5	ir à une annualisation négociée du	temps de travail afin d'adapter celui-c
27 5	nts et l'annualisation-réduction du	temps de travail sont aussi souvent créat
28 6	l'entreprise adopte une formule de	temps partiel de travail. Les syndicats
29 6	se de l'emploi. Aussi la notion de	temps de travail telle qu'elle est pratiq
30 6	r. La proposition de partage du	temps de travail néglige l'existence de
31 6	a permis de rouvrir le débat sur le	temps de travail. Mais la plupart des pro
32 6	convient donc que la flexibilité du	temps de travail ne soit ni encouragée n
33 6	ement des horaires, adaptation du	temps de travail, adoption du temps par
34 6	surtout de restaurer la liberté du	temps de travail. Pascal Salin est profe

35 7   es uns et par les autres de fixer le   temps de travail dans une entreprise à 3

36 7   monde de demain. Par exemple, le   temps de travail calculé par rapport à la

37 7   alariés en matière de salaires et de   temps de travail', souligne Philippe Sic

Appendice 2: MicroConcord search SW: temps CW: travail

Appendice 3

1. The new Government is today making the fight against unemployment its urgent priority.
2. But it knows full well that the jobs crisis is not due to the recession, it is also structural; and
3. clearly the French, like others, will have to learn to live with a high level of unemployment
4. for some years to come. France in theory is prosperous enough to be able to cope with this
5. and to guarantee those out of work a tolerable living. But if their hardship is to be reduced,
6. public attitudes too will have to evolve, so as to remove the stigma often attached to being
7. unemployed, in a nation that traditionally sets a high moral value on work. A parallel solution
8. is to share the burden more evenly, by shortening the working week so that more jobs are
9. available. As in some other EEC countries, the unions have been pressing for this: they want
10. a reduction from a 40- to a 35-hour week, without any drop in wages. In 1979-80,
11. tripartite negotiations on this never got anywhere, for the Patronat was hostile, predictably.
12. But now the Socialist Government is firmly backing the unions and has set the target of a
13. 35-hour week by 1985. It has even warned the Patronat that, if it still says 'no', it will
14. impose the scheme by legislation. So far, the Patronat is now being more conciliatory, and in
15. July 1981 it agreed to the initial step of reducing the basic working week from 40 to 39
16. hours without loss of pay. But many patrons are acutely worried about the extra costs
17. involved, in a time of low profits. And some business experts are predicting that, far from
18. creating new jobs, a shorter week for the same pay could well have the reverse effect: many
19. firms feel obliged to reduce their staff.

Appendice 3a: Extrait de 'France in the 80s' (J. Ardagh 1982: 107–8)

1. A TUC document published this summer setting out the case for a national minimum wage
2. carries as one illustration the photograph of a glum looking laundry worker pushing a trolley
3. laden with washing. As well it might. A recent analysis by the Low Pay Unit of the
4. Department's New Earnings Survey showed that of the 10 worst-paying jobs for men, that
5. of launderer ranks as number three. According to the LPU analysis, the average male
6. wage in the industry is £169.90 per week, including overtime, based on an hourly rate
7. of £3.80. Though well below the target minimum wage rate of £4.15 per hour espoused by
8. the LPU and some other campaigners, even that industry average is something Alan James
9. can only dream of. Alan, a 40-year-old divorced father of three, works for an industrial
10. aundry firm in the tough Millbay docks area of Plymouth. For a 39-hour week he is paid a
11. flat rate of £3.10 an hour – giving him a weekly take home pay, after deductions, of £101 if
12. he does not work overtime. Such a wage leaves little for the 'luxuries' that others may take
13. for granted and Alan, who lodges with friends in Plymouth, says many fellow workers at the
14. laundry have to work overtime just to make ends meet (…) Alan Swales, district secretary
15. for the Transport Workers Union, which represents the laundry's 60 employees, says
16. conditions in the cutthroat industry present the classic argument for a minimum wage.
17. 'People are paid very low wages, but the reality is that the industry is very competitive,
18. which does not allow employers to be generous,' he says. 'That is where the argument for
19. the minimum wage comes in. You can be the most efficient laundry going, but you can get

20. undercut by the ruthless employer who is not as efficient but makes savings by reducing

21. wages. It's a downward spiral. If the level of £4 was the base, this would allow all

22. companies to start from the same point and it would only be those companies that invested

23. in plant and equipment and efficiency that would be in a position to expand and progress (...)

Appendice 3b: Extrait de 'Poor victims of a cutthroat industry'
(G. Gibbs, The Guardian 9/9/95)

Appendice 4

3 **jectif raisonnable** 'et que **celui des 35** | **heures**, à terme, 'reste le bon'. Mais,
4   uatre jours. C'est-à-dire trente-deux | heures, à l'horizon de dix ans, un peu ap
5   par ailleurs', le passage de 39 à 33 | heures (15 %) devrait conduire à une a
6   qui sont passés progressivement à 37 | heures 30 avant de franchir, en octobre p
8   salarial. Le passage rapide aux 35 | heures (5 journées de 7 heures) pourrait p
19 osée, en 1982, avec le passage des 40 | heures aux 39 heures hebdomadaires. En t
20   Le Monde du 17 mars) ou même 32 | heures avec la semaine de quatre jours. L
21   rs que nos concurrents restent à 39 | heures avec moins de personnel. Cette m
22 **sant la durée légale du travail à 35** | **heures avec application au plus tard en**
25 le meilleur des cas, le passage aux 32 | heures dégage 2 millions d'emplois suppl
26   Pour ce faire, elle estime que les 37 | heures **d'ici à 1996 ou 1997** sont un 'ob
27   E) a testé les deux solutions, les 35 | heures d'un coup, avec partage des revenu
35 **9 février) : réduction à trente-sept** | **heures de la durée hebdomadaire du tr**
37 de se produire autour des trente-deux | heures de travail hebdomadaire ou ce q
39 le chômage, il suffit de **répartir ces** | **heures de travail** entre tous ceux qui son
51   ction du temps de travail 'trente | heures en 1990', **sans diminution de rev**
52   parti socialiste qui sera passé des 35 | heures en 1977 aux 37 heures... en 1997.
53 travail, qui pourrait être ramenée à 37 | heures en 1996 ou 1997.   Mme Martine
55 ry se prononce pour la semaine de 37 | heures en 1996 ou 1997 PUBLIE DANS
75 durée du travail passera à trente-cinq | heures hebdomadaires après épuisement
77 **de salaire et le passage de 38 à 35** | **heures hebdomadaires avec réduction**
126 hebdomadaire de travail sera de 33 | heures réparties sur 4 journées... 'Cha
131 e raisonnable vers les 37 puis les 35 | heures **sans baisse de salaire**. La mauvais
132 on de Lionel Jospin de passer aux 37 | heures **sans diminution de salaire** en 199
134 horaires hebdomadaires à trente-huit | heures **sans perte de salaire** et, le cas éc
145 duisant un recours plus modéré aux | heures supplémentaires de travail.   En
146 ps partiel généralisé voire annualisé, | heures supplémentaires 'récupérées ',
152 tendu. Tous ceux qui **prônent les 35** | **heures** tout de suite avec partage des rev

Appendice 4: MicroConcord search SW: heure

Appendice 5

1	emps partiel, toutes les formules ont	donc été acceptées, contrôlées, négociée
2	sieurs centaines de milliers… et a	donc évité, d'autant, une encore plus fort
3	multiplier les assurances privées (et	donc à différencier toujours plus les cla
4	produites dans le passé conduirait	donc à des incohérences. Rappelons-no
5	travail, socialement utile, qui doit	donc être reconnu comme tel par la sociét
6	re de leurs cadres. Ceux-ci doivent	donc avoir un souci constant de se poser l
7	age augmente inexorablement. Il est	donc bien clair que ces politiques ont éc
8	pas une évolution en cours, il s'agit	donc collectivement de trouver d'autres v
9	aucoup mieux. Ce chiffre apparaît	donc comme une contrainte, et cette contr
10	ins en moins de leur salaire direct (	donc de leurs efforts) et de plus en plus

etc.

Appendice 5: MicroConcord search SW: donc

Appendice 6

1	'industrie est, chez nous, inférieure de	30	% à ce qu'elle est en Allemagne
2	faveur du temps partiel de l'ordre de	15	% à 25 %. Ainsi, si nous souh
3	les salaires nets baissent en moyenne de	5	% (3 % pour les plus bas salair
4	accepteraient même une diminution de	10	% (3). Il nous semble pourtant
5	s le salaire minimum en sont exonérés à	50	%. A l'avenir, ce mécanisme devra
6	est aujourd'hui, chez nous, de près de	30	%, alors qu'il est à la moyenne n
7	salariés intérimaires avait diminué de	16	% au dernier trimestre 1992 (soi
8	ment, de près de 12 %, contre environ	3	% au Japon et 5 % dans l'ancienn
9	réduites de 10 % (la baisse atteindra	15	% au-delà et se chiffrera à 20 %
10	salaires est tombée de 70 % en 1973 à	58	% aujourd'hui. Les 10 % de sala
11	at, mais par une augmentation voisine de	1	%. Avec la possibilité de centain
12	onétaire de notre pays, car le chiffre de	3	% borne les prévisions à moyen t
13	a promis le niveau du baccalauréat pour	80	% d'une classe d'âge en l'an 2
14	choix aujourd'hui ne sont plus guère que	10	%, d'après les premiers résulta
15	au contraire que la croissance avoise	3	% dans les prochaines années
16	dans l'Europe du Nord (un peu plus de	14	% de l'ensemble des emplois en F
17	soit une majorité de 66 % représentant	55	% de l'ensemble du personnel. Co
18	iser, recruter (sans doute entre 10 % et	12	% de leurs effectifs initiaux) e
19	appellerons structurel, qui représente	8	% de la population active. Seuls
20	(1) a fait des comptes. Elle évalue à	6	% de la richesse nationale les d
21	ant, nos calculs prouvent que ça touche	4	% de nos effectifs, soit 1 000
22	ult-Reynolds SA de Valence (Drôme),	12	% des 454 salariés ont opté li
23	PEA ils représentent en France quelque	25	% des ménages (soit près de 6 mi

etc.

Appendice 6: MicroConcord search SW: %

Corpus-informed syllabus development: Parallel concordances and pedagogical grammars

Marie-Madeleine Kenning
University of East Anglia

1   Introduction

After being demoted and given a low profile in the early stages of communicative methodology, explicit grammar teaching has come back into the limelight with academic publications on the subject (e.g. King and Boaks, 1994, Engel and Myles, 1996, Goodfellow and Metcalfe, 1997), new or extensively revised grammar books, and projects such as the 'AFLS grammar initiative', an attempt by the Association for French Language Studies to initiate and encourage informed debate on grammar teaching through the wide distribution of pedagogical documents reflecting divergent approaches. At the same time the burgeoning field of corpus linguistics has brought to light the inadequacies of current language descriptions and shown that what is presented in textbooks differs substantially from actual native speaker usage (McEnery *et al*, 1997). As the debate on what to teach, when, and how, continues, this paper considers the application of corpus-informed syllabus design to the teaching of French, with particular reference to the use of parallel corpora and their analysis in the development of pedagogical grammars for advanced learners. Adopting Dirven's definition of pedagogical grammar as 'any learner-oriented or teacher-oriented description or presentation of foreign language rule complexes with the aim of promoting and guiding learning processes in the acquisition of that language' (Dirven, 1990: 1), the paper discusses three possible applications of parallel concordancers to syllabus development: as providers of information on usage and use, as providers of information on similarities and differences between the native and target language, and as means of introducing an element of syllabus negotiation. The discussion, which incorporates the results of recent investigations and experimental use, is illustrated with French/English output from MULTICONCORD, a multilingual concordancer developed with LINGUA funding (Johns, 21 December 1999).

2   Parallel concordancers as tools in syllabus design

Pedagogical grammars for advanced learners still bear surprisingly few traces of the debate surrounding syllabus design that has now been going on for some 30 years. While concepts such as frequency and difficulty have had a profound impact at beginners' level, the selection and ordering of the content of grammars for advanced learners still seem to rely far more on tradition and intuition than on specific external criteria. At any rate, the absence of detailed methodological information together with references to 'the influence of the work of those who have gone before' (Hawkins and Towell, xi) or to invented examples (Judge and Healey, xxxvi) suggests as much.

Admittedly, notions like frequency and difficulty are less easy to apply at advanced level: first, it has to be recognised that in so far as advanced learners must be able to cope with a wider range of language, the issue of frequency becomes less relevant; more importantly, however, our lack of knowledge about language acquisition/learning beyond the initial stages makes it hard to decide what is difficult and why. There are many questions on which we need more information, including whether there exist natural orders at advanced level, the precise influence of the native language, and the factors that promote or hinder internalisation, for example the impact of different types of sequencing. Nevertheless, in the absence of contrary information, it seems reasonable to give a high priority to frequency and difficulty, bearing in mind that the relative weight given to particular factors, and the overall organisation, will depend on the nature of the grammatical component, which may form part of a course, constitute an independent self-contained learning or teaching grammar, or be intended as a reference work. It will also be necessary to take into account whether grammar is being taught for comprehension or for production purposes.

Taken as a whole, the principles on which linguistic content is selected and sequenced can be divided into two main categories according to whether they arise from the target language itself, i.e. language usage and use, or from the language acquisition/learning process, with the concept of needs bridging the two. Frequency belongs to the first category, difficulty to the second. Both can be investigated using parallel concordancers.

Like monolingual concordancers, parallel concordancers are search and retrieval computer programs which enable the user to recover from a corpus all the instances of a given item in their immediate linguistic context. Parallel concordancers are used to examine corpora holding the same texts in different languages and the output displays both the search item in context and the corresponding segment of the translation. What follows is based on concordances produced with MULTICONCORD, which is associated with a corpus of translated texts in ten languages.

The main advantage of parallel concordancers in the context under discussion is to act as providers of data that can be used to guide development by helping decisions regarding the selection and ordering of the contents of a pedagogical grammar. However, as illustrated below, parallel concordancing can also be used to introduce an element of syllabus negotiation so that decisions are better informed by learners' needs. Indeed, the possibility of using parallel concordancers for investigating problems as they crop up makes them particularly valuable at higher levels, where the increasing diversity of individual needs militates against a generic approach. Last but not least, parallel concordancing provides a means of checking the validity of existing descriptions. The fact is that current grammars, pedagogical or merely descriptive, still contain a majority of statements derived from introspection backed up by observations involving limited, often unrepresentative, data. Descriptions are frequently second-hand and at variance with contemporary usage, while illustrative examples and practice materials are seldom drawn from real data. Thanks to the evidence gathered through concordancing, it becomes possible to verify whether accounts are a true reflection of the way in which language is actually used, to substantiate statements or improve their accuracy, and to include illustrations that reflect actual use.

3 Parallel concordancers as providers of information on linguistic usage and use

As already indicated, parallel concordancers are a means of gathering information on the frequency of a given form, structure, collocation, etc that can be used to inform decisions as to what to include in the syllabus, at what point, and with what prominence. Let us take relative pronouns as an example. It is a common observation that post-A level learners of French can usually handle *qui* and *que* fairly competently but experience difficulties with *dont* and are even less familiar with *duquel, de laquelle*, etc. Faced with this situation, one will probably want to focus on the two less well known pronouns but should one devote equal amounts of time and attention to each and deal with them in the same way? Or should one give priority to one, and if so, which and to what extent?

The answer will vary with circumstances, notably the objectives of the course. But it is bound to be influenced by the relative potential usefulness of the pronouns to learners, in other words by the likelihood of learners having to understand or compose sentences containing these pronouns. Here one might just rely on hunches. However, thanks to concordancers it is possible to obtain a more reliable estimate by looking at the frequency of the items under consideration in a corpus of texts similar to those to be read or produced. The results of such a search on the French/English section of the MULTICONCORD corpus (three chapters of a scientific book, a fictional work, a work of popularisation of academic writing and a second fictional work) are displayed in Table 1.

	dont	duquel	de laquelle	desquels	desquelles
file 1 (E/F)	15	0	0	0	0
file 2 (E/F)	9	1	1	0	0
file 3 (F/E)	154	1	2	1	0
file 4 (F/E)	5	0	0	0	0
Total	183	2	3	1	0

Table 1: Occurrences of dont, duquel, de laquelle, desquels, desquelles in 2 English/French and 2 French/English files of the MULTICONCORD corpus

As expected, the search reveals *dont* to be much more frequent than the *de* compounds put together, though the size of the difference, with 183 occurrences against 6, may come as a surprise. On the strength of this empirical data, it would seem reasonable, all things being equal, to spend considerably more time on *dont*; we may also feel inclined to get students to practise using *dont*, while confining ourselves, at least initially, to sensitising them to the prepositional context that calls for the use of duquel, etc.

The relative frequency of *ce qui, ce que, ce dont, ce à/en/sur quoi* in relative clauses and indirect questions is another area where one might feel the need for empirical evidence. Using the same files as before produces the results shown in Table 2.

	ce qui	ce que/ce qu'	ce dont	ce à/en/sur quoi
file 1 (E/F)	17	26	1	1
file 2 (E/F)	24	70	0	0
file 3 (F/E)	22	29	1	0
file 4 (F/E)	8	15	0	0
Total	71	140	2	1

Table 2: Occurrences of ce qui, ce que, ce dont, ce à/en/sur quoi in 2 English/French and 2 French/English files of the MULTICONCORD corpus

Again there are wide differences which, in this case, invite us to consider *ce qui* and *ce que* further, and to give them a higher priority in the syllabus.

It must be acknowledged at this point that Tables 1 and 2 are based on a small sample and that the results are unlikely to be representative of the language as a whole. It would be advisable therefore to check the findings against a larger corpus, which, in the absence of substantial parallel corpora, involves turning to a monolingual concordancer.

To illustrate the impact of the corpus on findings and the need to exercise caution, let us look at the context in which *dont* occurs in our data. First we note that using the selection and sorting facilities of MULTICONCORD on the same files as before reveals only 2 immediately obvious collocations: *façon dont* (3 occurrences) and *manière dont* (2 occurrences). On such evidence we may well regard these two strings as the only candidates for special highlighting in a pedagogical presentation. That it may not be advisable to stop there is shown by the results of two studies quoted in Blanche-Benveniste, 1996. The first, involving a corpus of conversations, shows dont co-occurring primarily with *parler* (48.4 % of occurrences), followed by *avoir besoin, faire partie, prendre conscience, sortir, dépendre, être question*, and *être convaincu*, these 9 verbs representing between them over 90% of the uses of dont (Blanche-Benveniste, 1996, 39). The second study, based on a corpus of articles from the newspaper *Le Monde*, also shows *parler* in first place, but with only 8,9 % of occurrences and in front of a different, albeit overlapping, list: *faire preuve, avoir besoin, dire, disposer, rêver, souffrir, sortir*, and *dépendre*. Furthermore in this case the first nine verbs only represent 45% of uses (Blanche-Benveniste, *op. cit.*).

Although puzzling at first, these discrepant findings are not too difficult to reconcile. For instance, one would expect a written corpus to include a wider range of lexical items and therefore to show less strong patterns of relationships between *dont* and its collocates than a spoken corpus. It goes without saying that the existence of this kind of variation is not without pedagogical implications. It invites us, in particular, to consider whether we should not approach grammar differently according to whether we wish to prioritise speech or writing, placing, for instance, more emphasis on the collocates of *dont*, especially *parler*, where our prime concern is to facilitate oral production.

As for the discrepancies between the studies reported by Blanche-Benveniste and our own, they can be seen to stem from differences in the focus of the analysis: our interest lay in the immediate environment of *dont* whereas the other studies considered longer stretches located to its right. Searching again in our files for the items mentioned in Blanche-Benveniste's paper reveals yet another pattern of co-occurrences: *parler* (1), *être question* (2), *disposer* (2), *dépendre* (1), *dire* (1), *rêver* (1), *souffrir* (1), *sortir* (1). Clearly, one cannot draw firm conclusions from such a smaller number of citations, but it might be noted that our results contain more items from the second list, in line with the written nature of the corpus.

While the smaller size of current parallel corpora may be a problem at times, and as such must be regarded as a shortcoming, restricted corpora are not without advantages. This is particularly true in a teaching/learning situation context where one may be content with broad indications, or where there may be didactic reasons for focusing searches on certain types of texts, genres or registers. Thus within a given course, the use of a corpus that reflects the type of texts that students are likely to encounter, or to have to create, in the near future, can serve to implement a strategy for moving towards greater complexity in a way that lets communicative needs determine the grammatical progression. For example, the high incidence of *soit... soit* and *soit* meaning *à savoir* in the same 4 files may well be a feature of the type of texts involved rather than a finding typical of general usage; this, however, does not prevent it from being a valuable discovery, if these are the kind of texts students have to deal with.

Above all, the presence of a translation, which constitutes the main distinguishing feature of parallel concordances, has the potential of bringing out patterns of variation much more sharply than the context alone, when, as is so often the case, the relationship between form and function/meaning happens to be different in the two languages. Correlations between meaning and word order are a case in point. Consider, for example, how much easier it is to infer the relationship between position and meaning with the help of a parallel text in the 3 concordance extracts which follow than in an output showing only the French:

---

il fallait que les règles en fussent impitoyables, même sur les bâtiments où la discipline s'était atténuée, pour qu'un condamné de droit commun, *ancien* terre-neuvier, ait lancé à la tête d'un gardien de prison brutal: 'Ici, on n'est tout de même pas à la grande pêche!'

Rules must have been pitiless, even on ships where discipline was relaxed, for someone sentenced by common law, a former Newfoundlander, to shout in the face of a brutal prison guard: 'We're not out big-time fishing, you know!'

j'habitais une maison *ancienne*

I lived in an old house

Différents observateurs… ne seront *pas toujours* d'accord sur la distance que la lumière aura parcourue	Different observers… will not always agree on how far the light travelled
L'Europe n'est *toujours pas* disposée à défendre ces taxations	Europe is still not minded to press for that
je ne *peux pas* le laisser partir	I cannot let it go
La découverte d'une théorie complètement unifiée, donc, peut ne pas venir en aide à la survie de notre espèce	The discovery of a completely unified theory, therefore, may not aid the survival of our species

From a pedagogical point of view, the fact that parallel concordances make it easier to grasp certain associations is not necessarily a recommendation. Given the controversies that continue to surround the use of the mother tongue in language teaching and the impact of depth of processing on retention, it may be argued that it is more beneficial to present students with several French examples and get them to work out the pattern or rule themselves. On the other hand, working things out without the help of the translation is likely to be more time consuming and may prove too cognitively demanding for some students. One way out of this dilemma might be to limit the exploitation of parallel output to cases where there are tight time constraints and/or to use it as a means of providing extra clues in a stepped approach.

To sum up, parallel corpora can be said to have a twofold advantage as far as linguistic usage and use are concerned: first, in providing a built-in comparator for one's interpretation, they facilitate and speed up the recognition of thorny areas; second, as a potential source of bilingual examples and teaching materials, they allow the inclusion in the grammatical syllabus of aspects which might otherwise be left out as being too difficult or of minor importance. In addition, though less obviously, they offer the opportunity of approaching problems laterally by investigating one language using another language as search language in order to resolve issues such as whether or not French stressed pronouns (e.g. *lui* in, for example, *sans lui*) can have inanimate antecedents (Kenning, 1998).

4 Parallel concordancers as providers of information on similarities and divergences between the two languages

Although the impact of the native language on the acquisition of another language is not as well documented as one might wish, there is widespread agreement that areas of divergence or partial correspondence tend to be more difficult to master than areas where the two languages operate in a similar way, and as such require particular attention. Returning to one of our previous examples, we may wish to concentrate on *façon dont*, not because it represents a frequent collocation, but because the use of *dont*, where English has *in which*, runs counter to common equivalence patterns and is therefore likely to take learners by surprise. Whether one alerts students explicitly to this difference is a matter of teaching strategy. The point is that parallel concordancers provide us with a tool for comparisons across languages and therefore for identifying and documenting similarities, differences and anomalies.

Here the choice of search language offered by parallel concordances proves to be a valuable asset which allows the corpus to be more thoroughly explored so as to achieve a fuller picture of the intricate web of relations between the two systems. In the case of the pair of languages under discussion, one can search the French data in the way illustrated above or start from the English texts. Since the two languages seldom behave in exactly the same way, the searches will usually unearth evidence of an overlapping or complementary nature. Typically, searches will bring to light one-to-many correspondences, so that those based on French will be more productive in the detection of cases in which a single French form, pattern or structure has more than one equivalent in English, whereas searches involving the English texts will show up imbalances in the other direction. In some cases one of the two languages will provide a more direct route to the evidence (e.g. *could = pouvait/ pourrait*), while in others, searching a particular language may bring to the surface phenomena which have not been noticed before and thus lead to genuine discoveries. Alternating the search language therefore represents both a useful means of gathering more complete evidence, and a fruitful research strategy.

As far as teaching is concerned, though, the choice of search language might well be influenced by the ultimate purpose of the tuition, that is to say whether one is primarily interested in the development of comprehension or production. The distinction between comprehension and production is one which is seldom made in relation to grammar teaching, possibly because most learners are known to want to acquire a language in order to act as addressers as well as addressees. It is not uncommon for points to be treated uniformly from a production perspective, as if learners necessarily needed to be able to produce everything they learn. It is argued here that grammar teaching should adopt a more discriminating, differentiated approach which takes account of considerations such as the extent to which the ability to produce a certain form/pattern/structure affects the learners' ability to communicate, whether there are alternative means of expression, the importance of the point for comprehension, the effect of mistakes, etc. Looking at the examples above, one can see that the implications of not knowing a particular point not only vary from case to case but are different for comprehension and production: for instance, not knowing *façon dont* is unlikely to cause comprehension problems. It is true that it may lead to the use of an incorrect relative pronoun (*dans laquelle*) when speaking or writing, but this is unlikely to interfere with communication. On the other hand, lack of familiarity with the variation in meaning of adjectives like *ancien, certain, propre*, or with the impact of word order in combinations of *toujours* and *pas*, or *ne pas* and verbs such as *pouvoir*, may create problems with regard to both comprehension and production.

In the main, lack of parallelism between the two languages poses a greater threat to production than comprehension, since in the case of comprehension help can often be obtained from the context. One major source of difficulties is those areas where the target language makes formal distinctions which are not made in the native language. This makes concordances involving the native language particularly relevant to production, and increasingly useful as overall proficiency develops and more emphasis is placed on accuracy and translation skills. The following extract from a concordance of *before* demonstrates both these points in as much as the existence of multiple equivalents is unlikely to interfere with comprehension, and the distinction between *avant* and *devant* is easier to grasp, as well as more important to master, than the requirement to use *avant de* and not *avant que* when the subject of the verb in the subordinate clause is the same as in the main clause.

Art galleries and antique dealers are generally not open *before* 10.30am	Les magasins d'antiquités ainsi que les galeries d'art n'ouvrent généralement pas avant 10h 30 le matin
Finally you will arrive *before* the town of Rostock	Enfin tu arriveras devant la ville de Rostock.
Before her was another long passage	Devant elle s'étendait un autre couloir
Nearly a century passed *before* this idea was taken seriously.	Presque un siècle s'écoula avant que cette hypothèse ne soit prise au sérieux.
After around twenty years in Bruges, the director of the Medici's offshoot had become adviser to Prince Charles *before* the prince became a duke;	Après une vingtaine d'années à Bruges, le directeur de la filiale des Médicis était devenu le conseiller du prince Charles avant que ce dernier ne devînt duc;
Arthur Rimbaud had never seen the sea *before* composing 'Le Bateau ivre'.	Arthur Rimbaud n'avait jamais vu la mer avant de composer 'Le Bateau ivre'.
For his part, Claude Debussy first benefited from contact with the sea in Cannes *before* staying in Russia at the home of the Tchaikovsky's patroness.	Claude Debussy, de son côté, bénéficia d'abord d'un contact avec la mer, à Cannes, avant de séjourner en Russie chez la protectrice de Tchaïkovski.

She thought it over *before* she made her next remark.	Elle y réfléchit un moment avant de demander.

Nevertheless, output of the kind illustrated below, taken from a concordance of yet, can enhance comprehension by helping to dispel expectations of one-to-one correspondences and by demonstrating the importance of the verbal context and effective parsing strategies.

And *yet* the Mediterranean was a means to salvation.	Pourtant la Méditerranée était une voie de salut.
The humble *yet* decisive role of fishermen, indispensable collaborators, has often been passed over in silence;	Le rôle, humble mais décisif, des pêcheurs, collaborateurs indispensables, a été souvent passé sous silence;
'That's the most important piece of evidence we've heard *yet*,' said the King, rubbing his hands;	'C'est la preuve la plus importante que nous ayons eue jusqu'ici', dit le Roi, en se frottant les mains.
Its *yet* uncompleted analysis opens an extraordinary perspective on the close ties of land traffic with maritime circulation	Son exploitation encore inachevée ouvre une perspective extraordinaire sur les liens étroits du trafic terrestre avec la circulation maritime.
The progress of cartographic techniques was filled with as *yet* unimagined, but real, possibilities.	Le progrès de la technique cartographique était porteur de possibilités alors insoupçonnées, mais réelles.

One of the main benefits of working with concordances of native language items is a better appreciation of the considerable demands made by production in, and translation into, the target language. The fact is that concordances often disclose many more equivalents than anticipated, thereby making one realise how many obstacles stand in the way of faultless production. To better appreciate this point, consider the amount of grammatical knowledge required to produce the correct equivalent of *what*, first on the basis of your knowledge of the two languages, and then in the light of the evidence provided by the following concordance extract:

At the end of the lecture, a little old lady at the back of the room got up and said: '*What* you have told us is rubbish.'	A la fin, une vieille dame au fond de la salle se leva et dit: 'Tout ce que vous venez de raconter, ce sont des histoires.'
The scientist gave a superior smile before replying, '*What* is the tortoise standing on?'	Le scientifique eut un sourire hautain avant de rétorquer: 'Et sur quoi se tient la tortue?'
There are even children, and I have met some of them, who want to know *what* a black hole looks like; *what* is the smallest piece of matter; why we remember the past and not the future	Il y a même des enfants, et j'en ai rencontrés, qui veulent savoir à quoi ressemble un trou noir, quelle est la plus petite parcelle de matière; pourquoi nous nous souvenons du passé et non du futur
What is the nature of time?	Quelle est la nature du temps?
It is not known exactly *what* length a stadium was, but it may have been about 200 yards	On ne sait pas exactement quelle était la longueur d'un de ces stades, mais il est probable que cela devait équivaloir environ à deux cents mètres
What lay beyond the last sphere was never made very clear, but it certainly was not part of mankind's observable universe.	Ce qu' il y avait au-delà de cette dernière sphère ne fut jamais bien précisé mais à coup sûr cette partie de l'univers n'était pas observable par l'humanité.

What did God do before he created the universe?	Que fit Dieu avant de créer l'Univers?
The classic example again is the Newtonian theory of gravity, which tells us that the gravitational force between two bodies depends only on one number associated with each body, its mass, but is otherwise independent of *what* the bodies are made of.	L'exemple classique est encore celui de la théorie newtonienne de la gravitation, qui nous dit que la force gravitationnelle entre deux corps ne dépend que d'un nombre associé à chacun, leur masse, et est indépendante de ce dont ces corps sont constitués.
They cannot therefore be influenced by *what* happens at P.	Donc, ils ne peuvent pas être affectés par ce qui arrive en P.

Finally, because parallel concordances show corresponding items in context, it is possible to arrive at a more reliable assessment of the impact of similarities, differences and anomalies on comprehension and production, either through careful consideration of the output and the probability of errors, or by using the concordance as a basis for experimental tests.

5 Parallel concordancers as means of introducing an element of syllabus negotiation

Parallel concordancers also provide means of involving learners in syllabus specification. Giving learners a say in what they study seems particularly important at advanced level since students who have followed different language courses are bound to have different needs. The problem may have been less acute in the past, when university courses recruited from a fairly homogeneous pool. However, the recent expansion of higher education has brought into advanced language classes a diverse population with a much wider range of ability, aptitude, and objectives. In such conditions, a common grammatical syllabus may not be sustainable and should be replaced by a system able to accommodate and cater for individual needs. This system is something that concordancers can help deliver.

The most extreme solution would be to train students to use concordancers by themselves and let them determine the syllabus. This would deliver individualisation and have the additional benefit of promoting self-managed learning. There are, however, serious obstacles to such an approach, due partly to poor metacognitive strategies on the part of the learners and partly to difficulties inherent in the task itself. Beginning with the former, it is an unfortunate fact that many students fail to pay attention to error correction and only engage superficially, if at all, in self-monitoring and self-evaluation. Consequently, they find themselves only partly aware of the gaps in their knowledge and unable to identify what they need to learn or practise. Under these circumstances the very flexibility of concordancers may prove a drawback rather than an asset: unless learners have their own sense of direction or access to some form of support and guidance, there is a real risk that they will be overwhelmed by the range of searches open to them. Furthermore, working with the raw data associated with hands-on experience is a difficult undertaking requiring a great deal of expertise. Indeed experience shows that even drawing inferences from cleaned out but relatively unmanipulated output can be too much for some students.

Another option, favoured by Johns, one of the main advocates of data-driven learning (1991a, 1991b), is exploration under the guidance of a teacher. This removes many of the problems mentioned above and operates well in the kind of post-graduate tutorial context in which Johns works, but is not a realistic proposition in the case of courses with large numbers of students.

A more feasible proposition is to use concordancers to prepare worksheets on a large number of topics, leaving students free to decide which to work on. This gives learners some control over what they engage in, but makes the selection easier by narrowing down the number of options. However, it does not meet the objection that the selection of topics reflects what the teacher/materials developer perceives as difficult, and may not coincide with actual needs and wants. A possible solution to this drawback is to involve students in the selection process. To this end, the author conducted a pilot study which consisted in giving a demonstration of MULTICONCORD to two post-A level students and getting them to read through *Help Yourself to French Grammar* (Marriott and Ribière, 1990) in search of areas they felt might be taught through concordances. Not all the points selected by the students lent themselves easily to concordancing. It is difficult, for instance, to conceive of a concordance transparent enough to explain the past historic and its use, as proposed by student B. Nevertheless the lists did provide pointers, suggesting that, repeated on a representative sample, the exercise might lead to better targeting (see Appendix).

In addition, one of the students went on to explore the uses of the subjunctive using *soit/soient*. Although her findings may partly reflect the nature of the data, and therefore need confirmation using other verbs, her conclusion is worth quoting:

The concordance search produced surprising results. The subjunctive is one of the most difficult tenses to master. The use of the concordancer helped to clarify when to use the subjunctive and also brought to light other uses of the words *soit* and *soient*. Interestingly, the most taught uses of the subjunctive were the least frequent (expressions of doubt, hope and probability) and indeed I discovered a very frequent use of *soit* (*soit... soit* meaning *either... or* and *que 'a' soit 'x' ou soit 'y'* meaning *whether 'a' is 'x' or 'y'*) which I had not been aware of.

Concordances lend themselves to the creation of diverse types of teaching materials, many of which have been described elsewhere (e.g. Johns, 1991b). Suffice it to say that materials based on parallel concordances provide a richer linguistic environment for the heuristics of learners to work on, thanks to the presence of a longer context (a whole sentence or even a paragraph) and the availability of the native language. The latter is very important in removing the shackles of vocabulary and permitting the inclusion of occurrences containing vocabulary unknown to the learner. This has a number of advantages: it extends choice, opening up the way for better and more interesting contextualisation, increases the chances of students picking things up by the way (serendipity learning), and encourages deeper processing through the use of longer and more complex sentences.

As such, materials based on parallel concordances have a training function. Despite the difficulties outlined above, hands-on experience can work provided the right conditions are met. There are in the end two basic requirements: clarity of purpose combined with the ability to process the output. Concordance-based materials, in so far as they call upon and develop learners' ability to sort, to recognise patterns, to draw inferences, and give learners a flavour of the applications of concordancers, can be seen as a preparatory stage to free exploration. However, they are unlikely to be sufficient by themselves and will need to be integrated into a framework that promotes autonomy. This may include encouraging focused investigations in relation to a learner's production errors (e.g. instructions to study the position of a word which the student has placed incorrectly, see Guillot, this volume) or supervised hands-on sessions in which the concordancer is used in conjunction with the study of a text. In this way it may be possible to ease the transition to exploratory learning and help learners make the most of the increasing accessibility of the foreign language.

6 Conclusion

In so far as parallel concordancers are tools for studying actual use, their integration into syllabus development offers the chance to move from a prescriptive approach to grammar teaching that relies on tradition and introspection and is associated with the use of invented decontextualised examples, to a descriptive approach based on and illustrated with data drawn from empirical evidence. Although parallel concordancers lend themselves to intralingual investigations, their main and distinctive advantage is to offer opportunities for contrastive studies that throw light on the relative degree of difficulty of particular areas.

Carrying out the sort of studies that have been delineated here on a large scale and in a systematic manner is a time-consuming enterprise. Comprehensive grammars based on actual use (along the lines of Quirk *et al*, 1985) may therefore seem a distant prospect. But the greatly improved opportunities for sharing ideas and information offered by the Internet make pulling advances together much easier and corpus-informed syllabuses may not be quite as far away as we might think.

References

Blanche-Benveniste, C. (1996) 'De l'Utilité du Corpus Linguistique', *Revue française de linguistique appliquée*, 1–2: 25–42.

Dirven, R. (1990) 'Pedagogical Grammar', *Language Teaching*, 23: 1–18.

Engel, D. and Myles, F. (eds.) (1996) *Teaching Grammar: Perspectives in Higher Education*, London: AFLS/CILT.

Goodfellow, R. and Metcalfe, P. (eds) (1997) 'CALL – The Challenge of Grammar', *ReCALL*, 9(2): 8–16.

Hawkins, R. and Towell, R. (1996) French Grammar and Usage, London: Arnold.

Johns, T. (1991) 'Should you be Persuaded – Two Samples of Data-driven Learning Materials', *ELR Journal*, 4: 1–16.

Johns, T. (1991) 'From Printout to Handout: Grammar and Vocabulary Teaching in the Context of Data-driven Learning', *ELR Journal*, 4: 27–45.

Johns, T. *Multiconcord: the Lingua Multilingual Parallel Concordancer for Windows*, http://web.bham.ac.uk/johnst/lingua.htm (21 December 1999)

Judge, A., and Healey, F.G. (1985) *A Reference Grammar of Modern French*, London: Edward Arnold.

Kenning, M-M. (1998) 'Parallel Concordancing and French Personal Pronouns', *Languages in Contrast*, I, 1: 1–21.

King, L. and Boaks, P. (eds) (1994) *Grammar! A Conference Report*, London: CILT.

Marriott, T. and Ribière, M. (1990) *Help Yourself to French Grammar*, Harlow: Longman.

McEnery, T., Wilson, A. and Barker, P. (1997) 'Teaching Grammar Again after Twenty Years: Corpus-based Help for Teaching Grammar', *ReCALL*, 9(2): 8–16.

Quirk, R., Grennbaum, S., Leech, G. and Svartvik, J. (1985) *A Comprehensive Grammar of the English Language*, Harlow: Longman.

Appendix

Grammar suggestions: student A

- Adjectives: meaning change according to where they are placed, before or after the noun (2.5, 14.1–10).

- *Depuis* and *pendant*: use of (4.7–9)

- Negatives: positioning of the 2 parts according to the tense they are being used in (5.2–4, 13.1–4)

- All relative pronouns: (6.1–4, 16.1–5)

- Subjunctive: (10.1–4, 15.1–7, 18.1–3, 25.1–2)

- *De*: in the various contexts that it is used in, i.e. how it is translated, as well as perhaps the others; *du, de la, des...* (12.8–11)

- *Si* +: the tenses that it combines with (12.12–14)

- Verbs that can take both *avoir* and *être*: (altering their meaning accordingly) + their various agreements in the past (13.7)

- 2 Verb constructions: testing to see whether student knows whether to put *à, de* or leave it blank (16.6–8, 21.4c)

Grammar suggestions: student B

1 Positions of adjectives – could the concordance be used to illustrate the way in which the position of certain adjectives i.e. *ancien, pauvre* affects their meaning?

2 Use of the subjunctive – a difficult tense to grasp, would the concordancer help people learn when to use the subjunctive? (*soit*)

3 To illustrate the different meanings in English of a single French word.

4 To explain the past historic tense and its use.

Current Issues in University Language Teaching

Published by the Association for French Language Studies (AFLS) in Association with the Centre for Information on Language Teaching and Research (CILT)

Series Editors: James A. Coleman   Gabrielle Parker
                   Aidan Coveney   Annie Rouxeville
                   Marie-Anne Hintze

The Association for French Language Studies, founded in 1981, has always believed in a close link between teaching and research, and in the insights each can bring to the other.

The *Current Issues in Language Teaching* series was conceived as a channel for disseminating research findings, theoretical developments and good practice in foreign language teaching and learning at university level. It also provides a focus for discussion of themes of topical or enduring concern to university language teachers.

The books are principally concerned with French, but since the outset have embraced all modern languages, and despite the focus on British higher education have welcomed contributions from the perspective of many different countries.

The AFLS Publications Committee and Series Editors would like to thank all those who have helped to assess and edit so many submitted manuscripts since the launch of the series in 1991.

Past and present membership of the AFLS Publications Committee is:

James A. Coleman (1991–)   Marie-Anne Hintze (1995–)
Aidan Coveney (1998–)   Marie-Madeleine Kenning (1999–)
Robert Crawshaw (1991–95)   Gabrielle Parker (1991–)
Dulcie Engel (1993–98)   Annie Rouxeville (1991–1999)

Acknowledgements

Other referees to whom we convey our thanks are:

Robin Adamson
Eve-Marie Aldridge
Nigel Armstrong
Gertrud Aub-Büscher
Kate Beeching
Jeremy Bradford
Noëlle Brick
Elspeth Broady
Inès Brulard
Peter Bush
Keith Cameron
Dora Carpenter
Janice Carruthers
Francine Chambers
Jean Compain
Aidan Coveney
Robert Crawshaw
Béatrice Dammame-Gilbert
David Drake
Lise Duquette
Peter Dyson
George Evans
María Fernández-Toro
Bob French
Raymond Gallery
Marie-Marthe Gervais-le Garff
Robin Goodfellow
Ruth Goodison
Terry Goodison
Geoffrey Hare
Brian Hill
Stella Hurd
Marie-Monique Huss

Douglas Jamieson
Anne Judge
Michael Kelly
Marie-Madeleine Kenning
John Kidman
Marie-Noëlle Lamy
Monique L'Huillier
Anthony Lodge
Ian Mason
Nicole McBride
Rosamond Mitchell
Florence Myles
Susan Myles
David Nott
Malcolm Offord
Martha Pennington
Charles Russ
Kamal Salhi
Rodney Sampson
Carol Sanders
Karen Seago
Penelope Sewell
Samuel Taylor
Ros Temple
Richard Towell
Jeanine Treffers-Daller
Robert Turner
Raynalle Udris
Richard Wakeley
David Walker
David Williams
Hilary Wise
Marie-Paule Woodley